EARLY CHILDHOOD CURRICULUM

Early Childhood Curriculum addresses current approaches to curriculum for infants, toddlers and young children, aged birth to eight. It provides a comprehensive introduction to the curriculum issues that student teachers and emerging practitioners will face and equips them with the decision-making tools that will ultimately enhance and promote young children's learning. The text proposes a cultural–historical framework to explore diverse approaches to early years education, drawing on research and examples of practice across a range of international contexts. It offers a clear focus on domain areas of the curriculum – the arts, health and wellbeing, literacy and language, science and maths, and information and communication technology – so that teachers are able to gain a breadth of understanding and effectively plan, design and implement curriculum strategy.

An essential text for undergraduate students throughout their pre-service teacher education, *Early Childhood Curriculum* is also a practical resource for early childhood teachers and carers, and a valuable tool for professional development programs. Important features include:

- curriculum pathway models to help students identify the core curriculum focus in each chapter
- reflective questions, hypothetical transcripts, and real-world examples to illustrate key points
- an accompanying website to support delivery of content and enhance student learning at www.cambridge.edu.au/academic/earlychildhood.

Claire McLachlan is Associate Professor, Early Years Education, Massey University College of Education.

Marilyn Fleer is Professor, Early Childhood Education, Faculty of Education, Monash University.

Susan Edwards is Senior Lecturer, Early Childhood Education, Faculty of Education, Monash University.

Early Childhood Curriculum

Planning, assessment and implementation

Claire McLachlan

Marilyn Fleer

Susan Edwards

CAMBRIDGE UNIVERSITY PRESS
Cambridge, New York, Melbourne, Madrid, Cape Town, Singapore,
São Paulo, Delhi, Mexico City, Tokyo

Cambridge University Press
477 Williamstown Road, Port Melbourne, VIC 3207, Australia

Published in the United States of America by Cambridge University Press, New York

www.cambridge.org
Information on this title: www.cambridge.org/9780521759113

First published 2010
Reprinted 2011

Cover design by Marianna Berek-Lewis
Printed in Australia by Ligare Pty Ltd.

A catalogue record for this publication is available from the British Library

National Library of Australia Cataloguing in Publication data
McLachlan, Claire.
Early childhood curriculum : planning, assessment and implementation / Claire McLachlan, Marilyn Fleer, Susan Edwards.
9780521759113 (pbk.)
Includes index.
Early childhood education.
Early childhood education-Curricula.
Curriculum planning.
Fleer, Marilyn.
Edwards, Susan.
372.19

ISBN 978-0-521-75911-3 paperback

CONTENTS

Figures

Tables

About the authors

Claire McLachlan is Associate Professor of Early Years Education at Massey University in Palmerston North, New Zealand. Claire became involved with early childhood education through the Playcentre movement as a young mother of three children, and became fascinated with how young children learn. She completed a doctorate on the topic of emergent literacy in New Zealand kindergartens. She has lectured on early childhood education at the University of Wisconsin in Madison, WI, at AUT University in Auckland and at Massey University in Palmerston North, New Zealand, as well as having had various roles as a teacher and manager in early childhood centres. Claire has a longstanding interest in curriculum, particularly literacy, and a number of publications on teachers' beliefs and practices as they relate to various aspects of early childhood curriculum. Since 2006 she has also been the co-editor of the journal *Early Education*, which is a publication aimed at early childhood practitioners.

Marilyn Fleer is Professor of Early Childhood Education at Monash University in Victoria. She has been a teacher in long day care, preschool and school. She has also been an adviser and curriculum officer for the Ministry of Education in Western Australia. In 2002 she was appointed as a Research Fellow for the Australian Government (then named the Department of Education, Technology and Youth Affairs). She has published nearly 300 works, 30 of which are books. She is the founder of the annual Australian Research in Education conference (commenced in 1993) and foundation editor for the *Journal of Australian Research in Early Childhood Education* (commenced in 1994).

Susan Edwards is Senior Lecturer in Early Childhood Education at Monash University. She has practised as an early childhood educator in long day care, occasional care and preschool settings. Susan completed a doctorate with a focus on how theory informs early childhood curriculum at Monash University. Susan coordinates the Bachelor of Education and Graduate Diploma degrees in early childhood education and supervises honours, masters and PhD research students. Susan has been actively involved in researching early childhood curriculum, particularly issues associated with teacher thinking, theories of development and the role of play in learning. She has published several key papers and book chapters nationally and internationally in this area.

Acknowledgments

It is impossible to write a book without the support and assistance of many other people. We would like to gratefully acknowledge the support, assistance and contribution of the following people:

1. Claire wishes to thank her husband, Simon Barton, for his amazing support, listening to many reports on how the writing was going and cooking beautiful dinners on a regular basis! Claire also wishes to thank her children – Daniel, Jeremy and Jessica Smith – who have provided such inspiration and food for thought over the years.
2. Marilyn wishes to acknowledge particular colleagues who have contributed to Chapters 3, 8 and 9 (see below) and to thank Debbie Lee, the commissioning editor, for her continued support for the conceptualisation, writing and publishing of this book:
   - The Department of Education, Employment and Workplace Relations provided funding for the development of a set of early learning resources that were discussed in Chapter 9. Consortium leaders were Professor Bridie Raban and myself. The overall results and theorisation are reported in: Fleer, M. and Raban, B. (2007) *Early childhood literacy and numeracy: Building good practice*. Early Childhood Australia: Canberra; Fleer, M. and Raban, B. (2006) A cultural-historical analysis of concept formation in early education settings: Conceptual consciousness for the child or only the adult? *European Early Childhood Education Research Journal*, 14(2), pp. 69–80.
   - The prestigious Margaret Trembath Research Scholarship fund provided financial assistance for the research reported in Chapter 3. Gloria Quinones provided invaluable support to this project by accompanying me on all field trips to the family home and in videotaping most of the school and centre observations. Carol Linney has supported this project by assisting with downloading tapes and undertaking some transcriptions of the video clips. The methodological approach to the coding was conceptualised by Professor Mariane Hedegaard, and is reported in: Hedegaard, M. and Fleer, M. (2009) *Study children: A cultural-historical approach to research*. UK: Open University Press. The findings of the study

are reported in: Fleer, M. and Hedegaard, M. (forthcoming) Development as participation in everyday activities across different institutions: A child's changing relations to reality, *Mind, Culture and Activity*.

- Chapter 8 was developed as a result of Amanda and Thomas taking me around their school and sharing their learning with me, and Esme Capp and Linda Sinadinos kindly agreed to being interviewed about the innovations within the school.

3. Susan wishes to acknowledge kind permission from Pademelon Press to use excerpts from *Early Childhood Education and Care: A sociocultural approach* in this book. She also wishes to acknowledge the work of teachers from the City of Casey and students from Monash University which are used in this book.

4. Draga Tomas from the Faculty of Education, Monash University, for carefully formatting the final draft.

5. The Cambridge University Press team, especially Debbie Lee, who followed up and persisted with the vision for this book.

6. Our employing institutions while we have been writing this text: Massey University College of Education and the Faculty of Education, Monash University.

7. Our colleagues at Massey University and Monash University, who have provided many helpful conversations, and the student teachers and children in early childhood and primary settings who have been its inspiration.

Chapter 1

Introduction

Setting: A university tutorial room

Participants: An international group of 3rd year BEd (Early Years) students and their lecturer

Subject: Curriculum in the early childhood setting

Lecturer: We've spent some time talking around the idea of a curriculum and I think we all have some ideas about what a curriculum is. In your reading today, Peter Moss argues that curriculum development is a political act. He says it is constructed – reflecting the values and beliefs of those involved at a particular point in time. He also says it is contested – there is no one agreed idea of curriculum, but rather multiple views of what it should be. What I'd like you to do in your groups is talk about what you think a curriculum is and what you think an early years curriculum should achieve for children. Take about 15 minutes to discuss this and then we will discuss it as a group. Get someone from your group to record your ideas, so that we can share them.

Students move off into groups of about six people and begin the task set by the lecturer.

Anna: I hate it when she asks these sorts of questions! I never feel like there is a right answer.

Kelly: Yes, it is annoying – hard to see what relevance this has to what happens in the reality of the classroom, but I suppose we'd better have a go at answering the question or she's bound to pick on us for an answer.

continued »

continued »

Kiri:	I don't see what all the fuss is about really, as we have two curriculum documents in my country that dictate what we should be doing: *Te Whāriki* and the *New Zealand Curriculum*.
Hui Lee:	In my context we only have one – *Nurturing Early Learners*. It's the framework for the kindergarten curriculum in Singapore.
Mandy:	We have just had our first document developed. It is a national early years learning framework for Australia – *Belonging, Being and Becoming*. But each of our states and territories has its own curriculum as well.
Kiri:	Most countries have some type of written curriculum document. Surely the people who wrote those documents knew what they were on about?
Gemma:	But aren't those documents just a guide to what we do in the classroom? I don't think that our curriculum – *Te Whāriki* – is very specific about the actual stuff I will do with children every day.
Kelly:	Isn't the curriculum how you plan the environment, and sort of based on your own national curriculum and the sorts of things it says that children should experience?
Anna:	But on my last teaching practice, my Associate Teacher told me that the curriculum was in her head and that she didn't take much notice of the curriculum she was using. She said that she just uses the curriculum as a source for ideas and then the real curriculum is designed on the trot as she interacts with children.
Arohia:	Yes, that's right. If you use the definitions in our curriculum – *Te Whāriki* – the curriculum is the sum total of the child's experiences. So isn't everything that happens to the child what the curriculum is?
Gwendolyne:	In Malawi, our curriculum is a guide to help the carers know more about children's development and what concepts they should be teaching.
Kiri:	But what about this idea of it being constructed and contested – how does that work if we have a written curriculum?
Gemma:	Isn't that when you talk to parents about what they want in the curriculum?
Anna:	I don't know and I don't understand how it fits with curriculum planning. How can you plan curriculum if you are using the emergent curriculum approach that some teachers use?

continued »

continued »

Kelly: I guess that's part of the curriculum design stuff, isn't it? That you work out what it is that you want children to be able to do and therefore you plan activities and work out in advance what you think they will achieve, so that you can assess whether it worked or not.

Arohia: But how does that fit with all these ideas around co-construction that our practicum lecturer has been talking about? How can I plan in advance, if I am trying to work with children to plan the curriculum?

Anna: And how does all this fit with what the Education Review Office, our overarching policy and assessment group, expect to see when they come in to do a review? Aren't there things that I have to do if I am in a licensed centre?

Sam: In Canada we have a similar group, and because our curriculum is so prescriptive in terms of content, it is a plus, but also a minus – so much paperwork!!!

Lecturer: Can you come back into the whole group now? First, can you tell me how your group defined what a curriculum is?

This brief scenario shows how hard it is for people in the field of early childhood education to work out exactly what a curriculum is:

- Is it a model?
- Is it a document?
- Is it the way the environment is organised?
- Is it the way in which people plan for children's learning?
- Is it the day-to-day decisions that teachers make about children and their learning?
- Is it what is negotiated with parents, community and external agencies?
- Is it what external evaluation agencies want to see?

All of these questions are approached at some level in this book; we hope it will help you identify your own understanding of what a curriculum for early childhood is or can be.

REFLECTION 1.1

Before we start to talk about early childhood curriculum in earnest, take a moment and think about what you understand by the term 'curriculum'.

Finding answers to these questions

> Educational acts are social acts. As social acts, they are reflexive, historically located and embedded in particular intellectual and social contexts. So knowledge about education must change according to historical circumstances, local contexts and different participants' understandings of what is happening in the educational encounter. And it is clear that the knowledge will to a very great extent be rooted in local historical and social contexts (Carr & Kemmis 1983, p. 47).

This statement by Carr and Kemmis about teacher knowledge, made some years ago, has been validated in an enormous body of research on the influence and importance of social, cultural and historical context on children's learning and development. Early childhood teaching therefore involves wrestling with some of the following issues:

- How can early childhood educators effectively plan curriculum for all children?
- How will the changing needs and interests of infants, toddlers and young children be met?
- How can children's domain knowledge be supported within a holistic curriculum?
- How can teachers effectively observe and assess children's learning if all children bring different social and cultural knowledge to their learning?
- How can teachers plan to support the learning of children who come from many different countries and cultures, speak different languages and are used to learning in different ways?

The answers to these sorts of questions are the purpose of this book. The subject of this book is current approaches to curriculum for children in the early years, and its overall purpose is to provide a comprehensive introduction to the curriculum issues that student teachers and emerging practitioners will face in the decisions they need to make to promote children's learning, and to explore current approaches to curriculum for children in the early years. We seek to work through the confusion that was shown in the vignette at the beginning of this chapter, as that conversation was typical of what can be heard across many countries, countries in which 'curriculum' is still a highly confused and confusing term.

In most countries, some form of curriculum has been designed by a government agency or the private sector. So why is it that the concept is so confusing and why is what is contained in the various curricula around the globe so different and highly contested? As Kiri said in the vignette, 'Surely the people who wrote those curriculum documents know what they are about?' Designing a curriculum document is a complex task and involves the use of a robust curriculum model which has been built upon a particular theoretical perspective. When you read through Chapter 2 you will be introduced to a range of curriculum theories and curriculum models. That chapter will help you as you think about and solve the issue of what is a curriculum document – at the macro level. In that chapter you will notice that there are indeed very different views on the theories that guide curriculum writers, and you will see that each writer selects a curriculum model – like a skeleton – that they use to frame how the content is introduced to the user.

In this book, we briefly introduce you to a broad range of theories and curriculum models. However, the focus of the book is on the use of cultural-historical theory for guiding curriculum design, implementation, assessment and evaluation. As such, more space has been devoted to this theory, as it is a relatively new and contemporary theory for guiding curriculum development in early childhood education. In Chapter 5 we specifically introduce you to how to interpret a curriculum, and Chapter 6 shows you a cultural-historical curriculum in action. These chapters will help you understand what a curriculum is and what a curriculum looks like when it is being implemented through teachers' programs.

Chapters 9 to 11 give working examples of curriculum in relation to the following content areas: maths and science; technology and environmental education; language, literacy and information and communication technologies; the arts, health, wellbeing and physical activity. By the time you read through these chapters, we hope you will feel you have answered Kiri's query about curriculum writers knowing what they are on about!

Anna raised an issue that faces many professionals in the field: the assessment and evaluation of a centre or classroom. She asked, 'How does all this fit with what the Education Review Office expects to see when they come to do their review?' Different countries have different expectations, of course, and different processes for reviewing how things are going in a centre or classroom. Basic requirements focus on whether or not the teacher or the school uses the curriculum documents for organising their teaching and learning, through to a comprehensive review that leads to a licence (or accreditation) to operate the early childhood education service. In Chapters 7 and 8 you will be introduced to the nuances between assessing children and assessing the outcomes of a curriculum through an evaluation of what is happening in a school or in a centre. In Chapter 8 you will read about how one curriculum leader evaluates the school's implementation of its curriculum. There you will see specific references to the issue identified by Anna about the relationship between what a teacher does and what a system expects in relation to the implementation and evaluation of a curriculum.

Finally, the confusion expressed by Kelly, Arohia, Gemma and Anna – is a curriculum the environment, is a curriculum what is in the teacher's head, or how they plan, or is a curriculum something that emerges in relation to children's interests – is addressed specifically in Chapters 2 and 4. Together, these chapters show that although there is a robust theoretical and modelling process used in curriculum design, what content is located within curriculum, and how decisions are made about 'what goes in' and 'what goes out' is highly contested. This is also evident in Chapter 3, where the concept of curriculum is discussed in relation to various theories of development. There it is argued that progression in curriculum is closely tied to what people believe about child development.

Through reading this book, you should come to understand what a curriculum is. You will then be able to resolve the issues raised by the student teachers in relation to curriculum.

We will return to these questions in the final chapter, where you will compare the reflective comments (Reflection 1.1) made here with what you have come to understand as a result of reading this book.

Whilst the chapters have been separated out, you should think about them as related to each other. The model below may help your thinking about how

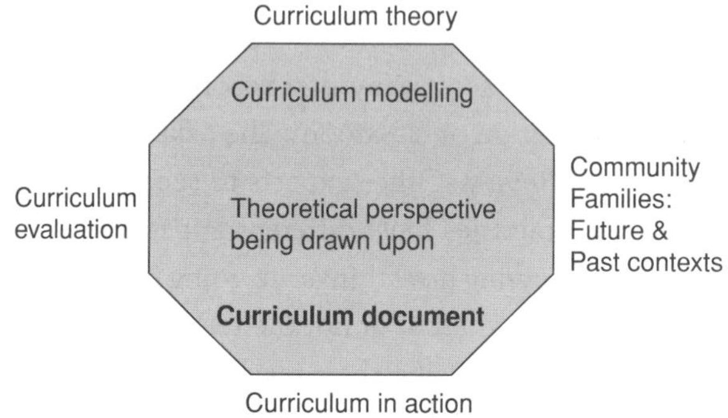

Figure 1.1 Curriculum development pathway

to engage with the chapters, separately and collectively. In each chapter, this icon will be used to show what the focus of attention is. However, the content of all the chapters should be considered as a whole, even though you can of course only read one chapter at a time.

REFERENCE

Carr, W. & Kemmis, S. (1983). *Becoming critical: Knowing through action research.* Melbourne: Deakin Press.

Chapter 2

Theory, research and the early childhood curriculum

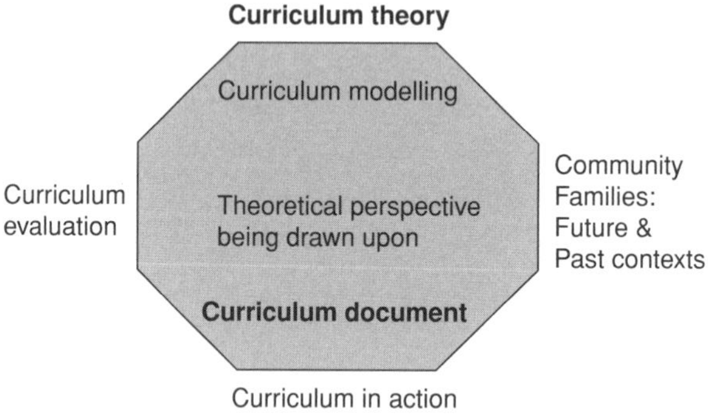

Figure 2.1 Curriculum development pathway – theories and models

In the first chapter it was noted that early childhood teachers are often confused by the term 'curriculum' because of the different ways this term is used, as noted by Kiri, Kelly, Gemma and Anna:

Kiri: Most countries have some type of written curriculum document. Surely the people who wrote those documents knew what they were on about?

Gemma: But aren't those documents just a guide to what we do in the classroom? I don't think that our curriculum – *Te Whāriki* – is very specific about the actual stuff I will do with children every day.

Kelly: Isn't the curriculum how you plan the environment, and sort of based on your own national curriculum and the sorts of things it says that children should experience?

Anna: But on my last teaching practice, my Associate Teacher told me that the curriculum was in her head and that she didn't take much notice of the curriculum she was using. She said that she just uses the curriculum as a source for ideas and then the real curriculum is designed on the trot as she interacts with children.

In this chapter we seek to unpack some of the ideas put forward by Kiri, Gemma, Kelly and Anna through introducing you to conceptual knowledge about curriculum, as well as through examining fundamental principles of curriculum design. The term 'curriculum' is defined and the major philosophical and theoretical positions that underpin modern conceptions of early childhood curriculum are examined. Because knowledge is not static, we ask you to consider the importance of research as a driver for change and continued professional development. This chapter will also include an analysis of how the efficacy of a curriculum can be evaluated. This is a long and quite theoretical chapter, but there are working examples of all the concepts either in this chapter or in the others in this book.

WHAT IS A CURRICULUM?

According to Scott (2008), a curriculum can be defined in the following way:

> A curriculum may refer to a system, as in a national curriculum; an institution, as in a school curriculum; or even to an individual school, as in the school geography curriculum (p. 19–20).

This definition begins to make it clear why the word 'curriculum' can be so confusing to people.

REFLECTION 2.1

When you think about the curriculum you are using, or that you see professionals use in your local community, how would it be classified: As a national document? As an institution? As a school-developed curriculum? As a regional child care centre document? Or . . . ?

Emma suggested that the curriculum she uses is 'not very specific about the actual stuff she does with children every day'. When you examine curricula from around the world, there is indeed great diversity in what is presented – some are specific, some quite general. According to Scott (2008), a curriculum can be organised specifically to include four dimensions:

> aims or objectives, contents or subject matter, methods or procedures, and evaluation and assessment. The first dimension refers to the reasons for including specific items in the curriculum and excluding others. The second dimension is content or subject matter and this refers to knowledge, skills or dispositions which are implicit in the choice of items, and the way that they are arranged. Objectives may be understood as broad general justifications for including particular items and particular pedagogical processes in the curriculum; or as clearly defined and closely delineated outcomes or behaviours; or as a set of appropriate procedures or experiences. The third dimension is methods or procedures and this

> refers to pedagogy and is determined by choices made about the first two dimensions. The fourth dimension is assessment or evaluation and this refers to the means for determining whether the curriculum has been successfully implemented (pp. 19–20).

So the four crucial elements which apply to curriculum in any teaching and learning setting from early childhood through to tertiary education are:

1. **Aims, goals, objectives or outcome statements** – what do we want this curriculum to achieve, what would we expect to be the outcomes as a result of participating in the implementation of this curriculum?
2. **Content, domains, or subject matter** – what will we include or exclude from our curriculum?
3. **Methods or procedures** – what teaching methods or approaches will we use to achieve these goals or outcomes?
4. **Evaluation and assessment** – how will we know when we have achieved them?

Emma's concern about her curriculum not being specific enough clearly relates to her wishing the document to prescribe learning activities. Scott's assessment of what is a curriculum shows that a curriculum must be broadly conceived. It gives guidance about general concepts, but it gives information only in general terms on how the learning will be specifically organised.

What a community expects its education system to achieve is a strong force in determining curriculum content within particular countries. In South Korea, for instance, curriculum writers have stated that children will achieve the following:

Table 2.1 Ministry of Gender and Community Services (2003). *Parents' and Caregivers' Guide for Household and Communities: Child development practices.* Republic of Malawi (Fleer 2010)

Country	Learning to perform	Learning to make meaning	Learning to participate	Learning to be	Other concepts
Korea (kindergarten)	Sensory skill and physical cognition; fundamental movement competence; health; safety.	Listening, speaking; becoming interested in reading and writing; scientific inquiry; logical-mathematical inquiry; creative inquiry.	Basic living habits; personal life; family life; group life; social phenomena and environment; exploration; expression; appreciation.	Appreciation; creative inquiry.	

REFLECTION 2.2

Examine the content of your curriculum documents. What kind of knowledge is valued? Can you find content to fit under the headings given by Scott – aims, content, methods, and evaluation/assessment?

To this point we have learned that a curriculum can be defined as a national document, a school-based document, or a document for a geographically defined area larger than a school but smaller than a nation. It is likely to be made up of Scott's four basic elements – aims, content, method and evaluation/assessment. But what governments or society at large wants for its youngest citizens will vary depending upon the community. For instance, Bernstein (1996) argues that there are essentially two models of curriculum and that all curricula fall into one or the other category. He states that curriculum is oriented to either ***performance*** or ***competence*** and that ***performance*** models of curriculum are the most dominant around the world.

The ***performance*** model has its origin in the behavioural objectives movement:

> It is a model that clearly emphasises marked subject boundaries, traditional forms of knowledge, explicit realisation and recognition rules for pedagogic practice and the designation and establishment of strong boundaries between different types of students (Scott 2008, p. 4).

Implicit in this model is the sense that explicit criteria would save teachers and students from muddle and confusion. For example, the Canadian (Ontario) curriculum is quite explicit about the content it expects teachers to cover during the year before starting school:

Table 2.2 Ministry of Education (2006). *The Kindergarten Program.* Ontario (Fleer 2010)

Country	Learning to perform	Learning to make meaning	Learning to participate	Learning to be	Other concepts
Ontario (kindergarten)	Large and small muscle development and control.	Language, mathematics; science and technology; health and	Personal and social development (self-awareness and	Personal and social development (self-awareness);	*(cont.)*

Table 2.2 *(cont.)*

Country	Learning to perform	Learning to make meaning	Learning to participate	Learning to be	Other concepts
		safety practices; the arts (problem-solving strategies when experimenting; basic knowledge and skills across arts); awareness of surroundings.	self-reliance; social relationships).	communicate ideas through various art forms; awareness of selves as artists.	

In contrast, the ***competence*** model suggests that learners have some control over the selection, pacing and sequencing of the curriculum. ***Competence*** models have been more common in early childhood education. New Zealand's early childhood curriculum, *Te Whāriki* (Ministry of Education 1996) is a good example of this sort of curriculum. However, the dominance of competence models of curriculum in early childhood education is changing in some countries; the *Foundation Stage* curriculum in the UK (Aubrey 2004), for example, has clearly defined curriculum outcomes for very young children:

Table 2.3 Department for Education and Employment (2000). *Curriculum Guidance for the Foundation Stage*. London (Fleer 2010)

Country	Learning to perform	Learning to make meaning	Learning to participate	Learning to be	Other concepts
England (nursery and reception aged children)	Physical development.	Communication; language and literacy; mathematical development; knowledge and understanding of the world.	Personal, social and emotional development.	Creative development.	

REFLECTION 2.3

Examine your curriculum and determine if it is based on a competence model or a performance model. Is the sequence of content detailed and prescriptive or is it general, requiring a great deal more teacher judgment about what to introduce and when?

There is another important dimension of curriculum that has been noted in the literature, and that is the ideology that underpins its design. Schiro (2008) argues that there are four dominant ideologies which shape curriculum practice in the United States, and we would argue that these models have also been influential in many other countries, including New Zealand and Australia. These four ideologies are:

1. The scholar academic ideology;
2. The social efficiency ideology;
3. The learner-centred ideology; and
4. The social reconstruction ideology.

The **scholar academic** ideology is based on the notion that our culture has accumulated knowledge over the centuries which has been organised into academic disciplines within universities. For example, science has a long tradition, and scientists would argue that there is an accumulated body of knowledge in this area which children need to become familiar with in order to engage in contemporary society. The OECD (2006) has classified any early childhood education and development curriculum that follows this ideology as the 'pre-primary approach', because the content of the curriculum mirrors what we might see in primary school. An example of this is shown in Table 2.2 (*Ontario Early Childhood Curriculum*). Followers of this ideology believe that the academic disciplines, the world of the intellect and the world of knowledge are loosely equivalent. The central task of education is to extend this equivalence on both the cultural and individual planes; to discover new truths for the former and to acculturate individuals into their civilisation in the latter. For example, through observations of the world, learners note patterns, and see causal links, and can make predictions. This is a form of empirical knowledge. We might see this being promoted through a teacher planning to look at the concept of water displacement using a specific activity in the water trolley.

In this ideology, an academic discipline is made up of a hierarchy:

- the inquirers into the truth (the university academics);

- teachers of the truth (those who disseminate truth); and
- learners of the truth (the students whose job it is to learn).

For example, teachers have gained the scientific knowledge of displacement whilst at university, their role is to teach this knowledge (as determined in the early childhood curriculum), and it is the job of the children to learn it when using the water trolley equipment and engaging in the activity that the teacher has planned.

The vision of the child in this ideology is of the child as incomplete, a 'neophyte', an immature member of the discipline, who is capable of developing intellect, memory and reasoning, shaped by the discipline (Schiro 2008). This view sees the child as a 'blank slate' or 'empty, needing to be filled with knowledge. Learning is viewed as a function of teaching: the teacher is a transmitter and the child is a receiver. Although no formal theory of learning using this model is espoused by most curriculum developers, there is an understanding of readiness which supports Jerome Bruner's statement that 'any subject can be taught effectively in some intellectually honest form to any child at any stage of development' (1963, p. 529).

The three major teaching methods used are didactic discourse, supervised practice and Socratic discussion. Didactic discourse is usually presented as formal or informal lectures, supported by written textbooks. Supervised practice means applying theoretical knowledge gained to problem solving, in an appropriate context (such as a chemistry laboratory). Socratic discussion is a pattern of interrogative questioning used to help children to think clearly, critically and analytically. Assessment and evaluation in this ideology are objective rather than subjective, often based on tests and examinations of children, teachers and curriculum materials. Most people will recognise many elements of their own secondary and tertiary education in this ideology. In the early childhood field this can be loosely translated into demonstrating to children, as might happen in a science experiment. The teacher shows the children the experiment and the children watch and listen, and are then quizzed on their understandings.

The **social efficiency** ideology is based on the writings of Franklin Bobbitt, and in particular his book *The Curriculum*, published in 1913 and further developed by Ralph Tyler in 1949 in *Basic Principles of Curriculum and Instruction*, in which both authors declared that educators should learn to use the scientific techniques of production developed by industry to improve the outcomes of education. In this ideology, the school is the equivalent of a factory and the child is the raw material. The adult is the finished product and the teacher is the factory worker, who runs the machines. A teacher in this model must determine what the consumer wants as a finished product and what the most efficient way of producing that product is. Bobbitt (1918) proclaimed that the educational 'task preceding all others is the determination of... a scientific technique' of curriculum design (in Schiro 2008, p. 51). Tyler (1949) proposed that educators must be able to answer the following questions:

1. What educational purposes should the school seek to have?
2. What educational experiences can be provided that are likely to achieve these purposes?
3. How can these educational experiences be effectively organised?
4. How can we determine whether or not these purposes are being achieved?

Social efficiency educators devote much time to developing objectives in behavioural terms: as observable skills, capabilities for action, activities to be performed – demonstrable things people can do. For instance, a behavioural objective in sport might be 'Physical development: That the child can throw a beanbag towards a target and over a distance of 3 metres'.

Here we see that the action is clearly stated – throwing a bean bag – and the measurement of success is determined – at a target and over 3 metres. In this model, only observable and therefore easily measurable things count.

An efficient curriculum is defined as one in which children experience a controlled learning environment, in which content is carefully sequenced and efficiently organised. This is often called a programmed curriculum. For example, the curriculum would be organised so that teachers could plan their teaching programs for incremental success: throwing a beanbag at the target over 1 metre, then 2 metres, and finally 3 metres. Assessment and evaluation are used to determine the changes in children's behaviour that are taking place. Is success determined by the direction of the throw, or the distance? The curriculum developer's role is that of 'behavioural engineer' (Holland 1960).

There are several assumptions about teaching and learning in this ideology. First, there is the assumption that changed behaviour is a response to stimulus and would have otherwise not have taken place. For example, giving the child increasingly small beanbags to throw, or increasing the distance to be thrown. Second, there is also an assumption that learning only occurs through practice of the behaviour children are to learn, such as practising throwing the beanbag regularly. Third, there is an assumption that learning consists of acquiring specific responses to particular stimuli, rather than general responses to vague stimuli. That is, setting up a target and placing beanbags at predetermined locations will of itself stimulate children to practise hitting the target. Fourth, there is a belief that complex behaviours are acquired by building on repertoires of simpler ones over time: accuracy of aim, and strength of throw, for example, increase with time and practice. Finally, there is an assumption that all aspects of learning can be dealt with in this way. This approach to curriculum development supports the teaching method of planning for observable and directly measurable objectives.

Education is seen as a shaping process in this ideology, preparing children to create a better society. Children are seen as potential members of the adult society and as workers capable of putting energy into the education endeavour. Through learning how to throw more accurately, children can children participate better in organised support, and they have the eye-hand coordination skills and strength to operate equipment in industry and in service professions. The teacher is the 'manager of the conditions of learning' (Gagne 1970, p. 324). As Schiro (2008, p. 86) argues:

> the job of teaching is to fit the student to the curriculum and fit the curriculum to the student. It involves stimulating students to run the curriculum and adjusting the curriculum to the capabilities of students. This entails knowing students and taking into account their idiosyncratic natures. The curriculum developer designs curriculum for a standard student; the teacher makes adjustments for particular students.

In this model, teachers are implementers of curriculum, not designers of it. The curriculum is thus perceived to be protected from the vagaries of individual teaching skill. In this model, teaching can be evaluated in terms of how efficiently the teacher has ensured student achievement.

Learner-centred ideology is based on the idea of an ideal school, or what John Dewey (1915) called 'the school of tomorrow'. These sorts of schools are particularly common in early childhood, although they exist in all levels of education. Current models which typify this ideology include Montessori preschools and Reggio Emilia schools. In learner-centred ideology, the needs of the individual child dominate, rather than the needs of teachers, school subjects, school administrators or community groups. For example, a child who is very active, and comes from a sporting family, is likely to show great interest in physical activity. In a school with a child-centred curriculum, a teacher will draw upon a curriculum that is loosely organised around goals such as 'Building individual competence and sense of self' to plan a sports-inspired program for building that child's competence and sense of self, because that child is someone who values physical activity. Within this ideology, a curriculum is focused on children having hands-on experiences of things themselves. Activity is a key term – physical, social, verbal and emotional (Schiro 2008) – and it will take place both inside and outside the classroom. The history of these ideas can be seen in the ideas of several key thinkers: Comenius (1592–1670), who argued that learning moves from concrete experience to abstract thought; Jean-Jacques Rousseau (1712–78), who believed that the purpose of education was to nurture children's innate goodness and that learning should result from direct experiences with nature and sensory experiences with concrete objects; Johann Heinrich Pestalozzi (1746–1827), who argued that children should be free to pursue their own interests and advocated for the freedom of the 'whole child'; and Friedrich Froebel (1782–1852), who invented the kindergarten, which was based on the education of children's senses and the use of 'gifts' and 'occupations' that allowed children to perceive the order and beauty of nature as a result of interacting with it. Also associated with this ideology are G. Stanley Hall (1844–1924), the founder of the child study movement at Clark University in the United States, and John Dewey (1859–1952), the American educational philosopher, who argued that 'children learn by doing'.

A curriculum based on these ideas uses an integrated curriculum, based on education of the 'whole child'. It uses interdisciplinary approaches to academic disciplines and assumes that children will actively integrate their own knowledge. For example, learning about mathematics might be introduced to a child through sport – keeping score during a game. There are few fixed periods of learning in a learner-centred school; children will initiate and terminate activities at their own will and children will have opportunities to participate in many activities at any given time. For instance, in many early education programs, children will join an activity – in the home corner, say – and will leave and move on to other activities when they wish. Finally, an integrated curriculum attempts to integrate children's home and school lives, so that the world is not viewed as fragmented.

The learner-centred ideology is humanist in orientation – the fundamental principles are about human growth, the potential for self-actualisation and the need for personal autonomy. Learning is seen to occur through the child's interaction with the environment and the dominant learning theory used is constructivism, often using Jean Piaget's theory (see Bredekamp 1987). Piaget's theory proposed that children are active learners, and their interaction with the physical world provides the main constraints on and contributions to the development of their intelligence: children learn and construct meaning as they act upon objects in space and time.

More recently, social constructivism, based on Lev Vygotsky's theories, has also been expressed within this ideology (see Bredekamp & Copple 1997). Project approaches to learning are typical in this ideology – teachers help children scope and sequence learning and enable children to move from personal, concrete and physical learning experiences to abstract, verbal and intellectual understandings (Schiro 2008). In this ideology the teacher is not a transmitter, but carefully observes the children and sets up environments to support learning. The teacher may also intervene between the child and the environment to assist learning. Many of you will recognise various elements of the early childhood settings you have previously encountered in this description.

Curriculum developers who follow a learner-centred ideology present their curriculum in ways which integrate knowledge with children's growing sense of themselves as members of their society. The Swedish curriculum is one that exemplifies a learner-centred ideology:

Table 2.4 National Agency for Education (2006). *Lpfo 98* (Curriculum for preschool), Stockholm, Sweden (Fleer 2010)

Country	Learning to perform	Learning to make meaning	Learning to participate	Learning to be	Other concepts
Sweden (preschool)	Motor skills, ability to co-ordinate, awareness of their own body.	Health and wellbeing; differentiate shades of meaning in concepts; understand the surrounding world; use spoken language, communicate and express their thoughts; develop vocabulary and concepts; play with words, show interest in written language; build, create and design using different materials and techniques; use mathematics; use concepts of number, measurement and form and	Norms and values (openness, respect, solidarity and responsibility); take account of and empathise with others and be willing to help; participate in own culture, and feel respect for other cultures; understand that everyone is of equal value; respect and care for surrounding environment; function individually and in group; handle conflicts, understand rights, obligations and	Identity; curiosity and enjoyment at the same time as ability to play and learn; self-autonomy and confidence; work out own position on different ethical dilemmas and fundamental questions of life; express themselves creatively; understand cultural identity; be able to listen, reflect and express views.	

Table 2.4 *(cont.)*

Country	Learning to perform	Learning to make meaning	Learning to participate	Learning to be	Other concepts
		time and space; appreciate nature and simple scientific phenomena.	common rules; express thoughts and influence own situation; exhibit responsibility; understand democracy.		

The Swedish early childhood curriculum clearly positions the learner as central to the curriculum. For instance, the statement 'identity; curiosity and enjoyment at the same time as ability to play and learn' demonstrates that knowledge and a sense of the learner's identity, curiosity and enjoyment are to be brought together. In this way, learning is directly related to the learner, and it is the role of the early childhood professional to know as much as possible about the learner in order to know how learning experiences can be framed for each child's individual and collective sense of self.

The **social reconstruction** ideology is premised on the idea that our society is threatened by many problems and that education can provide the cure. Henry Giroux's (2006) writing typifies this approach to curriculum:

> Educators need to assume the role of leaders in the struggle for social and economic justice . . . Educators must connect what they teach and write to the dynamics of public life . . . and concern for . . . democracy (p. 9).

Teaching and learning in this ideology is based on where the children are and what the issues are in their community. For instance, we note in the Swedish curriculum that children are not just exposed to some of these big ideas, such as human rights; they are actively engaged as learners with issues – for example, one of the curriculum goals is 'work out own position on different ethical dilemmas and fundamental questions of life'. Learning is based on experiences that intellectually and emotionally involve the children. Group discussion is a key instructional method, and values, feelings, injustices, alternatives and solutions are explored. The teacher is seen as a colleague, who has experiences to share with the children, rather than as an expert. Schools are seen as institutions of change, in which children are prepared to change society for the better. Children are not seen as children, but as products of society, as social actors and as potential contributing members of society who can aid reconstruction (Schiro

2008). Children are viewed as 'meaning makers': active learners who perceive, interpret and organise their own reality. In examining the Swedish national curriculum, it is possible to see social reconstruction ideology firmly built into it. Very few other early childhood education curricula within our global community so clearly deal with social reconstruction. However, it is possible to find early childhood professionals who have adopted a social reconstruction ideology in their own centres, as part of their worldview about teaching and learning.

REFLECTION 2.4

Go back through the curriculum extracts introduced in this chapter and note any goals which foreground a social reconstruction ideology. What do you notice?

REFLECTION 2.5

In your own experiences of education, can you name any examples of these four ideologies in practice?

Another useful model, this time from a British point of view, is provided by Scott (2008), who argues that there have been overlapping episodes in thinking about curriculum, but that there are seven predominant episodes:

- scientific curriculum making;
- intrinsic worthwhile knowledge;
- innovative pedagogical experimentation;
- sociocultural learning;
- critical pedagogy;
- instrumentalism; and
- school effectiveness/school improvement.

These approaches to curriculum may arise, persist and reconstitute themselves or re-emerge in different guises and through different practices over time.

REFLECTION 2.6

Use Scott's (2008) model to analyse the curriculum extracts provided in this chapter to here (not *Te Whāriki*, which follows). Can you categorise the curricula?

continued »

Reflection 2.6 continued »

Are there some categories that were difficult to use? Were some curricula difficult to categorise? You will return to this activity later in the book, as you gain more understanding of the different theoretical traditions that have informed curriculum development. This task is designed to sensitise and orient you to the different ways in which curriculum developers have been informed by theory.

Scientific curriculum emerged from the curriculum movement in the United States in the early part of the 20th century, with the application of scientific method to the study of curriculum and its implementation. It equates to what Schiro (2008) calls 'social efficiency ideology'.

Intrinsically worthwhile knowledge emerged in the 1970s and 1980s, based on the notion that learning should be for its own sake, rather than from any prescribed list of knowledge and skills. Advocates of this approach include Paul Hirst (1974), who argued for curriculum as initiation into social practices and proposed seven forms of knowledge: logico-mathematical; empirical; interpersonal; moral; aesthetic; religious; and philosophical. Hirst believed that the curriculum should reflect these foundations of knowledge and that the child should be initiated into the ways of thinking about them. A liberal education is proposed as the way to become an autonomous being.

Innovative pedagogical experiment is based primarily on the work of John Elliot (1998), who argues that all curricula are experiments concerning the interface between curriculum and pedagogy. Elliot argues that the task for the teacher is to find cultural resources which will support people to meet the demands of changing and diverse circumstances and that the behavioural models do not leave room for individuals to use culture as a medium for learning.

Sociocultural models of learning originally emerged in Bruner's (1960, 1996) study of the intrapsychic processes of knowing and learning, as expressed in his model of spiral curriculum, and his three modes of understanding: enactive, iconic and symbolic. His later work developed a theory of cultural psychology based on meaning, narrative and interpersonal communication, echoing the earlier work of Vygotsky (1978, in Bruner 1996). Vygotsky's influence on curriculum in recent years has been enormous. He described his theory as cultural-historical. By this he meant that mind, cognition and memory can only be understood as functions that are carried out with other people and in society. Both Bruner and Vygotsky foregrounded society and culture as key dimensions of learning.

Critical pedagogy is underpinned by the belief that schools and curriculum are designed to legitimate some ideas and suppress others. Critical pedagogy is designed

continued »

Reflection 2.6 continued »

to disrupt and undermine the conventional forms of understanding, which serve to reproduce undemocratic, racist, sexist and unequal social relations. Implicit in this ideology is the idea of student centredness and student empowerment. The writings of Michael Apple (1979, 1982), Henry Giroux (1981, 1989) and Michel Foucault (1977) are all significant. Apple's writing concerned social reproduction by schools, student socialisation, the 'hidden curriculum' and inequalities perpetuated by curriculum. Giroux was more concerned with 'emancipatory citizenship' and postmodernist conceptions of knowledge. Foucault, although not a curriculum theorist, has had his writings extensively used to support discussion of knowledge–power discourses in curriculum and schooling.

Instrumentalism as an ideology means that a curriculum can be justified in terms of what virtues or experiences children should have in order to lead a fulfilled life. The writings of those interested in lifelong learning fit into this ideology, including John White's (1982) notion of autonomy, in which children and adults are able to make decisions which allow the possibility of a good life. There are tensions, however, between leading an autonomous life and leading a fulfilled one.

School effectiveness/school improvement models of curriculum are separate but often linked by theorists, so that knowledge developed by school effectiveness research is translated into prescriptive school improvement practices.

Clearly, many curriculum documents are blends of ideologies and thinking stemming from the range of episodes of thinking about curriculum outlined above. Let's return briefly to the key questions about curriculum identified at the beginning of this chapter and analyse some current curriculum documents that we are familiar with.

Table 2.5 provides an analysis of the curriculum document, *Te Whāriki* (Ministry of Education 1996), which is used by all licensed early childhood centres in New Zealand. The purpose of the analysis is to identify whether some of the ideologies and models we have discussed so far can be seen in the various aspects of the curriculum, and if the questions discussed on p. 3 can be answered. What is clear from the analysis is that this curriculum is influenced by more than one ideology, but there is clearly a dominant ideology in operation.

Table 2.5 Current curriculum models: The interesting case of *Te Whāriki* (Ministry of Education 1996)

Key questions about curriculum	Case study: *Te Whāriki*	Analysis and links to ideologies and models
Aims or objectives – what do we want this curriculum to achieve?	• Aspirations for children: 'to grow up as competent and confident learners and communicators, healthy in mind, body and spirit, secure in their sense of belonging and in the knowledge that they make a valued contribution to society (Ministry of Education 1996, p. 9). • Aimed at children from birth to school entry (typically 5 years in New Zealand). Curriculum focused around three age categories: infant (birth to 18 months); toddler (1–3 years); and young child (2.6 years to school entry). • Aimed at building on learning that children bring from home and extending learning. • Conceptualised as a woven mat (or *whāriki*) which weaves together the principles of empowerment, holistic development, family and community and relationships, with the strands of wellbeing, belonging, contribution, communication and exploration. • Each strand has named 'learning outcomes: knowledge, skills and attitudes' for each age category.	• Links to 'social efficiency' ideology in that the purpose of the curriculum is to help children make a contribution to society. • Clear links to 'learner-centred' ideology, as the curriculum is focused on children having hands-on experiences and actively experiencing things themselves. • A 'competence model' of curriculum in orientation as children are seen to have control over content and sequencing of curriculum. • Links to developmental theory, with indications of aged-linked learning outcomes, which has links to both 'learner-centred' ideology, with the notion of curriculum being based on ages and stages, and 'social efficiency' models of curriculum, in terms of measuring learning against learning outcomes.
Content or subject matter – what will we include or exclude from our curriculum?	• Definition of curriculum: 'The term "curriculum" is used in this document to describe the sum total of the experiences, activities and events, whether direct or indirect, which occur within an environment designed to foster children's	• Named link to Bronfenbrenner's (1979) ecological systems model of human development (see p. 19). Links with 'learner-centred' ideology, which links learning at home and at school.

(cont.)

Table 2.5 *(cont.)*

Key questions about curriculum	Case study: *Te Whāriki*	Analysis and links to ideologies and models
	learning and development' (Ministry of Education 1996, p. 10). • Te reo Māori (Māori language) version of the curriculum is included in the document. All teachers are encouraged to understand Māori views on child development and the role of family and community in children's learning. • Child is seen to develop holistically – cognitive, social, cultural, physical, emotional and spiritual dimensions of development are integrally interwoven: 'curriculum takes up a model of learning that weaves together intricate patterns of linked experience rather than emphasising the acquisition of discrete skills' (p. 41). • Subject content areas are embedded within principles and strands, but are explicitly linked with essential learning of the New Zealand curriculum in Part D. • Inclusive of different cultural perspectives on ECE such as indigenous Kōhanga Reo or various Pacific Island language immersion centres. • Inclusive of different philosophical emphases, such as Montessori, Playcentre or Rudolf Steiner. • Inclusive of organisational differences such as kindergarten or child care. • Inclusive of children with special needs.	• Inclusion of diverse philosophies of teaching and learning, consistent with 'learner-centred' ideology. • Implicit, but not named links to Vygotsky's theory and sociocultural theory, through reference to 'scaffolding' children (see p. 43 for example) and explanation that children will learn through social interaction and 'responsive and reciprocal relationships' (see p. 43). • Constructivist approaches are apparent in many references to children being active in their learning.

(cont.)

Table 2.5 *(cont.)*

Key questions about curriculum	Case study: *Te Whāriki*	Analysis and links to ideologies and models
Methods or procedures – what teaching methods will we use to achieve these goals?	• Experiences, activities and events may be planned, or may evolve in response to a particular situation. • Teaching methods must be flexible to account for different age categories and individual differences in children. • Role of the teacher in all categories is to provide a safe, secure and predictable environment, with challenges to extend learning. • Planning is based on observation of children's interests, strengths, needs and behaviours. • Planning can be based on the environment, the setting, particular age groups or on groups of children or individuals. • 'Planning should help adults . . . to understand what young children are learning, how the learning happens and the role that both adults and children play in such learning' (p. 28).	• No theory of teaching and learning is explicitly espoused, probably because the curriculum is designed to be inclusive of diverse philosophies. • Clear links to 'learner-centred' ideology, as in this curriculum the teacher is not a transmitter, but is involved with careful observation of children and setting up environments to support learning.
Evaluation and assessment – how will we know when we have achieved our goals?	• Purpose of assessment is to give useful information about children's learning and development to the adults providing the program and to children and their families. • Assessment involves intelligent observation of the children by experienced and knowledgeable adults for the purpose of improving the program. • Continuous observation provides the basis for more in-depth assessment and evaluation. Adults need to be	• Observation is the primary assessment method used. No other methods are named. • Links to 'social efficiency' model of curriculum, as assessment and evaluation are designed to provide feedback on the effectiveness of the program and achievement of learning outcomes. • Links to 'learner-centred' ideology as assessment and evaluation are framed around the effectiveness of

(cont.)

Table 2.5 *(cont.)*

Key questions about curriculum	Case study: *Te Whāriki*	Analysis and links to ideologies and models
	wary of generalising from single observations. • Assessment contributes to evaluation, revision and development of the program. • Children are encouraged to make self-assessment of achievement of learning goals. • Needs of children, not assessment, determine the curriculum. • Assessment of the early childhood environment (safety, routines, regulations, resources, and people) is integral to evaluating the potential of the setting and program.	the curriculum and the environment for meeting children's needs.

Research as a driver for change in early childhood curriculum

The purposes of this brief review of what a curriculum is are twofold: first, it is important to be able to identify what sort of curriculum is being espoused; and second, it is important to be able to identify the strengths and weaknesses of the approach taken. No model of curriculum is perfect, which is why so many teachers use eclectic models, which include key ideas from many models, and it is consequently very hard to evaluate the effectiveness of the approach taken.

Clearly, in contemporary early childhood education around the world, many curriculum models have drawn on the learner-centred ideology and many have used constructivist theories of learning, drawing on either Piaget's or Vygotsky's theories of how children learn through active participation. This text will draw most heavily on cultural-historical theory as a framework for curriculum design, assessment and implementation, and the strengths and weaknesses of this approach will be explored.

Much of our current understandings of 'what counts' for quality in early childhood curriculum is based on the outcomes of longitudinal studies of children in early childhood settings. Most of these studies (e.g. Abecedarian Project 1999; Osborne & Millbank 1987; Schweinhart & Weikart 1999; McCain & Mustard 1999) demonstrate clear links between the quality of an early childhood program and children's later educational achievement. They also demonstrate positive long-term social outcomes, as well as short-term cognitive gains (Golbeck 2001). Barnett, Jung, Jarosz, Thomas, Hornbeck, Stechuk and Burns (2008) argue that it has been difficult to draw solid conclusions about the effectiveness of one model of curriculum design over another because there have been few studies which used random assignment to groups, and non-experimental studies have often confounded curriculum differences with other program characteristics or the characteristics of the children attending the program. Barnett et al. cite some exceptions to this, where well-designed, randomised controlled trials of different approaches to curriculum, from which conclusions can be drawn, have been carried out. From these studies it can be concluded that direct instruction models produce larger gains on achievement in subject content knowledge over the first couple of years, but that these gains do not persist over time. There is also some evidence that curriculum effects differ according to child characteristics, specifically gender and ability at program entry, but this is not found in all studies. Finally, curricula produce differences in social and emotional outcomes, which may be more persistent than the cognitive outcomes. In particular, direct instruction models have been found to produce worse social and emotional outcomes for children than learner-centred models, which has implications for behavioural difficulties. In their evaluation of the use of the 'Tools of the Mind' curriculum, based on the cultural-historical writings of Vygotsky and Luria, Barnett et al. found that the curriculum improved children's classroom experiences, social development, and cognitive development; however, they expressed little confidence in this outcome. They propose that other curricula, which reflect key principles of Vygotsky's theory, such as Reggio Emilia in Italy, are likely to have similar outcomes. In their analysis of a curriculum based around intentional learning principles, they also conclude the following:

> Moreover, our findings suggest that polarized debates – about academics versus play, child-initiation versus direct instruction, academic skills versus curiosity, and cognitive development versus socialization – pose false choices and are inadequately conceptualised (p. 310).

In a similar vein, Golbeck (2001) states that there are three enduring conflicts which shape decision making around early childhood curriculum:

1. short-term v long-term outcomes;

2. child-centred v teacher-centred; and
3. cognitive development v character development.

However, she argues that a resolution of these enduring conflicts is possible if the next generation of early childhood research addresses how the following issues can be integrated into effective models of curriculum:

- child-regulated learning;
- teacher-guided learning;
- an understanding of the disciplines;
- a scientific model of learning and development; and
- the ecology of the child's learning and development, which includes the child herself, the school or centre setting, and the child's family and community.

Fleer (2003) argues that early childhood teachers have a specialised discourse, which is not readily open to critique, in which prevailing models of child-centred ideology have been reified. There have been a growing number of critiques of learner-centred ideologies, which draw on constructivist understandings of child development and learning (e.g. Dahlberg, Moss & Pence 1999; Woodhead 1998). Much of this critique is based on cross-cultural research, which highlights that the research based on a minority of children from North American and western European countries is not relevant to children from all cultures and that assumptions about children can be challenged (see, for example, Rogoff 1990, 1998; Dahlberg, Moss & Pence 1999; Goncu 1999). In western conceptions of childhood, the idea of 'learning by doing' – children having hands-on opportunities for learning – is sacrosanct, and is a key tenet of learning for most early childhood practitioners. Yet recent research highlights that this is not the case in all cultures and that learning through observation of others is much more common in other cultures (Rogoff 1990; Fleer & Williams-Kennedy 2002).

Much recent writing has effectively merged cultural-historical theory and critical pedagogy approaches to curriculum in order to understand how children are the product of the society and culture in which they are raised and that their development and learning may have differing trajectories, based on the experiences, values and understandings that each community provides. Hohepa and McNaughton (2007), talking about the education of Māori children in New Zealand, argue that teachers need effective strategies to add to the experiences that children bring from home and also to add to their classroom practices:

> The challenge facing educators is to have strategies that enable effective collaborations between professional and family knowledge. With this

> knowledge, two strategies are possible: to add to the proper literacies of family and to add to the effectiveness of classroom instruction (p. 227).

In a similar vein, Mejia-Araz and Rogoff (2001) state:

> Children's personal and family histories of participation in different forms of learning need to be recognised and understood in order to build on the children's familiar ways of learning. Teachers, and other adults whose aim is to foster children's learning can help children learn new ways of learning and also strengthen familiar traditional ways, by recognising and adapting school practices to cultural variations in the traditional modes of learning (p. 20, in Fleer 2003, p. 77).

Fleer (2003) considers that the way forward for early childhood education is to build a new 'community of practice', using Wenger's (1998) terminology, in which teachers use a range of cultural tools to work with children and their families to build on the social and cultural strengths that they bring to their learning. Cultural-historical theory, based on Vygotsky's theory and the more recent work by Rogoff, Lave, Wenger, Fleer and others provides a useful theoretical framework, which includes the personal, interpersonal, social, historical and cultural influences on children's learning. Fleer (2005, p. 6) argues that:

> the term 'cultural-historical development of children' more closely captures the dynamic and complex nature of the interlacing (Vygotsky 1997) of institutional structures, cultural belief systems and the dynamic processes of children engaged in daily activity with other people (p. 6).

REFLECTION 2.7

1. Thinking about early childhood centres or junior school classrooms you have been in recently, can you identify the dominant model of curriculum used in this setting?
2. What did you perceive as the strengths of this approach to curriculum?
3. What were the roles of teachers and children in this curriculum?
4. Were there any weaknesses to the approach that you could identify, and how could they be rectified?
5. Is there a dominant view of curriculum noted? If there is, what does this mean for the cultural diversity of the group of children?

Summary

In this chapter we have examined the question 'What is a curriculum?' and have sought to present the range of ways in which curriculum can be classified. The categories that were introduced, and that were field-tested on international curricula, gave insights into the kinds of models, theories and approaches that sit under a particular curriculum. We learned that curriculum contains four essential components: Goals/Outcomes; Content; Methods/Approaches; and Evaluation/Assessment. We also problematised curriculum in relation to the diversity of cultures across and within communities. We have added some informed content to the confused discussion on curriculum that was had by Kiri, Gemma, Kelly and Anna. In the next chapter we examine curriculum modelling, and specifically examine a curriculum model which was built upon cultural-historical theory.

References

Abecedarian Project (1999). (http://www.fpg.unc.edu).

Apple, M. (1979). *Ideology and the curriculum*. Boston: Routledge & Kegan Paul.

Apple, M. (1982). *Education and power*. New York: Routledge.

Aubrey, C. (2004). Implementing the Foundation Stage in reception classes. *British Educational Research Journal*, 30(5), pp. 633–56.

Barnett, W.S., Jung, K., Yarosz, D.J., Thomas, J., Hornbeck, A., Stechuk, R. & Burns, S. (2008). Educational effects of the Tools of the Mind curriculum: A randomized trial. *Early Childhood Research Quarterly*, 23, pp. 299–313.

Bernstein, B. (1996). *Pedagogy, symbolic control and identity: Theory, research, critique*. London: Taylor & Francis.

Bobbitt, F. (1918) [1913]. *The curriculum*. Bouston: Houghton Mifflin.

Bredekamp, S. (1987). *Developmentally appropriate practice in early childhood education programs: Serving children from birth through aged 8*. Washington DC: National Association for the Education of Young Children (NAEYC).

Bredekamp, S. & Copple, C. (1997). *Developmentally appropriate practice in early childhood education programs* (revised edn). Washington DC: NAEYC.

Bruner, J. (1960). *The process of education*. Cambridge MA: Harvard University Press.

Bruner, J. (1963). Needed: A theory of instruction. *Educational Leadership*, 20(8), pp. 523–32.

Bruner, J. (1996). *The culture of education*. Cambridge MA: Harvard University Press.

Dahlberg, G., Moss, P. & Pence, A. (1999). *Beyond quality in early childhood education and care: Postmodern perspectives*. London: Falmer.

Department for Education and Employment (2000). *Curriculum guidance for the Foundation Stage*. London: Department for Education and Employment.

Dewey, E. & Dewey, J. (1915). *Schools of tomorrow*. New York: E.P. Dutton.

Elliot, J. (1998). *The curriculum experiment: Meeting the challenge of social change*. Buckingham: Open University Press.

Fleer, M. (2003). Early childhood education as an evolving 'community of practice' or as lived 'social reproduction': Researching the 'taken for granted'. *Contemporary Issues in Early Childhood*, 4(1), pp. 64–79.

Fleer, M. (2005). Developmental fossils – unearthing the artefacts of childhood education: The reification of 'Child Development'. *Australian Journal of Early Childhood*, 30(2), pp. 2–7.

Fleer, M. (2010). *Early Learning and Development: Cultural–historical concepts in play*. Melbourne: Cambridge University Press.

Fleer, M. & Williams-Kennedy, D. (2002). *Building bridges: Researching literacy development for young indigenous children*. Canberra: Australian Early Childhood Association.

Foucault, M. (1977). *Discipline and punish: The birth of the prison*. New York: Vintage.

Gagne, R.M. (1970). *The conditions of learning* (2nd edn). New York: Holt, Rinehart & Winston.

Giroux, H. (1981). *Ideology, culture and the process of teaching*. London: Routledge.

Giroux, H. (1989). *Schooling for democracy: Critical pedagogy in the modern age*. London: Routledge.

Giroux, H. (2006). *America on the edge*. New York: Palgrave Macmillan.

Golbeck, S.L. (2001). Instructional models for early childhood: In search of a child-regulated/teacher-guided pedagogy. In S.L. Golbeck (ed.), *Psychological perspectives in early childhood education*. Mahwah NJ: Lawrence Erlbaum Associates (pp. 3–34).

Goncu, A. (ed.) (1999). *Children's engagement in the world: Sociocultural perspectives*. Cambridge: Cambridge University Press.

Hirst, P. (1974). *Knowledge and the curriculum: A collection of philosophical papers*. London: Routledge & Kegan Paul.

Hohepa, M. & McNaughton, S. (2007). Doing it 'proper': The case of Māori literacy. In L. Makin, C. Jones Diaz & C. McLachlan (eds), *Literacies in childhood: Changing views, challenging practices*. Sydney: MacLennan & Petty (pp. 217–29).

Holland, J.G. (1960). Teaching machines: An application of principles from the laboratory. *Journal of the Experimental Analysis of Behaviour*, 3, pp. 275–87.

McCain, M. & Mustard, J.F. (1999). *Early years study: Reversing the real brain drain*. Final report to the Government of Ontario, Canada (http://www.childsec.gov.on.ca).

Ministry of Education (1996). *Te Whāriki. Early Childhood Curriculum*. Wellington: Learning Media.

Ministry of Education (2007). *The New Zealand Curriculum*. Wellington: Learning Media.

Ministry of Education (1999). *The National Kindergarten Curriculum*. Republic of Korea. Korea (translated by Ki Sook Lee and Eunhye Park).

Ministry of Education (2006). *The Kindergarten Program* (Revised). Ontario, Canada (retrieved February 2009: http://www.edu/gov.on.ca).

Ministry of Gender and Community Services (2003). *Parents' and Caregivers' Guide for Household and Communities: Child development practices*. Republic of Malawi.

National Agency for Education (2006). *Lpfo 98* (Curriculum for preschool). Stockholm: National Agency for Education.

OECD (2006). *Starting Strong II. Early childhood education and care*. Paris: Organisation for Economic Co-operation and Development (OECD).

Osborne, A.F. & Millbank, J.E. (1987). *The effects of early education*. Oxford: Oxford University Press.

Rogoff, B. (1990). *Apprenticeship in thinking: Cognitive development in social context*. Oxford: Oxford University Press.

Rogoff, B. (1998). Cognition as a collaborative process. In D. Kuhn and R.S. Siegler (eds), *Handbook of child psychology*, Vol. 2, 5th edn (pp. 679–744). New York: John Wiley.

Schiro, M.S. (2008). *Curriculum theory: Conflicting visions and enduring concerns*. Los Angeles: Sage.

Schweinhart, L.J. & Weikart, D.P. (1999). The advantages of High/Scope: Helping children lead successful lives. *Educational Leadership*, 57(1), pp. 76–78.

Scott, D. (2008). *Critical essays on major curriculum theorists*. London: Routledge.

Stone, C.A. (1993). What's missing in the metaphor of scaffolding? In E.A. Forman, N. Minick and C.A. Stone (eds), *Contexts for learning*. New York: Oxford University Press (pp. 169–83).

Tyler, R. (1949). *Basic principles of curriculum and instruction*. Chicago: University of Chicago Press.

Vygotsky, L. (1978). *Mind in society*. Cambridge MA: Harvard University Press.

Vygotsky, L.S. (1997). The history of the development of higher mental functions. In R.W. Rieber (ed.) (trans. M.H. Hall), *L.S. Vygotsky: The collected works of L.S. Vygotsky*, Vol. 4. New York: Plenum Press.

Wenger, E. (1998). *Communities of practice: Learning, meaning and identity.* Cambridge: Cambridge University Press.

White, J. (1982). *The aims of education revisited*. London: Routledge & Kegan Paul.

Wood, D., Bruner, J. & Ross, G. (1976). The role of tutoring in problem solving. *British Journal of Psychology*, 17, pp. 89–100.

Woodhead, M. (ed.) (1998). *Cultural worlds of early childhood*. London: Routledge.

Chapter 3

Development and learning – how views of development shape how curriculum is framed

In this chapter we will explore the concepts of 'development' and 'learning' in relation to curriculum development. It will be argued that how we think about these concepts shapes how we develop curriculum for the early years. Development, defined as an internal and evolving process, will be examined in relation to 'Developmentally Appropriate Practice' and development as a cultural-historical interaction will then be discussed in the context of changing views on early childhood curriculum.

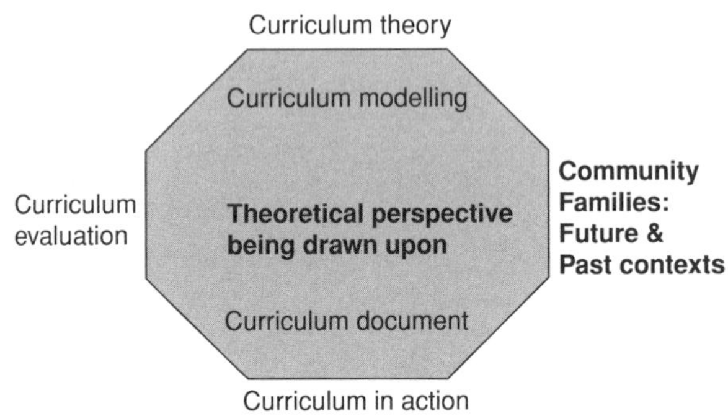

Figure 3.1 Curriculum development pathway – child development and learning

Development and curriculum

REFLECTION 3.1

What assumptions do we have about children, childhood, learning and development?

When we look at curriculum documents prepared by early childhood professionals from a range of countries we notice differences in what they value in terms of:

- development and learning.
- children and childhood.

These values are reflected in what they want their curriculum to do, and thus in what the outcomes for children and society will be. Three examples of curriculum statements are given below.

In the first example, Carlina Rinaldi (2006) is being interviewed about her views on curriculum in the context of the important work being done in Reggio Emilia, Italy for early childhood education:

> As a reaction against people who classify us in Reggio as working with an emergent curriculum, I have been thinking about a concept that might be called a 'contextual curriculum'. Our interpretation of the concept of curriculum starts from the assumption that children have a stunning mastery of many languages and an appreciation that 'other minds' can share their own different beliefs and theories . . . *If* the curriculum is conceived as a path or journey, it will be a path or journey that has, in our opinion, to sustain these competences as fundamental values for knowledge and for life (p. 205).

REFLECTION 3.2

What assumptions do you think underpin the curriculum developed in Reggio Emilia? Record your views.

The second example is drawn from the Nordic region. Einarsdottir and Wagner (2006) highlight the main principles that underpin curricula and childhood values in the countries of Denmark, Sweden, Norway, Iceland and Finland, and the regions and provinces of the Aaland Islands, Farore Island, and Greenland:

> Child and family policies are based on Nordic ideology and traditions, emphasizing democracy, equality, freedom and emancipation, solidarity through cooperation and compromise, and a general concept of the 'good childhood,' or what life should be like for all children . . . Nordic people generally view childhood as important in its own right, not simply [as] a platform from which to become an adult. Among the practical

> exemplars of this viewpoint is that Nordic children typically begin formal school later than children in most other parts of the industrialized world, so they have both time and freedom during the early childhood years to play and to explore the world around them, unencumbered by excessive . . . supervision and control by adults (pp. 4, 6).

REFLECTION 3.3

What do you think would be the main focus for the curriculum content developed in the Scandinavian countries? Record your views.

In the final example, an extract has been taken from position papers produced by the National Association for the Education of Young Children (NAEYC) in the United States. These papers result from a highly consultative process with the early childhood community about what they believe is important for young children, curriculum, and the professionals who work with families and children to deliver the curriculum outcomes. In the extract, a summary of what early childhood professionals believe is important for curriculum is given. As you read this extract think about what the US community values in relation to children and childhood development:

> Construct comprehensive systems of curriculum, assessment, and program evaluation guided by sound early childhood practices, effective early learning standards and program standards, and a set of core principles and values: belief in civic and democratic values; commitment to ethical behavior on behalf of children; use of important goals as guides to action coordinated systems, support for children as individuals and members of families, cultures, and communities; partnerships with families; respect for evidence; and shared accountability. Implement curriculum that is thoughtfully planned, challenging, engaging, developmentally appropriate, culturally and linguistically responsive, and comprehensive, and likely to promote positive outcomes for all young children (NAEYC 2003, p. 1).

REFLECTION 3.4

What assumptions do you think underpin the curriculum developed by NAEYC? Record your views.

What we notice in these statements from the US, the Nordic region and Reggio Emilia is a range of views about children and about what is important for their learning and development. Reggio Emilia has positioned children as capable and competent learners who are part of the collective community, and the curriculum must be built with these assumptions in mind. In the Nordic countries, children are highly valued and should be given time and space in which to play and be children. The curriculum must be respectful of the youngest citizens in their communities. In the US, children are to be respected as individuals with needs and democratic rights. The curriculum must cater for and engage children in developmentally appropriate ways, but be responsive to cultural diversity.

REFLECTION 3.5

Think back to the ideologies and examples of curriculum outlined in Chapter 2. Try to identify the theoretical influences that are under each of these curricula.

REFLECTION 3.6

Local curriculum

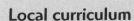

- How are children viewed in the document? What language is used to describe them?
- What content is valued? – e.g. democracy, subject knowledge, domains such as social and emotional.
- How is knowledge framed? – e.g. divided into areas, holistic, absolute, general, detailed and specific, related to community, politically oriented, culturally diverse.
- How is progression organised (or not)? – e.g. stages, journey, community defined and embedded, related to school-based curricula, development as traditionally defined through ages and stages.
- Who decides on the content? – e.g. government, licensing agencies, community, professional associations, the early childhood professional delivering the program.

Use the responses to these questions as a basis for determining the relationship between your curriculum and how children are positioned in your community. An analysis of a country's curriculum documents gives great insights into how children and childhood are perceived. An important and basic assumption, upon which these constructions are based, is child development. In the next section, the concept of child development will be examined and discussed in relation to curriculum.

CURRICULUM AND CHILD DEVELOPMENT

In this section we will look at two different theoretical examples of the concept of child development in relation to curriculum development. The first example (introduced earlier, in the NAEYC position statement), is known as Developmentally Appropriate Practice (DAP). This view of development has been influential in early childhood education across a number of English-speaking countries for at least 20 years. The second example draws upon cultural-historical theory, and has progressively gained more attention over the past 5–10 years. The latter theory is less well understood, and as such, slightly more explanation about this theory is given.

DAP view of development

In their 1997 position paper on curriculum the NAEYC stated:

> Because we define developmentally appropriate programs as programs that contribute to children's development, we must articulate our goals for children's development. The principles of practice advocated in this position statement are based on a set of goals for children: what we want for them, both in their present lives as they develop to adulthood, and what personal characteristics should be fostered because these contribute to a peaceful, prosperous, and democratic society (p. 4).

The paper argues that the curriculum and the practices that result from curriculum planning are based on knowledge of child development and learning, of the needs, strengths and interests of individual children, and of the social and cultural context of children.

Development as expressed in the NAEYC paper focuses on a view that children evolve incrementally. Here the age of children is significant. What can be expected of a 2-year-old will be different from what can be expected of a 5-year-old. This view of development is quite common in many communities of European heritage, and can be found in many documents related to young children, particularly in the US, Australia, and the UK. You can see how this is used to frame understandings about children's development. Conduct a search of the term 'Developmentally Appropriate Practice' and you will see how development is viewed as something occurring within the child. According to this perspective, developmental trajectories are predictable, and stable, unless there is some biological problem (internally generated or mediated from the external world).

DAP as a perspective for framing curriculum development suggests that practices must meet the developmental expectations that have been identified as occurring in relation to children's ages and stages of development. Curriculum which is built on this view will frame outcomes for children in ways which highlight different ages. For instance, curriculum for infants will be very different from the curriculum for 5-year-olds. Work by Allen and Morotz (1989) exemplifies this very clearly:

> Developmental milestones are major markers or points of accomplishment in children's development. They are made up of important motor, social, cognitive and language skills. They show up in somewhat orderly steps and within fairly predictable age ranges. Essentially, milestone behaviors are those that mostly normally developing children are likely to display at approximately the same age. . . . The failure of one or more developmental milestones to appear within a reasonable range of time is a warning that a child may be developing a problem and should be observed closely (p. 5).

Rogoff (2003) offers an alternative perspective. She argues that schooling structures reinforce the importance of age in curriculum through having classes of children who are all the same age. However, she reminds us that having classes of the same age is not related to children's development, but is instead an educational practice that was introduced in a particular historical period as a result of the effects of industrialisation on communities and families:

> With the rise of industrialization and efforts to systemize human services such as education and medical care, age became a measure of development and a criterion for sorting people. Specialized institutions were designed around age groups. Developmental psychology and pediatrics began at this time, along with old-age institutions and age-graded schools (p. 8).

The practice of separating children into classes and 'rooms' (i.e. the babies and toddlers room) in terms of their age became an accepted educational practice and is something that is usually not questioned. This particular organisational structure is generally consistent with curriculum that draws upon DAP for its framing and implementation. This view of development provides a strong basis for curriculum organisation because it relates development to age and suggests that children and curriculum are related according to developmental age.

In recent times, the NAEYC has included direct references to culturally appropriate practices, in recognition that variations in children's development will arise due to cultural practices and beliefs. This view was added to the first version of the NAEYC position statement. It added to DAP the idea that practice should also be culturally appropriate and linguistically sensitive to children's life experiences. This meant the NAEYC position statement continued to frame development in terms of children's ages, but suggested that variations in children's development from this framework could be expected. Researchers have argued that this positions many cultural groups as being bolted onto the dominant European heritage developmental trajectories and practices (Dahlberg, Moss & Pence 1999; Mallory & New 1994; Rogoff 2003).

A significant body of cultural research challenges the idea that development is defined by age. This research therefore also challenges the idea that development and age can be used for defining and constructing curriculum. For instance, Nsamenang and Lamb (1998), in their study *Nso children in the Bamenda Granfields of Cameroon, West Africa*, suggest that in that area:

> children are progressively assigned different roles at different life stages depending on their perceived level of social competence rather than on their biological maturation (p. 252).

These expectations are not based upon the age of the children or on what they can or cannot do. Children with greater social competence are those who have had more life experiences at an earlier age. These life experiences will in turn have an impact on their development. It is clearly important to identify the full range of theoretical views of development which can inform curriculum in early childhood education.

A cultural-historical view of development

Vygotsky (1998) suggested that a child's chronological age was not a reliable criterion for determining a child's development. He argued that 'development as a continuous process of self-propulsion is characterized primarily by the continuous appearance and formation of the new which did not exist at previous stages' (Vygotsky 1998, p. 190). Whilst the developmental perspective has dominated psychology and early childhood education for the past century, Vygotsky has argued that this perspective sees development as a linear path, where deviations from 'the normal path' can be considered as 'diseases' of development (1998, p. 191). Educators look for and expect particular behaviours, and when they are not forthcoming, concern is expressed about the individual.

In his time, Vygotsky argued for a different perspective. He suggested that development is a dialectical process 'in which a transition from one stage to another is accomplished not as an evolving process but as a revolutionary process' (1998, p. 193). He argued that a dialectical approach invites the teacher to be continually projecting learning beyond the child's current capacities, in ways which connect with the child's growing sense of themselves in their communities/institutions. This perspective encourages early childhood professionals to examine context as well as the children's zones of proximal development when making judgments about children and when planning for learning. Thinking of development as a revolutionary transition provides an alternative conceptual framework to the more traditional ideas used in documents such as the NAEYC position statement on DAP. It helps us move beyond the present developmental age-oriented conceptual framework for informing curriculum. This cultural-historical view of development highlights the contexts the child participates in (e.g. early childhood centres, family) and the specific child's lived experience. An example of what this looks like in practice shows us how participation in the family provides opportunities for development, and compares this to what children experience in educational settings, such as childcare centres:

> *At home:* It is 6.00 pm and the Peninsula family are preparing their evening meal. The father cooks a meat and pasta dish. He then retreats from the kitchen and the mother serves up the meal into four bowls. Lizzy, who is 16 months, is seated in a highchair. She is given a bowl and spoon. Andrew, who is five, Nick, who is four, and JJ, who is three, all sit at the table. The mother leaves the kitchen and the children begin eating. Andrew makes long and very loud howling noises. He moves about the table between the children's bowls, squirting tomato sauce into the bowl of anyone who wishes the sauce. Nick takes his food and moves into the lounge room and continues to eat, whist watching TV. JJ eats a small portion of his food and then walks around the house whilst eating. Lizzy is left in the kitchen, strapped into her highchair. She eats for a short period and then makes soft sounds, as though indicating she would like to be let out of the highchair. The parents occasionally appear in the kitchen for brief periods, but are generally busy with their own activities elsewhere in the house (Fleer 2010).

> *In the childcare centre:* All the children are seated at tables waiting for their lunch meal to be served. JJ is sitting under an easel in close proximity to the lunch tables. He moves backwards and forwards beneath the easel. The teacher goes over to JJ and takes his hand and physically moves him to the table. He is compliant. He sits for a short moment and then raises his body, in a standing up position, shuffling his chair five metres from the tables, and back to the table when asked by the teacher. The food arrives and he sits facing the table, with his feet lying across the table next to his lunch bowl. He is asked to take his feet off the table by his teacher. He does so (Fleer 2010).

There are few demands placed upon the children in the Peninsula family at meal times when they are at home. They are free to move about whilst eating. Although the family meal begins in the kitchen at a table, there is no expectation that the children need to stay there or to be seated whilst eating. This is the family practice for the children. However, when the children attend an early childhood centre or school the practices and expectations are very different. The children are expected to sit and wait for their meals at the table, to stay seated, and to sit in a particular manner whilst eating. Whilst the family does not demand this of them, the institutions they attend do make these demands. At home the children experience a kind of geographical grazing. They are able to effectively and easily combine eating with other activities. They are able to physically manage eating their meals whilst walking, talking and attending to other activities. Though they do drop a small amount of food, they expertly manage their food and the other activities. In the institutional settings, they meet new demands – waiting, sitting still, and fixed point eating. This is very different from geographical grazing, and creates a development opportunity for the children. When we examine the institutions that children participate in we learn about different opportunities for learning and development that are generated across families. These different demands upon the children generate different developmental opportunities. This is a cultural-historical view of development, where the child's interaction with their social and physical world, as mediated by the family or the institutions the child attends, determines the developmental trajectory. Development is not viewed as being located within the individual child and related to how old they are, but as something that foregrounds the relations between the child and their social and physical world – and their changing relationship to it.

Having a revolutionary transitional perspective on development allows teachers **to foreground the social situation of development** rather than focusing on ages and stages of development:

> The social situation of development represents the initial moment for all dynamic changes that occur in development during the given period. It determines wholly and completely the forms and the path along which the child will acquire ever newer personality characteristics, drawing them from the social reality as from the basic source of development, the path along which the social becomes the individual. Thus, the first question we must answer in studying the dynamics of any age is to explain the social situation of development (Vygotsky 1998, p. 198).

The social situation of a child is dependent on the society and cultural context in which the child lives. Different cultural contexts foreground particular social situations, which in turn position children to actively engage and take up particular ways of learning and participating within their communities (see Fleer 2010 for further explanation of this view of development).

A universal view on child development positions some children from some families in deficit. As suggested by Rogoff, Mosier, Mistry and Göncü (1998), we need to begin to understand 'the development of children in the context of their own communities' and this requires the 'study of the local goals and means of approaching life' (Rogoff, Mosier, Mistry & Göncü 1998, p. 228). In the example of the Peninsula family, development is viewed in the context of family life and life within early childhood centres and schools.

Hedegaard (2005) has researched the construction of childhood and development within the framework of the institution (for example, school, child care, preschool, family, clubs, sporting groups), the society and the individual. She argues that development is not something that exists within the child, but rather something that takes place when the child participates in the activities of their cultural community. When the development of the child within their cultural community does not match what is expected or accepted as the 'normal' developmental trajectory by an institution such as a school or an early childhood centre, conflicts arise. She argues that the **problem lies not within the child, but rather within the institution**. In this situation, the teacher is blind to the possibilities of both the diversity among children and the potential for creating different developmental trajectories within the institution. Hedegaard (2009) argues that when children enter a new societal or institutional context, where expectations and practices are unfamiliar, children experience demands which result in a crisis situation. She outlines three main perspectives (see Figure 3.2):

- the *societal perspectives* that set up the conditions for institutional practice, both through political material conditions and through traditions that can be found in the dominating value positions in a society;

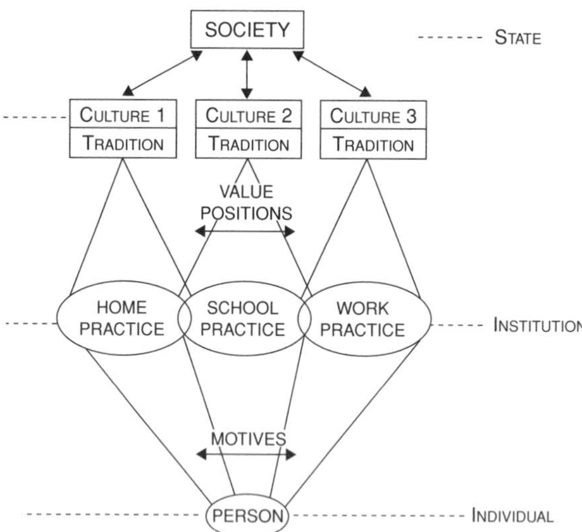

Figure 3.2 A model of children's learning and development through participation in institutional practice (Hedegaard 2009)

- the *institutional perspectives* with their different practices, such as the ones we find in home and school; and
- the *person's perspectives* (i.e. the child, the mother, the father, or the teacher), which are reflected in the person's motives and personal values.

Hedegaard's model can be more easily understood if we examine a practical example of a common institutional practice. Group time is common in early childhood centres and schools. Children are expected to participate in group time in a particular way. That is, they must sit still, pay attention to the person speaking (usually the teacher) and not engage in anything else whilst doing this. For example, they are not usually allowed to hold something in their hands or talk to the children near them, as such activities are deemed to distract from the main purpose of the group. This is an institutional practice which does not necessarily reflect what occurs in children's homes. Children must learn this institutional practice in order to engage in it effectively. In schools, children experience group time in many different ways: they may be gathered together as a group when they arrive at school, they are usually asked to be seated at desks for extended periods of time, and they usually move to different activities as a group, as shown below in Figure 3.3.

We can see the significance of these demands on children when we compare the amount of movement at home with the amount in school. In Figure 3.4 we see that for the Peninsula family at home, there is a great deal of movement over a 50-minute period. In contrast, Figure 3.5 is an observation of Andrew at

Figure 3.3 Activity at school captured through video technology (Fleer 2009)

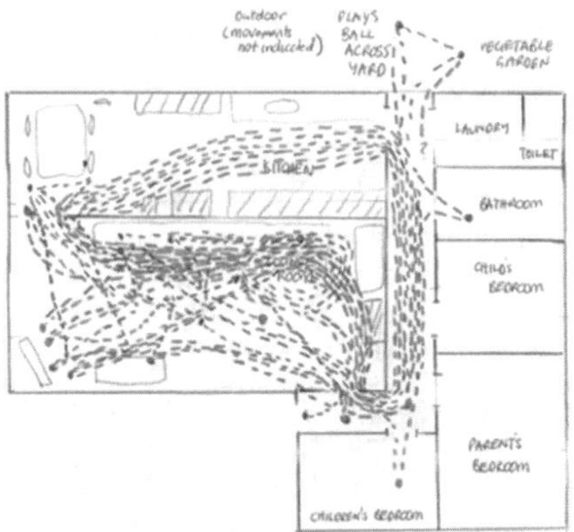

Figure 3.4 Movement at home (Fleer 2008)

school over a 90-minute period. We note very little movement at school when compared with what occurs at home. This represents a significant difference in practice for Andrew. He would require great effort to sustain limited movement for that period, and it puts significant demands upon him.

We can learn more about children's development when we focus on the institutions that children participate in, and consider the demands and possibilities that are generated through activity in those institutions. A cultural-historical perspective on development examines the relations between the child and the institutions the child participates in, including the family. This is a very

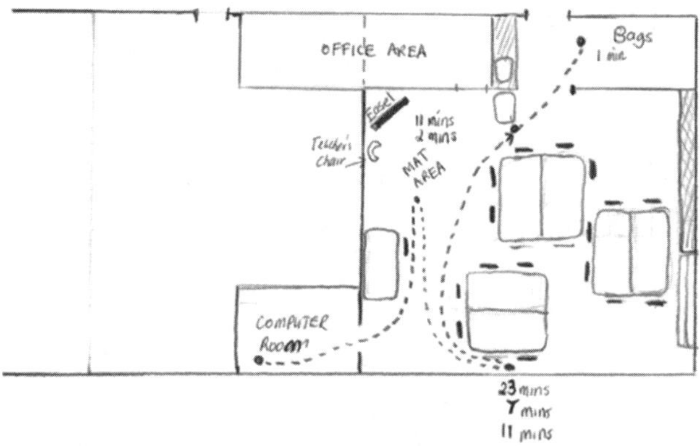

Figure 3.5 Movement at school (Fleer 2008)

different view of development from that of an evolving internal process, where the focus of attention is usually just on the child. This newer perspective views development as possibilities and demands across institutions in relation to the child. The relations between cultural and natural elements – the child's biological process of development and the cultural experience of development – are dialectically related: the cultural and natural elements are thought of as two sides of the same coin. This view of development is different from more traditional thinking, and must be considered when thinking about curriculum development.

REFLECTION 3.7

A cultural-historical curriculum

Imagine that you are a curriculum writer. Your task is to create a curriculum document that uses cultural-historical theory of development to frame the content.

- How would children be viewed in your curriculum?
- What language would be used when describing them from a cultural-historical perspective?
- What content would be valued in your cultural-historically derived curriculum?
- How would knowledge be organised?
- How would progression be presented in your curriculum?
- Who decides on the content?

There are further examples of curriculum and child development throughout this book. The examples in this chapter illustrate the link between how a curriculum document is written and framed and particular perspectives on child development. It is always important to be mindful of what view of child development underpins the curriculum being used. Understanding this relationship helps teachers engage with and critique curriculum innovations that emerge (and they will) over the course of their careers. This means teachers are able to interpret curriculum, rather than simply be consumers of it. You will explore more of these ideas in the following chapter, where we focus on interpreting curriculum.

Summary

This chapter has been about recognising the assumptions held in relation to child development within the curriculum. How child development is theorised is significant because it acts as the backbone on which the curriculum content is placed. It frames what we pay attention to in terms of curriculum knowledge, how we conceptualise progression, and how we implement the curriculum. These ideas can be seen in the following three quotations. We began with three views on curriculum, all from different countries. The chapter concludes with three statements from these same authors and countries. These quotations show how curriculum development is a neverending process.

Imperatives in curriculum: Reggio Emilia, Italy

> My attempt to develop the idea of 'contextual curriculum' arises from my wish to be understood by those who use the language of curriculum and believe in the importance of curriculum. For us in Reggio, *progettazione* is a word that is very dear to us, and is something different from curriculum. *Progettazione* is a strategy, a daily practice of observation-interpretation-documentation. When I speak of 'contextual curriculum', I am really attempting to explain the concept of *progettazione* (Rinaldi 2006, p. 206).

Imperatives in curriculum: Nordic countries

> However, increasing emphasis on academic learning (which many Nordic scholars and practitioners view as an 'invasion' from other countries) encroaches on both the value and the time for childhood play, as each

> Nordic country in turn produces national curriculum guidelines and restructures early childhood teacher preparation, often to more closely mirror professional preparation of elementary school teachers (Einarsdottir & Wagner 2006, p. 6).

Imperatives in curriculum: NAEYC Position Statement (1993: currently under review)

The common elements defined what all early childhood professionals must know and be able to do. They include:

- demonstrate an understanding of **child development** and apply this knowledge in practice;
- **observe and assess children's behavior** in planning and individualizing teaching practices and curriculum;
- establish and maintain **a safe and healthy environment** for children;
- **plan and implement developmentally appropriate curriculum** that advances all areas of children's learning and development, including social, emotional, intellectual, and physical competence;
- establish supportive relationships with children and implement developmentally appropriate techniques of guidance and group management; establish and maintain positive and productive **relationships with families**;
- support the development and learning of individual children, recognizing that children are best understood in the context of **family, culture, and society**; and
- demonstrate an understanding of the early childhood profession and make a commitment to **professionalism** (pp. 5–6).

References

Allen, K.E. & Marotz, L.R. (1989). *Developmental profiles: Birth to six*. New York: Delmar Publishers Inc.

Dahlberg, G., Moss, P. & Pence, A. (1999). *Beyond quality in early childhood education and care: Postmodern perspectives*. London: Falmer Press.

Einarsdottir, J. & Wagner, J.T. (2006). *Nordic childhoods and early education: Philosophy, research, policy and practice in Denmark, Finland, Iceland, Norway, and Sweden*. Greenwich CT: Information Age Publishing.

Fleer, M. (2008). Keynote paper presented at the ISCAR pre-conference workshop on *Cultural-historical approaches to children's development*, 8 September 2008, San Diego (http://www.iscar.org/section/chacdoc).

Fleer, M. (2009). Using digital video observations and computer technologies in a cultural-historical approach. In M. Hedegaard & M. Fleer (eds), *Studying children: A cultural-historical approach*. Maidenhead UK: Open University Press (pp. 104–17).

Fleer, M. (2010). *Early Learning and Development: Cultural–historical concepts in play*. Melbourne: Cambridge University Press.

Hedegaard, M. (2005). Strategies for dealing with conflicts in value positions between home and school: Influences on ethnic minority students' development of motives and identity. *Culture and Psychology*, 11, pp. 187–205.

Hedegaard, M. (2009). Children's development from a cultural-historical approach: Children's activity in everyday local settings as foundation for their development. *Mind, Culture and Activity*, 16, pp. 64–81.

Mallory, B. & New, R. (1994). Introduction: The ethic of inclusion. In B. Mallory & R. New (eds), *Diversity and developmentally appropriate practices: Challenges for early childhood education*. New York: New York Teachers College Press (pp. 1–13).

NAEYC (1993). *A position statement of the National Association for the Education of Young Children: A conceptual framework for early childhood professional development* (http://www.naeyc.org/about/positions.asp, accessed 17 October 2008).

NAEYC (1997). *A position statement of the National Association for the Education of Young Children: Developmentally appropriate practice in early childhood programs serving children from birth through age 8* (http://www.naeyc.org/about/positions.asp, accessed 17 October 2008).

NAEYC (2003). *A position statement of the National Association for the Education of Young Children Early childhood curriculum, assessment, and program evaluation* (http://www.naeyc.org/about/positions/cape.asp, accessed 17 October 2008).

Nsamenang, A.B. & Lamb, M.E. (1998) Socialization of Nso children in the Bamenda Grassfields of Northwest Cameroon. In M. Woodhead, D. Faulkner & K. Littleton (eds), *Cultural worlds of early childhood*. London: Routledge (pp. 250–60).

Rinaldi, C. (2006). *In dialogue with Reggio Emilia: Listening, researching and learning*. New York: Routledge.

Rogoff, B. (2003). *The cultural nature of human development*. Oxford: Oxford University Press.

Rogoff, B., Mosier, C., Mistry, J. & Göncü, A. (1998). Toddlers' guided participation with their caregivers in cultural activity. In Woodhead, Faulkner & Littleton (eds), *Cultural worlds of early childhood* (pp. 225–49).

Vygotsky, L.S. (1998). *The collected works of L.S. Vygotsky*, Vol. 5, R.W. Rieber (ed.), M.H. Hall (trans.). New York: Kluwer Academic/Plenum Press.

CHAPTER 4

CURRICULUM AS A CULTURAL BROKER

This chapter highlights how early childhood practices are enacted in different cultural communities and related to curriculum decision-making processes. These examinations will be used to show how different curricula are informed by alternative perspectives on development and learning, and by their political contexts. A case study of teacher practice will be used to show how this process is related to a cultural-historical perspective. Research emerging from the use of cultural-historical theory as an informant of the early childhood curriculum will then be used to discuss curriculum as a cultural construction affecting a range of stakeholders, including teachers, families, children, communities and policy makers.

REFLECTION 4.1

In this chapter we will examine the issues raised by Kiri, Hui Lee and Mandy. Do you share their concerns?

Kiri: I don't see what all the fuss is about really, as we have two curriculum documents in my country that dictate what we should be doing anyway: *Te Whāriki* and the *New Zealand Curriculum*.

Hui Lee: In my context we only have one – *Nurturing Early Learners. A framework for a kindergarten curriculum in Singapore*.

Mandy: We have just had our first document developed. It is a national early years learning framework for Australia – *Belonging, Being and Becoming*. But each of our states and territories has its own curriculum as well.

Four-year-old Ava was very interested in *Dora the Explorer*. Ava had many of the *Dora the Explorer* DVDs and her preferred bedtime reading was usually a *Dora*

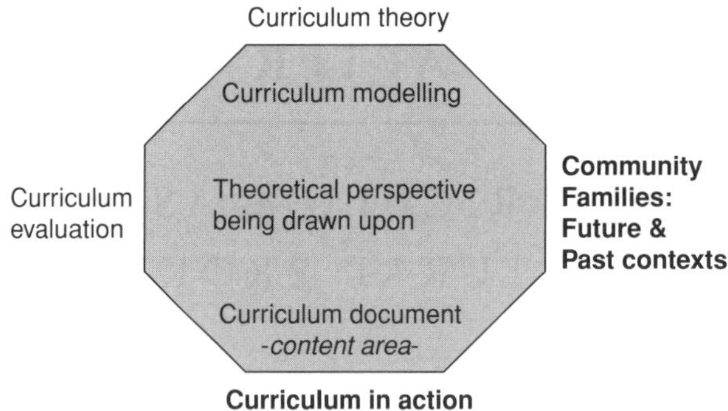

Figure 4.1 Curriculum development pathway – cultural broker

the Explorer book. When grocery shopping with her father, Ava always selected the *Dora the Explorer* flavoured yoghurt, and at home she played with her *Dora the Explorer* craft materials and building blocks. Ava brushed her teeth with her *Dora the Explorer* toothbrush and slept under her *Dora the Explorer* blanket doona. Ava also enjoyed listening to music on her *Dora the Explorer* CD player, and would play online games on a *Dora the Explorer* website, which is designed for young children. On her first day at kindergarten Ava took her *Dora the Explorer* backpack and wore her favourite *Dora the Explorer* dress. She wanted to take a *Dora the Explorer* DVD and book to share with the other children, but her father said she wasn't allowed. The enrolment letter from the kindergarten had stated quite clearly that children were not to bring toys, books, DVDs or other materials from home. The letter said this was because the children could lose or break their toys, and because they might have trouble sharing them with the other children. The kindergarten also said that it was important for the children to experience a range of different activities at the centre, and that they should not be distracted from their learning by toys brought from home. Ava thought this was an unfair rule, but her father pointed out that she was still allowed to use her *Dora the Explorer* backpack and wear her *Dora the Explorer* dress. When Ava arrived at kindergarten she quickly made friends with two other girls, both of whom had *Dora the Explorer* bags and were wearing *Dora the Explorer* clothes.

Dora the Explorer was an important part of Ava's life. Ava had quite a sophisticated understanding of Dora, and she readily identified with the other girls at her kindergarten who also shared her interest. However, one of Ava's first experiences at kindergarten, through her father's interaction with the enrolment letter, suggested that her interest in *Dora the Explorer* was not something she could bring into the centre.

This example raises questions about how the early childhood curriculum operates as a cultural broker in early childhood education, a 'broker' being someone or something that communicates (or 'mediates') between parties. In business, a 'broker' might mediate between a buyer and seller (for example, when people sell their houses they use a real estate agent to mediate the purchasing relationship). Educationally, the phrase 'curriculum as a cultural broker' refers to the idea that the curriculum has the potential to mediate children's cultural experiences with what they learn at their centres or schools. In Chapter 5 we will discuss the idea of 'dual socialisation' (Wise & Sanson 2000), where children experience and learn to manage social and learning expectations that differ between home and centres. Thinking about the curriculum as a cultural broker is a way of addressing the issues that can arise from dual socialisation, allowing us to think about how the curriculum can work to mediate children's home and centre learning experiences.

An important part of thinking about the curriculum as a cultural broker is reflecting on the beliefs and values we have about what and how young children learn in early childhood programs and the early years of school. Some teachers see value in using the curriculum as a cultural broker to support children's learning. However, other teachers may be more like Ava's teacher, and believe that children should not be distracted from what the teachers see as the core work of early childhood education by artefacts brought from children's own 'cultural worlds'. These teachers might believe that toys derived from television programs such as *Dora the Explorer* do not provide appropriate learning experiences for young children. These are important debates for teachers to have, as they affect how teachers design and implement curriculum. In the future, this particular debate could well become increasingly important as the lives of families, children and communities continue to change. In recent years we have already witnessed enormous change in how young children are positioned in society. In part, this change has derived from advances in technology, but it is also related in many countries to the rise of consumerism and the idea that young children are viable markets for companies wishing to sell their wares (Edgar & Edgar 2008). When combined with the increasing cultural and socio-economic diversity experienced by many communities, we can see that it is important to reflect on the role that curriculum has in relation to what and how young children are growing up and learning, both within their homes and communities, and within their early childhood centres and schools. As Cannella (2005) argues, teachers need to engage critically with their assumptions about what it is that they are attempting to achieve in centres and schools. As she states:

> The various professionals in the field of early childhood education can join together to take immediate political action regarding the material and political conditions in which the field is functioning and as directly related to the everyday lives of children. First, we can explore, learn about and accept diverse forms of knowledge from the children and communities within which we work. Until we appreciate the physical bodies, experiences and knowledges of the traditionally marginalised, our concerns for children will never be realised. Second, we should develop practices in care and education settings that are critical in nature, that continuously ask the questions: Whose knowledge is being taught? Who decided that the knowledge was important? What happens to individuals and groups within the use of this knowledge or these methods? How are various individuals and peoples being represented? Who is being helped? And who is hurt? (p. 33).

Reflecting on the broker: What should the curriculum mediate?

Some teachers were discussing the idea of using the curriculum as a cultural broker. They were talking about whether or not they should welcome the artefacts children bring from home as a basis for learning. In Box A you will see that one teacher thought it was important to recognise these artefacts, whilst another teacher felt the curriculum could be offering the children other opportunities.

BOX A

Teachers discussing the idea of using the curriculum as a cultural broker

Teacher 1: If the thing that is really interesting them is this McDonald's toy, you could still look at it and say, 'OK, what else can you do with that toy?' Do you want to take it over and paint it, or make a replica in clay or do you want to take it to

continued »

Box A continued »

the sandpit?' Because anything that the child brings in, if it is of value of to them, I think we should be allowing the child to use it appropriately. Just whizzing it around is not so good, but try to encourage them to use that as a stimulus for something that is appropriate. But then again, maybe they might need a little bit of time to just whiz it around because Mum doesn't let them do it either, so perhaps that can be appropriate at times too.

Teacher 2: I am selective at what I greet warmly, creatures and things I believe have potential for learning, but McDonald's toys, I believe there are other things they could be doing and there are lots of things they could learn about. It is about what you value as play and learning (Edwards 2009, p. 67).

These teachers engaged in some thoughtful reflection about how they saw the role of children's cultural artefacts in the early childhood curriculum. Teacher 1 believed that if an artefact was of value to the children, she should try to think of ways to use it as a basis for learning. Teacher 2, however, felt quite strongly that the kindergarten was a place for the children to participate in other types of activities, for example, learning about 'creatures' rather than playing with toys they have collected from McDonald's. Both of these perspectives are valid, and both are drawn from the beliefs the teacher holds about how children learn. When engaging in this type of debate it can be useful to draw on theoretical knowledge about children's development and learning to further inform our beliefs. In this way we can work from a theoretically informed perspective to explain why we are making particular curriculum decisions.

One such theoretical perspective which can be useful in this situation is provided by cultural historical theory, which describes how children's development evolves in relation to the social and cultural activities their communities have developed over time (other teachers might find other perspectives useful, including, for example, constructivism or poststructuralism. These are ideas which we discussed in some detail in Chapter 3). Working from a cultural historical perspective means teachers can use these ideas about children's learning and development in a cultural context to understand the processes and outcomes associated with learning. Because cultural-historical theory values the historically developed knowledges and practices within communities as central to learning and development, teachers using this approach can think about the curriculum as working to mediate children's cultural experiences, in addition to offering the more traditional experiences often found in early childhood settings. McNaughton (2002) argues that a curriculum should recognise the familiar, while being wide enough to also recognise the unfamiliar, so that the teacher acts as a broker between familiar and unfamiliar cultural knowledge.

Mediating culture and curriculum: A cultural-historical perspective

An important idea in Vygotsky's cultural-historical theory is that a child is born into a world that already contains all the knowledge, beliefs and practices that the community developed over time prior to the child's birth. This is easier to think about when we consider our own time of birth, or perhaps that of our children, siblings or other family members. Take your own time of birth and reflect on what type of technologies were available at the time and the beliefs and practices that surrounded childbirth and the care of infants. For example, 40 years ago in many western births, infants were taken away from their mothers and cared for in nurseries in the hospital, and mothers fed their babies according to quite rigid 4-hourly schedules. More recently, many infants 'room-in' with their mothers from the moment of birth and mothers feed their infants on demand. Clearly, knowledge about, and practices of, caring for newborn babies have changed over time within the community. In part, this is where the notion of 'cultural-historical' comes from. This idea is important to cultural-historical theory because it suggests that the collective historical knowledge of the community is what a child actually begins to learn from birth, and this learning in turn drives their development. We can see this in the following quote from Vygotsky (1987), about how an infant develops into adulthood:

> How does the organised and rational behaviour of man develop from the chaos of uncoordinated movements of the child? As far as we can judge by today's scientific data, it develops from the planned, systematic and autocratic influence of the environment in which the child happens to be. His conditional reactions are organised and formed under the predetermining influence of elements of the environment (p. 158).

In our earlier example, the 'predetermining influence of the elements of environment' might refer to an infant rooming-in with their mother after birth. From the moment of birth, the activities and cultural practices of their community begins to organise their interactions with their mother (and others). This is a very important idea, because it reminds us that what and how children develop and learn changes over time. This is why we can see differences in development and learning over generations. Think back through your own family over a number of generations and consider the activities your great grandparents might have participated in as a child compared with those you participated in.

In cultural-historical theory, children's participation in cultural experiences promotes learning and leads to development. Through participation in the cultural community, children carry forward the cultural knowledge they have acquired, but also transform this knowledge and use it in new ways within the community for themselves and others. For example, when she was born, Ava had no existing knowledge of *Dora the Explorer*. However, the community in which she lived did, and so through participating in this community (watching DVDs, reading stories, etc), Ava acquired knowledge about *Dora the Explorer* which she carried with her when she first went to kindergarten. Ava attempted to use this knowledge within the kindergarten setting when she began to make friends with two other children she recognised as also having the same knowledge. This is where we can think about how cultural-historical theory might help teachers reflect on how to use the curriculum as a cultural broker. For Ava and the other girls, an important set of cultural knowledge was derived from their experiences of *Dora the Explorer*. Their experience of *Dora the Explorer* was set within a broader social and cultural experience, in which the consumption of goods, such as DVDs, books, clothing and other items is encouraged through mass marketing and considered an economic imperative by many governments. If we look at the girls' knowledge and experience from this perspective we can see that their interest in and commitment to *Dora the Explorer* is an outcome of their participation within a particular community. If the curriculum is to act as a cultural broker for these girls, it might need to include *Dora the Explorer* as a basis for learning, rather than treating *Dora the Explorer* as a potential 'distraction' from learning. This approach to curriculum was implemented by some teachers who used a child's interest in *Thomas the Tank Engine* to structure a series of learning experiences for the children (Yelland, Libby, Lee, O'Rourke & Harrison 2008, p. 123). You can read about this example in Box B.

BOX B

The curriculum as a cultural broker

Brendan loved the Brio train set at preschool and he brought in his much-cherished *Thomas the Tank Engine* DVD from home. We used this as an opportunity to build shared connections as well as literacy learning. We explained to the children that later in the day we would watch the DVD. We talked about going to the movies and what happens and what you need. Some children then wanted to make tickets so they cut up paper and some added letters and numbers and others drew pictures of trains. Another child was interested in food at the movies and said 'We need popcorn!' and so we made some popcorn and the children helped put this in paper bags for later. At the end of the day the children were invited to come to the movies if they wanted to. Some of the children helped the teachers set up chairs in rows. The tickets were distributed to those who wanted to go. We lowered the blinds to reduce the light and then asked the children to hand in their tickets. At times these roles were undertaken by the children and the smell of the popcorn and the physical environment helped to create an atmosphere of excitement. The children were captivated by the experience and some didn't want to leave when their parents arrived to take them home. These parents then delayed going and joined in the experience.

This example shows how an artefact from the child's participation in popular culture can be used to teach children socially valued skills and knowledges, such as those associated with various forms of literacy. Here the teachers used the curriculum as a cultural broker to mediate between Brendan's home experiences of *Thomas the Tank Engine* and his classroom experience of literacy learning.

Brokering curriculum for the future?

The example provided in Box B is useful because it draws on one of the key ideas of cultural-historical theory, which is that the artefacts of a child's community work to shape their development and learning. However, when considering the idea of 'curriculum as a cultural broker', it is also important to think about how else the curriculum is related to the broader social and cultural situation in which children, families and teachers are involved. Two further ideas from cultural-historical theory which can be helpful when considering this aspect of the curriculum are related to what is called 'social situation' and 'joint-collective enactment in social activity' (Davydov & Kerr 1995, p. 15).

'Social situation' refers to they way in which children's development can be further promoted when they begin to attend school, kindergarten or child-care because they have broadened or changed their social situation in a way that exposes them to other people, practices and knowledge. 'Joint-collective enactment in social activity' is about the way children's development is furthered when children and adults are able to bring their collective knowledges and interactions together in order to learn in ways that change both the adult and the child. In Box B, we saw one example of how the curriculum can be used to mediate a child's learning by drawing on his interest in *Thomas the Tank Engine*. However, it is important to remember that this interest in *Thomas the Tank Engine* is located within a broader social and cultural situation in which consumerism features as both a way of life and as dominant model for the distribution of material wealth. We saw this in relation to Ava, who had an in-depth cultural knowledge of *Dora the Explorer* as a figure who was popular in her community. The sheer number of artefacts associated with *Dora the Explorer* (including yoghurt, toothbrushes and underwear sets, for example) which are available for Ava and her family to purchase highlights the extent to which these items themselves are related to a focus on the consumption of material items.

Many people are beginning to question the social, economic and environmental sustainability of consumerism as a social practice and how its continuation might impact on future generations. This concern poses an educational problem: it is argued that today's children need the skills, knowledge and attitudes to critically engage with consumerism as an economic model and work towards the development of sustainable economic, technological, environmental and social practices (Kalantzis & Cope 2008).

In Box B we saw how the curriculum could be used to mediate Brendan's home and centre learning. However, teachers could use their understanding of cultural-historical theory to extend the notion of 'curriculum as a cultural broker' and focus on 'brokering the curriculum for the future'. Teachers working in this way would draw on the idea that kindergarten is a change in social situation for children through which their participation in the broader community could be examined. This change in social situation provides a context for joint collective engagement between children and adults to occur in ways that allow children and adults to share their perspectives on cultural artefacts such as *Thomas the Tank Engine*. For example, this might mean using the children's interest in *Dora the Explorer* to examine with children where these stories come from, where their money goes when they purchase these items, and what happens to their toys when they have finished with them. In this example, the curriculum moves beyond mediating children's home and school experiences towards helping children interpret and respond to the social situations that are shaping their lives and will impact on them into the future. Box C gives an example of some adults and a child engaged in joint collective engagement around the Wiggles.

BOX C

Joint collective engagement around the Wiggles

The parents of two young children were particularly keen to help their children become aware of how marketing was used to create the desire to purchase particular toys and other artefacts. One day when changing the youngest child's nappy, the older boy discovered a small series of Wiggles stickers which fell out of the empty packet of nappies. Although not a fan of the Wiggles, the older boy peeled the stickers from the label and began sticking them on items of furniture around the home. His father and mother asked him why he was using the stickers and he said he didn't know. His parents then discussed how the Wiggles and the people who produced Wiggles products were interested in children liking them, because the more children liked them the more they would buy Wiggles products and so get more money. The boy thought this was unfair and that the Wiggles should not try to get children's money. Then the family discussed why the stickers might have been placed in the bag with the nappies. Was it to make children happy or to remind children about the Wiggles? Together, they discussed how they would be reminded about the Wiggles every time they looked at their own furniture if the stickers remained where they were. The boy decided to remove the stickers from the furniture. He thought he might give them to a friend instead.

Thinking professionally about brokering curriculum for the future

In the example in Box C, the adults and child engaged in joint collective activity around the Wiggles stickers and were able to examine how the stickers worked as a cultural artefact towards a particular aim within the child's and the adults' social world (i.e. to prompt the family to consume more Wiggles products). This way of looking at children's learning and thinking about the curriculum as a cultural artefact is challenging. When presented to some teachers attending a conference on Curriculum for the 21st Century, these ideas generated much discussion and debate (Edwards 2009). Some teachers felt that it was timely for them to change their practices and consider new ways of engaging with contemporary experiences of the children and families they worked with. Others felt that traditional approaches and practices should be maintained because otherwise children might not have access to experiences such as sand play, using paint or experiencing 'nature'. Another teacher raised a very important question: she asked if it was appropriate for teachers to broker curriculum for the future when the children's family might value and enjoy engaging with consumerism-orientated practices? These are important ideas and questions that early childhood educators need to grapple with.

Interestingly, cultural-historical theory recognises that the past is carried into the present, and the present is carried into the future (Davydov & Kerr 1995). How a community engages with the ideas, knowledges and practices that are carried forward will continue to define what and how young children will learn. This means the field of early childhood education has two tasks to carry out when considering the idea of brokering a curriculum for the future. The first is how children's and families' experiences are defining their current and future learning needs. The second is how traditional ideas in early childhood education have been carried into the present and are defining existing approaches to curriculum. What will be interesting for the field to consider is how these two tasks are related to each other and whether or not there truly is need for early childhood education to begin the process of brokering curriculum for the future.

Summary

This chapter has talked about the term 'curriculum as a cultural broker' and used cultural-historical theory to suggest that one way this can occur is by using children's home learning experiences to mediate learning in the centre or school. The chapter has also considered the need to look at children's learning and development beyond the home and to see how broader social and cultural practices are related to what and how young children are learning. This broader perspective suggests that children need to acquire a range of skills so that they can participate in contemporary and future society. A cultural-historical perspective shows how education and interactions with people within education can create opportunities for children to develop these skills. How the field of early childhood education works towards the idea of brokering curriculum for the future depends on how children's learning and development is currently perceived and the relationship existing approaches to curriculum have to these questions.

References

Cannella, G.S. (2005). Reconceptualising the field (of early care and education): If 'western' child development is a problem, then what do we do? In N. Yelland (ed.), *Critical issues in early childhood education*, Maidenhead UK: Open University Press, pp. 17–39.

Davydov, V. & Kerr, S. (1995). The influence of L.S. Vygotsky on education, theory, research and practice. *Educational Researcher*, 24(3), pp. 12–21.

Edgar, D. & Edgar, P. (2008). *The new child: In search of smarter grown-ups*. Melbourne: Wilkson Publishing.

Edwards, S. (2009a). *Early education and care: A sociocultural approach*. Sydney: Pademelon Press.

Edwards, S. (2009b). Curriculum for the twenty-first century. Crèche and Kindergarten Association Centenary Conference, Gold Coast, Queensland.

Kalantzis, M. & Cope, B. (2008). *New learning: Elements of a science of education*. Melbourne: Cambridge University Press.

McNaughton, S. (2002). *Meeting of minds*. Wellington: NZCER Press.

Vygotsky, L. (1987). *The Collected Works of L.S. Vygotksy*, Vol. 3, R.W. Rieber & J. Wollock (eds). New York: Plenum Press.

Wise, S. & Sanson, A. (2000). *Childcare in cultural context: Issues for new research*. Australian Institute of Family Studies Research Paper No. 22. Melbourne: Australian Institute of Family Studies.

Yelland, N., Libby, L., O'Rourke, M. & Harrison, C. (2008). *Rethinking learning in early childhood education*. Maidenhead UK: Open University Press.

CHAPTER 5

INTERPRETING EARLY CHILDHOOD CURRICULUM

This chapter will refocus attention on the ideas examined Chapters 1 to 4, positioning teachers in relation to their centres or classrooms as cultural communities, their positions in the broader cultural community and their reading of early childhood education as a cultural practice. The ways in which teachers construct curriculum in relation to document, time, history and place will be explored. The need for teachers to actively engage in ongoing professional learning is highlighted.

REFLECTION 5.1

In this chapter, we will explore the issues raised by Gwendolyne and Kiri about the relationship between teachers' knowledge about child development and curriculum documents.

Gwendolyne: In Malawi, our curriculum is a guide to help the carers know more about children's development and what concepts they should be teaching.

Kiri: But what about this idea of it being constructed and contested – how does that work if we have a written curriculum?

Take a few moments now and think about your own view of how children learn. How does it relate to your local curriculum document?

Jill is a teacher who participated in a research project about teachers' interpretations of the early childhood curriculum (Edwards 2004). As part of this project Jill was asked to reflect on her understanding of the curriculum. Jill has worked in early childhood education for over 20 years and during this time developed an interpretation of curriculum which emphasises the relationships she sees

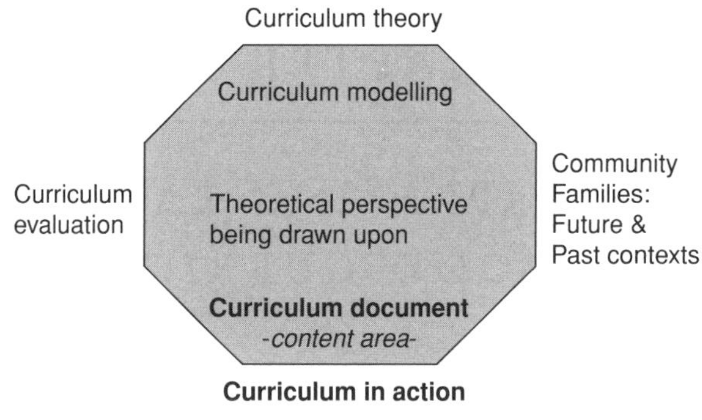

Figure 5.1 Curriculum development pathway – interpreting curricula

between children's participation in their communities and their learning in the classroom. Jill's comments are presented in Box A.

BOX A

Jill's interpretation of the early childhood curriculum

Well people talk about curriculum, but I think perhaps I have defined my own curriculum over a period of time, and as I mature and see needs within the society. I am certainly looking at our society as very egocentric, where the rights of the individuals are being put forward predominantly, often to the disadvantage of the group, and one person impacting on an entire group of others can cause detrimental effect. I see that we need to develop small societies where we look at the care and concern for all, and as part of a Christian school with that as a base to its philosophy then we develop that within our program – a program of care and concern. So I am developing a small society within the area of the preschool.

Jill's thoughts remind us that the early childhood curriculum is not interpreted in a social or cultural vacuum. By describing the society she sees children inhabiting, and noting the particular religious affiliation of the school she works in, Jill highlights how curriculum is influenced by the contexts in which it is developed and implemented. We know from Chapter 2 that curriculum frameworks draw on various differing perspectives of childhood, learning and development to promote what they consider to be important for children's learning. Furthermore, Chapter 3 presented examples from Italy, the Nordic region and the US to show how each region valued different aspects of learning and development because of the way they related to its communities' goals. Some of the goals cited referred to democracy, solidarity and cooperation, and others focused on support for children as individuals and members of families. Interpreting the curriculum always involves reference to the social, cultural and community contexts in which curriculum is created and implemented.

Working with early childhood curriculum frameworks

Many countries, states and territories have formal curriculum frameworks for young children. For example, Hong Kong has the *Guide to the Pre-Primary curriculum* and New Zealand has *Te Whāriki*. Documents such as these are intended to guide early childhood professionals in the development of curriculum for young children. Some frameworks are quite detailed and outline what children should be able to do at particular stages and how teachers can support this learning. The UK's *Early Years Foundation Stage* is an example that clearly outlines goals for children's development in areas such as social participation and literacy learning. Other frameworks are less specific, and suggest instead broad values and goals associated with children's participation in early childhood education. For example, Sweden's *Curriculum for the Pre-School* has a series of goals and guidelines that focus on what the preschool environment should provide children with to support their participation in the community.

Early childhood curriculum frameworks are usually text-based, and even when presented online they can seem like static documents far removed from the reality of working with children. However, it is important to remember that the implementation of a curriculum framework is actually a dynamic process that involves teachers interpreting how the curriculum will be used in their classrooms. This process depends on how teachers read particular ideas about learning and development as they are presented in the documents they use. The Singaporean curriculum *Nurturing Early Learners: A framework for a kindergarten curriculum in Singapore* is presented in a series of sections. One of these sections is titled 'How young children learn'. Box B provides the definition of learning that is used in the Singaporean curriculum.

BOX B

Definition of learning used in the Singaporean early childhood curriculum framework

Young children are natural and active learners. They enjoy observing, exploring, imagining, discovering, investigating, collecting information and sharing knowledge. Adult and peer support are vital to this process [learning] as children extend their individual skills and knowledge of the world to more elaborate and complex ways of learning, doing and understanding (Pre-school Education Unit, Ministry of Education, Singapore 2003, pp. 10–11).

The definition presented in Box B might be interpreted in practice as providing opportunities for children to engage with information and ideas in a group context with their peers and other adults. Teachers might plan learning experiences that see children exploring particular concepts through play, through discussion with others, and by drawing on more formal resources such as books, posters or charts. When the written definition of learning is interpreted in this way the curriculum begins to emerge as a process involving children and adults in the construction and sharing of knowledge.

The Scottish document, *A Curriculum Framework for Children 3 to 5*, is also presented in sections. This document considers key aspects of children's development and learning and suggests that these occur in domains of development. One of the domains covered is Communication and Language. Box C outlines how this aspect of development is considered in the Scottish curriculum.

BOX C

Definition of language development used in the Scottish early childhood curriculum framework

The development of children's skills in language is central to their abilities to communicate in relationships and learning, to understand ideas and to order, explore

continued »

Box C continued »

and refine their thoughts. From birth, children are part of a communication and language system that includes the body language of gesture, facial expression and movement as well as verbal language. Children will bring their own experience of understanding and using language in the home and community to the pre-school setting. Their home language should be valued and encouraged so that children can respond confidently to adults and other children, and express their own needs, thoughts and feelings. It is important to allow children to express themselves in a language in which they are comfortable during free play and social activities (Scottish Consultative Council on the Curriculum 1999, p. 15).

A teacher interpreting the definition provided in Box C might read this as meaning that language for very young children should be seen as non-verbal as well as verbal, written and oral. A teacher might use this definition of language to build on the developing language capacities of an infant as they begin to point at different objects. For example, when sharing a book with the baby the teacher might ask the infant what she can see and discuss with her the different objects presented as the baby points to them. Another teacher might interpret the definition as meaning that children's home languages should be supported and used in the preschool setting. This might involve the teacher becoming familiar with some key words in the child's language or seeking to find resources that are provided in the home language. The way in which the definition of language learning is interpreted means the curriculum begins to take shape, in practice, in a particular way. It is important to remember that the definitions are also usually informed by the beliefs about children, childhood and learning that informed the writing of the curriculum framework in the first place.

Whilst we can see how teachers interpret the curriculum through their actions with children we can also see proof of curriculum interpretation in the different documents teachers use and develop to support their work with young children. An example of a curriculum document created by students participating in a unit of study about babies and toddlers is presented in Figure 5.2. These students created a document which reflected their interpretation of how routines could be enacted with babies and toddlers in ways that were responsive and reflective of the children's cultural experiences.

MAKE ROUTINES FUN!

讓日常生活更有趣!!!

Handwashing! 洗手

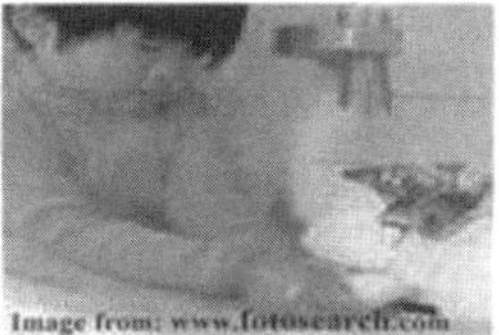

Nappy Change! 換尿布

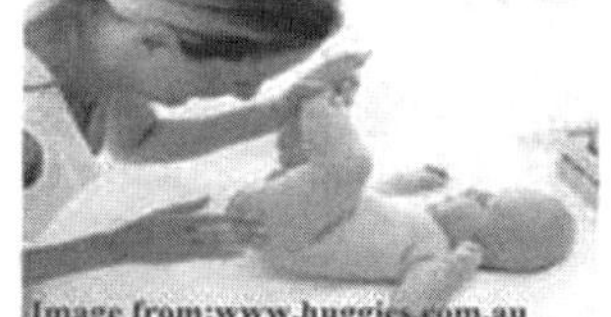

Wash your Hands!
Wash, wash, wash, your hands
Play our handy game
Rub and scrub, scrub and rub
Germs go down the drain HEY!

The Nappy Song
There's a nappy in the sink
There's a nappy on the chair
There's a nappy in the freezer
We are never unprepared
Every corner, ever closet
Every cupboard in the place
Has a nappy waiting just in case

Infants Counsellor

Meal Times! 吃飯

Sleep Times! 睡覺

Pat a Cake
Pat a cake, pat a cake
Baker's man!
Bake me a cake
as fast as you can.
Pat it, and prick it,
and mark it with a

Hush-a-bye Baby
Hush-a-bye baby,
on the tree-top,
When the wind blows
the cradle will rock;
When the bough breaks
the cradle will fall,
Down will come baby,
bough, cradle, and all.

'Singing songs makes routines Respectful, Responsive and Reciprocal!'

歌唱使日常生活受到恭敬、響應和互惠。

Figure 5.2 Documents created by teachers also reflect particular interpretations about curriculum (created by Wan Yang and Michelle Addamo, Monash University 2008)

REFLECTION 5.2

Select a curriculum document for examination (your own or that of another country). Consider the way different aspects of the curriculum present key ideas such as learning and development. How would you interpret these definitions in practice? Compare your interpretations with those of your peers. What similarities and/or differences do you note?

So far we have examined how curriculum frameworks are influenced by the contexts in which they are developed. We have also considered how particular definitions of learning and development might be interpreted in practice by different teachers. Another important aspect of interpreting early childhood curriculum and curriculum frameworks involves understanding how the curriculum can be related to the experiences of children and families in their local communities.

Relating early childhood curriculum to children, families and communities

Research suggests that children's learning and development are best supported when strong relationships are created between children's home and educational experiences (Fleer & Williams-Kennedy 2002). When these relationships are absent from children's educational experiences they are exposed to what Wise and Sanson (2000) call 'dual socialisation'. Dual socialisation occurs when what children experience in their families and communities differs significantly from what they experience in their educational settings. We saw an example of a child experiencing dual socialisation in Chapter 3: at home, Andrew engaged in significant amounts of physical activity and movement, whilst at school he was required to limit his movements and spend time in transitional activities, such as lining up and waiting for his turn. Chapter 3 explained how both home and school were 'institutions' that had expectations of Andrew, and that contributed to his development and learning.

Being aware of the notion of dual socialisation is important because children participate in a range of institutions that work to define how they develop and what they learn. Recognising that early childhood education is one of these institutions helps teachers use their curriculum to create learning experiences that build on children's existing strengths. It is important to remember that attempting to build bridges between home and school experiences does not mean focusing only on children's home practices. Rather, it means using children's existing skills and knowledge practices as a base for furthering their knowledge and increasing their abilities to engage with ideas. Hedegaard and Chaiklin (2005) discuss this idea:

> The task of the teacher who is going to create conditions for learning, so that the learning will be developmental, is to help the child move from the perspective of local events and capacities of everyday life to the perspective of possible events and capacities (p. 65).

Box D provides an example of a teacher working from a Developmentally Appropriate Practice (DAP) (Bredekamp & Copple 1997) approach to curriculum. This teacher developed her learning plans for the children around specific developmental areas, including social, language, cognitive and physical learning development. Whilst valuing the guidance provided to her through the use of such a curriculum, this teacher was aware of the importance of using the curriculum to create a strong relationship between a child's home learning experiences and those in the centre.

BOX D

Example of a teacher creating conditions for learning within the curriculum

Noah is a 3-year-old boy who attends a long day care centre one and half days a week. His parents value lots of discussion in the family home and spend a great deal of time talking about different topics, such as insects and bugs, the human body. The family often visit the local library and enjoy reading together. Noah's home experiences mean that he is very capable of participating in long and detailed conversations about a range of scientific concepts. One day Noah took some library books about the solar system to his childcare centre to show his teacher and the other children. To Noah's delight his teacher used the books and his knowledge about the solar system in her curriculum planning. One of the activities involved each of the children representing one of the planets. The teacher showed the children by using their bodies how the planets rotated around their own axis to create day and night-time, and also how the planets also circled the sun to create a year. The next time Noah was reading the books with his parents he was able to discuss the location of the planets within the solar system and talked about the distance of each planet from the sun. One evening whilst on a family walk he commented on the setting sun and said, 'The sun does not go to bed, the earth turns around.'

In this example we can see that the teacher acknowledged the child's and family's interest in science and learning. Although the teacher worked within a developmental curriculum, she did not reject Noah's interest in the solar system as inappropriate for a 3-year-old child. Instead she used his expertise and knowledge to inform the curriculum and to provide Noah and the other children with some scientific knowledge. Importantly, Noah was able to take this knowledge home and to use his learning with his parents as they re-read the books before returning them to the library. This example shows how a curriculum framework can be interpreted in relation to family practices around learning to extend children's conceptual knowledge.

The role of professional learning in curriculum interpretation

Interpreting curriculum involves teachers in constant professional learning. Professional learning is important for early childhood teachers because it can help teachers learn more about the latest theoretical perspectives in early childhood education and explore how these might relate to the children, families and communities they work with.

There is, however, growing research evidence around the challenges that teachers can face in changing their beliefs and practices. For example, McLachlan, Carvalho, Kumar and de Lautour (2006) found that over 50 per cent of the teachers in their study of how teachers support children's literacy had not changed their beliefs and practices since the advent of *Te Whāriki*, instead drawing on previously held understandings of how children learn. As Nuttall (2005) has argued, teachers do not simply apply a curriculum document:

> Instead, curriculum construction is most usefully thought of as an ongoing social construction, constantly reiterated through teachers' syntheses of reflection on their own and others' experiences (particularly those of children and families), constructs drawn from available curriculum frameworks (such as *Te Whāriki*), their own beliefs and value systems, and theoretical informants found in programmes of teacher education (p. 20).

Nuttall (2003) also states that several things need to be taken into account when thinking about teachers implementing curriculum: their initial training; their awareness of various curriculum traditions and models in early childhood education; and their ideas about which aspects are part of the teacher's role. Mitchell and Cubey (2003) have identified several features of effective professional development in their 'Best evidence synthesis': it builds on teachers' existing knowledge; it includes alternative theoretical knowledge and practices; it involves investigation and analysis of data by teachers in their own settings; it involves critical reflection; it includes diversity; it challenges beliefs and practices; and it enhances teachers' insight into their own thinking and actions. An example of this learning process in action is provided through the work generated by the City of Casey teachers.

The City of Casey is a large metropolitan region in Victoria, Australia where groups of teachers are employed by the local municipality to deliver the prior-to-school kindergarten year for 4- and 5-year-old children. These teachers engaged in a professional learning program over two years in which they considered their existing interpretations of curriculum and then engaged in some professional learning about cultural-historical theory to develop alternative ways of working with young children and their families. Initially, most of the City of Casey teachers interpreted learning and development from a developmental perspective and used a form of curriculum that draws on many of the ideas represented in DAP guidelines (Bredekamp & Copple 1997). You can see the teachers' ideas about children's learning as represented in the curriculum in Box E, which provides some examples of how they interpreted curriculum prior to their participation in the professional learning program.

BOX E

Developmental perspectives on learning and development informing teachers' interpretations of curriculum (cited in Edwards 2007, p. 94)

The curriculum is child-centred, initiated, directed, and adult-supported. It considers all developmental areas – social, emotional, cognitive and physical. It should be flexible.

continued »

Box E continued »

My philosophy is that all children have individual needs and develop at different stages. This means the curriculum comes from the children. Their interests/needs/wants are met by planning play-based experiences.

The program is play-based and based on the observed needs, interests and developmental progress of the children.

In these examples we can see a relationship between the particular view of development the teachers are using and their interpretation of curriculum. The teachers understand development to occur in different domains and to occur in particular stages. They use these ideas to plan curriculum that is matched to the children's observed needs, interests and developmental abilities. As the teachers participated in professional learning sessions they learned more about cultural-historical theory and how it differs from developmental theory. The teachers were encouraged to think about theories as different explanations for how children learn and grow. The idea that a theory is not a truth about all children's learning and development was discussed by the teachers. For example, one teacher reflected in her journal that she was not encouraged to question developmental theory at university, and that the theory she was using was never presented as a theoretical perspective – it was a presented as 'fact' about children's development (Edwards 2007).

This example shows how important professional learning is to interpreting curriculum. This teacher had previously viewed developmental theory as fact. Her view of development influenced how she interpreted the curriculum and meant she provided learning experiences based on the children's observed needs and interests. By participating in the professional learning this teacher was able to reflect on how theories are used in early childhood education and became more aware that developmentalism was not necessarily the truth about development. This meant the teacher was able to consider an alternative theoretical perspective for use in her practice.

The teachers in the City of Casey learned more about cultural-historical theory and started trying to use ideas from this theory in their practice. They attempted to observe children in groups and looked for how learning was co-constructed between children and adults instead of focusing on individual developmental domains. The teachers also tried to think more broadly about the cultural experiences children had at home and how these related to their participation in the centres. The teachers began to develop new ideas about children's development, which influenced how they began to interpret the early childhood curriculum. Examples from the teachers' emerging ideas are presented in Box F.

BOX F

Teachers' ideas on learning development after participating in a professional learning project about cultural-historical theory (cited in Edwards 2009)

I now have a greater emphasis on understanding knowledge construction. Otherwise we just used to look at behaviours and make assumptions about it. Observing from a sociocultural perspective is richer; it tells us more about what is happening. We did not used to record the rapport between children.

I now focus more on the quality of interactions between children and adults. I now believe in looking and observing children in groups rather than individually. Looking at my prior notes I didn't really take into account how important and vital the interactions with their peers are.

The interactions are important, to write down what they are doing. I am looking more at what they are doing, what is the other child doing, looking beyond the individual.

From these examples we can see that the City of Casey teachers were beginning to work with new ideas about children's learning and development. The teachers began to interpret the curriculum in new ways, and started to plan learning experiences that were designed to include group learning. The work conducted by the City of Casey teachers highlights the importance of professional learning in interpreting curriculum. Professional learning contributes to ongoing thinking about how different theories of learning and development shape interpretations of curriculum in early childhood education. As one of the Casey teachers suggested, participating in professional learning challenges established ways of thinking and helps teachers interpret curriculum in new ways.

Summary

Interpreting early childhood curriculum is a complex and dynamic process. Some teachers work from government-mandated early childhood curriculum frameworks. Others develop their own curriculum for children based on their understandings of how children learn and develop. Whichever way teachers work, it is important to remember that the early childhood curricula are informed by particular perspectives on childhood, learning and development, and that their goal is to promote learning and developmental outcomes that are valued by the community. Interpreting the early childhood curriculum involves reflecting on these perspectives and considering what they might look like in practice. An important part of interpreting curriculum is considering ways to make links between the curriculum and the home, family and community experiences of children. Curriculum interpretation is also strongly linked to professional learning, which provides opportunities for teachers to reflect on how various theories of learning and development relate to the ways they interpret curriculum for young children.

References

Bredekamp, S. & Copple, C. (1997). *Developmentally appropriate practice in early childhood programs.* (Revised edition.) Washington DC: NAEYC.

Curriculum Development Council (2006). *Guide to the pre-primary curriculum.* Hong Kong: The Education and Manpower Bureau HKSAR.

Department for Children, Schools and Families (2008). *Practice guidance for the Early Years Foundation Stage*. London: Crown.

Edwards, S. (2004). Teacher perceptions of curriculum: Metaphoric descriptions of DAP. *Journal of Australian Research in Early Childhood Education*, 11(2), p. 88–98.

Edwards, S. (2007). From developmental-constructivism to sociocultural theory and practice: An expansive analysis of teachers' professional learning and development in early childhood education. *Journal of Early Childhood Research*, 5(1), pp. 89–112.

Edwards, S. (2009). *Early childhood education and care: A sociocultural approach.* Sydney: Pademelon Press.

Fleer, M. & Williams-Kennedy, D. (2002). *Building bridges: Literacy development for young Indigenous children*. Canberra: Australian Early Childhood Association.

Hedegaard, M. & Chaiklin, S. (2005). *Radical-Local teaching: A cultural historical approach*. Denmark: Aarhus University Press.

McLachlan, C.J., Carvalho, L., Kumar, K. & de Lautour, N. (2006). Emergent literacy in early childhood settings in New Zealand. *Australian Journal of Early Childhood*, 31(2), pp. 3–41.

Ministry of Education (1996). *Te Whāriki. He whāriki matauranga mo nga mokopuna o Aotearoa: Early childhood curriculum*. Wellington: Learning Media.

Ministry of Education and Science in Sweden and National Agency for Education (2001). *Curriculum for the pre-school (Lpfo 98)*. Sweden: Graphium Vastra Aros.

Ministry of Education, Singapore (2003). *Nurturing Early Learners: A framework for a kindergarten curriculum in Singapore*. Singapore: Preschool Unit.

Mitchell, L. & Cubey, P. (2003). *Characteristics of professional development linked to enhanced pedagogy and children's learning in early childhood settings: Best evidence synthesis*. Wellington: Ministry of Education.

Nuttall, J. (2003). Exploring the role of the teacher within *Te Whāriki*: Some possibilities and constraints. In J. Nuttall (ed.), *Weaving Te Whariki: Aotearoa New Zealand's early childhood curriculum in theory and practice*, Wellington: NZCER, pp. 161–86.

Nuttall, J. (2005). Looking back, looking forward: Three decades of early childhood curriculum development in New Zealand. *Curriculum Matters*, 1, pp. 12–28.

Scottish Consultative Council on the Curriculum (1999). *Curriculum Framework for Children 3 to 5*. Scotland: Learning and Teaching Scotland.

Wise, S. & Sanson, A. (2000). *Childcare in cultural context: Issues for research*. Australian Institute of Family Studies Research Paper No. 22. Melbourne: Australian Institute of Family Studies.

Chapter 6

Cultural-historical curriculum in action

In the previous chapters of this book it was proposed that teachers need to understand how curriculum is constructed: by teachers in collaboration with children, families and communities. We begin here with a discussion of the ways teachers make decisions about curriculum. Cultural-historical theory is used as a framework for supporting educators' work with young children in culturally respectful ways. We examine the importance of moving beyond notions of multiculturalism to understandings of how development and learning are enacted in different cultural communities, and the need for early childhood curriculum to enable learning for all children. This chapter also explains how teachers need to have an understanding of the knowledge children bring to their learning and be able to identify opportunities for extending children's learning.

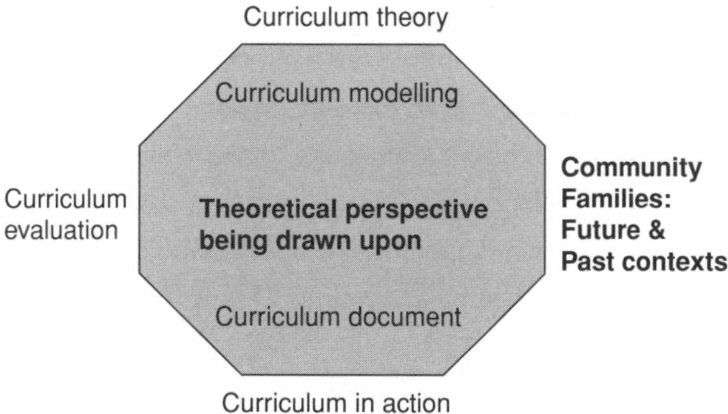

Figure 6.1 Curriculum development pathway – curriculum in action

This chapter will help you answer the question posed by Gemma about curriculum in our opening scenario: 'Isn't that when you talk to parents about what they want in the curriculum?'

Some students studying for a Bachelor of Education were participating in a class preparing for a practicum placement with babies and toddlers. As part of this class the students were examining how cultural-historical theory could be used to develop curriculum experiences for very young children. They participated in a role-play activity where they pretended to be teachers engaged in a professional conversation about the relationship between theory and practice. Box A is a transcript of this role play.

BOX A

Role-play transcript

Kate: How is everyone going observing and planning using a sociocultural approach?

Samantha: I am attempting to get a handle on it. I feel that in all my observations so far I focus on the individual and their interactions, looking at what they are doing and planning to extend and support their interests.

Jacinta: I have only ever used checklists and anecdotal observations before.

Sarita: What do you think of checklists? Do you think it is appropriate for observing children?

Jacinta: Yes I do, because it tells me what the children can't do so I can work on things they are deficient in.

Samantha: What areas of development do you focus on using checklists? Are you willing to try something new?

Bev: I don't think teachers should use a checklist. It's such negative form of marking them, rather than focusing on what the children are doing.

Kate: They may be helpful for monitoring some behaviours, but how do they assist you with planning?

Jacinta: I focus on their development in domains. Don't they need to reach the milestones? Their parents want to know that they are developing normally.

Samantha: What is 'normal'?

Kate: What about their social development?

Jacinta: I guess what I am reading about development in social and cultural contexts means that there could be lots of ways to describe normal. But if I am not focusing on the domains in my curriculum planning what should I focus on when I write up the plan?

continued »

Box A continued »

Kate: I like to focus on interests whilst still trying to extend their skills.

Sarita: I try to focus on the interactions between peers.

Kate: And by skills I don't just mean fine and gross motor skills; I also mean skills such as observing, questioning, social and problem-solving skills.

Samantha: If a child cannot cut with scissors by the time they leave kindergarten, would you as the teacher, Jacinta, feel that it was important to plan fine motor skills activities to 'fix' this developmental area, or would you rather focus on the social interactions, meaning that the child may very well learn to use the scissors by watching and by assistance from peers?

Jacinta: Well perhaps instead of focusing on what they can't do, I could observe: a) what they can do; b) who they do it with; and c) the interactions they have to help each other learn. I guess that includes me, then?

Kate: Exactly!

Jacinta: But even if I observe in this way, how would I develop a curriculum plan?

Kate: I've got a good example: yesterday during an outdoor session a child approached me with a bottle which had a dry sponge in it. They asked me to get it out, which I was eventually able to do. The child then attempted to get it back in, and with my assistance the child was able to bend the sponge in a way that allowed him to fit it back in the bottle. He then continued to ask me to take it out and then he would bend it and put it back in. Reflecting on this, I think I am going to plan an experience with items in bottles and plastic tongs. This can be the basis for my curriculum planning. We can start to talk about the properties of different materials. Which things bend to fit into the bottle and which things don't?

Jacinta: So we are extending the development. Is it the potential learning I plan for?

Kate: That's how I approach it. But it is not only planning for the potential 'skill development'. It's also to promote the interactions between the children and the teachers.

Samantha: Good luck with your observations and planning. It is important for educators to have an open mind and try new approaches.

Understanding cultural-historical approaches to curriculum

Cultural-historical approaches to curriculum focus on how learning occurs between children, teachers and the environment. As Jacinta, Samantha, Kate, Sarita and Bev discussed in their role play, this involves looking at the learning and development that happens in the classroom rather than focusing on particular domains of development, or even thinking about developmental 'norms'. Cultural-historical approaches to curriculum recognise that what is considered 'normal' development depends very much on the experiences children have in their families and communities. Cultural-historical approaches to curriculum use children's existing cultural practices and strengths to work towards particular educational and learning goals. Sadikeen and Ritchie (2009), in their discussion of a Centre of Innovation research project which examined ways to make meaningful links with families and communities, identified working closely with a local Māori elder (kaumātua) in the Taranaki district as enabling the kindergarten teachers to form closer links with families, encourage greater involvement of families in the kindergarten and develop more meaningful learning opportunities for children and families. Their research identified that teachers need to go well beyond tokenistic inclusion of Māori culture, language and knowledges in the curriculum:

> Key ingredients in the Brooklands journey are seen in the dedicated leadership and shared team commitment, the involvement of kaumātua with whom longstanding close relationships have been fostered and nurtured, the daily enactment of welcoming and other spiritual rituals of inclusion and celebration, and the fostering of connection to local iwi (local Māori tribes) and heritage. This validation of the local Māori context can be seen to create bridges towards awakening appreciation and respect for the increasingly diverse and complex cultural heritages converging within our early childhood education communities.

A further example of this in practice is presented in Box B. In this example, a kindergarten teacher reflects on how she used to view independence in the classroom as a desired 'norm' and 'outcome' for children. She goes on to discuss how learning about cultural-historical theory and using this as a basis for curriculum planning changed the way she went about providing materials for the children, and how this led to new learning outcomes for both herself and the children.

BOX B

Curriculum planning from a sociohistorical perspective

Our centre is quite multicultural; however, as a society we value independence. In the Sri Lankan community it is the mother's role to be doing things for children, so these mothers would be neglectful if they didn't spoon-feed their child and help them get dressed. In our centre we are saying to families [that helping children] is not teaching them to be independent, although helping is something they value. We stopped insisting the children put their smocks on themselves. It became less of an issue. Before we would be going, 'Why can't they do it themselves?' Now we just step back and think it is not such an issue. Before we used to say, 'Put the smock on and get to work.' Now it is not a big deal anymore, we just help with that. I think it is probably a more genuine acceptance of other cultures and differences. I think it is very easy to say we accept individual differences and cultural differences without really caring. Like, 'We accept them – but put your smock on yourself.' This is different from tolerance because with tolerance you think 'we tolerate it' but you are not necessarily compassionate about it (cited in Edwards 2007; see also Edwards 2009).

In this example, when the teacher stopped trying to 'teach' independence and worked instead with the children's cultural experience of interdependence, she found that she could more readily help the children access the curriculum. This teacher realised that working in cultural-historical way meant genuinely accepting different ways of learning and being. Instead of saying 'cultural difference is tolerated here', she learned to enact an understanding of cultural difference in her practice. Being able to understand and reflect on the many ways children learn allows teachers to plan for learning in ways that are not only culturally respectful, but relevant to children's lives.

Enacting cultural ways-of-knowing in practice was a key theme emerging from research conducted by Fleer and Williams-Kennedy (2002). In this project Fleer and Williams-Kennedy worked with Indigenous families to video record the many forms of learning that occurred within their homes, families, communities and schools (including child care and formal prior-to-school settings). Families were able to discuss the importance of the 'forms of learning' that occur in their homes and communities. They highlighted how traditional Australian approaches to learning in early childhood education did not necessarily meet the needs of all children. For example, the families discussed how children entering child care maintained their strong connection to family, community, cultural beliefs and expectations: rather than the child operating as an individual unit within the centre, the child was seen to take their family (and obligations to the family) with them when they entered the centre (Fleer 2004). Fleer suggested that recognising the importance of family to these children and communities would mean teachers reconsidering how to connect the curriculum to the children and their experience of family. Important starting points might be around how everyday routines such as picking up and dropping off children are enacted, or how family contributions to the centre are invited, supported and maintained (Fleer 2004).

Beyond multiculturalism: Using cultural practices and engagement to support learning

Understanding how children learn in their families and communities is central to enacting a cultural-historical perspective, because it takes children's cultural knowledge and ways of knowing as a basis for practice. This approach is not the same as focusing on multiculturalism in early childhood education. In the past, teachers have tried to be respectful of children's cultural heritage by acknowledging the role of multiculturalism in society. This resulted in practices which saw centres having 'cultural days' and so forth, where the centre would celebrate particular cultures for a day. Usually this involved eating the food of the selected culture, perhaps reading stories related to the community or learning about the geographical location of that cultural group. This approach to multiculturalism has been termed the 'tourist approach' (Derman-Sparks 1989), because it focuses on 'visiting' different cultural groups throughout the year. The tourist approach has been criticised for emphasising the differences between cultural groups in ways that continue to make mainstream early childhood practices the norm:

> Tourist curriculum is likely to teach about cultures through celebrations and through such 'artefacts' of the culture as food, traditional clothing and household implements. Multicultural activities are special events in

> the children's week, separate from the ongoing daily curriculum. Thus, Chinese New Year is the activity that teaches about Chinese-Americans; a dragon is constructed, and parents are asked to come to school wearing 'Chinese' clothing to cook a 'Chinese' dish with the children, who have the opportunity on this one day to try eating with chopsticks. Paradoxically, the dominant, Anglo-European culture is not studied as such. Christmas is not perceived as an 'ethnic' holiday coming from specific cultural perspectives, but is treated as a universal holiday (Derman-Sparks 1989, p. 7).

Research suggests that when teachers focus on the differences between cultures that they can confuse cultural-historical curriculum with multiculturalism. This means teachers might try to recognise diversity by having cultural days, rather than by understanding that the many ways children learn and develop in their communities shape and impact on the way they interact with the curriculum (Edwards 2006). Remember the teacher from Box B, who shifted her focus from trying to make the Sri Lankan children fit her model of independence to working within the community's model of interdependence. By acknowledging and enacting the cultural and community values around interdependence this teacher moved beyond recognising multiculturalism to working with an understanding of what cultural-historical theory means in action. A further example is provided in Box C, which outlines how a Centre of Innovation kindergarten in Aotearoa New Zealand responded to the question 'To what extent does our entranceway reflect the cultural heritage of this community?' In this example, the teachers, children and local community members worked together to understand how local legends related to their own context and could be used in their centre to provide meaning to the act of entering and leaving the centre.

BOX C

How one kindergarten enacted cultural and community values

A kindergarten survey of parents suggested that families found the entrance and exit to the centre congested. The teaching staff had recently participated in professional learning about enacting bicultural practices and learned how everyday events and

continued »

Box C continued »

objects convey cultural meaning that is just as important as celebratory occasions. The staff decided to work with the children, families and community to develop a new entranceway:

We decided to ask whānau and local iwi about the history of the area (facilitated by our committee president) and to use the information from our term evaluations as a prompt for discussion. During the term we created opportunities to discuss the children's perspectives on the entranceway and recorded this information. For example, when children were changing, putting their shoes away, or getting their lunchboxes, we talked about the most appropriate places for putting their things. We considered these in relation to what we now understood to be appropriate bicultural practice, such as separating hats and shoes from food.

Local iwi and whānau sourced information about the local legends for us and we learned about a local legend of the three whales. This was shared with the children through story, drama, and art experiences. Whānau invited children, teachers and families to visit their property, which is in a location where the mountains that represent the three whales are visible. A grandmother shared her stories about the significance of the property and its situation. We visited our local marae, where the significance of the legend of the three whales and its relationship to the kindergarten were shared with the children and families/whānau. The legend soon became both significant and relevant to us all.

We looked at the data from the evaluation forms again and saw that the comments mentioned the fact that the lockers were right in the doorway and that the doorway served as an exit and an entrance. This had not been mentioned by many parents, but we felt this could have been a result of the questions we had asked and we were reluctant to dismiss the issue. At an end-of-term committee meeting, we summarised the information we had gathered and realised we had developed an understanding of the significance of the legend of the three whales to our cultural heritage. We considered how to represent this legend as one that we felt belonged to us all and that we honoured. Our local iwi endorsed our ideas.

Many different images of whales were represented in our kindergarten throughout this time. Children were dramatising and representing images of whales in their artwork and storytelling. The children made three images out of hardboard that they asked to be hung in the entranceway. These images provoked a great deal of interest from parents and children alike.

Adapted from: http://www.lead.ece.govt.nz/Publications/SelfReview/Appendix1/Kindergarten.htm.

Play and a cultural-historical early childhood curriculum

Traditional approaches to European heritage early childhood curriculum have focused on using play as the vehicle for children's learning. According to this perspective, children learn about the world and acquire conceptual knowledge by participating in freely chosen and open-ended play (White, Toso, Rockel, Stover & Ellis 2007). Curriculum development has involved teachers providing open-ended play-based experiences for children so that children can discover their own learning. This perspective forms a very large part of many western approaches to early childhood education and is still valued by many early childhood professionals for the potential it has to contribute to children's learning. However, in recent years, international research has suggested that open-ended play can be culturally loaded in favour of western-heritage children who typically experience free play in their home environments (Dachyshyn & Kirova 2008). This idea is illustrated by Chang (2003), who talks about how early childhood curriculum has changed in Taiwan due to teacher educators attending western universities. She discusses how open-ended approaches to learning are not necessarily valued by parents or adopted in early childhood programs because they conflict with traditional beliefs around the importance of formal education:

> During the past decade, many Taiwanese teacher educators have acquired their graduate degrees in Western universities and have introduced Western theory of early education to Taiwan, especially seen in the promotion of the value of play for young children. Even though the importance of play has been acknowledged by professors in early childhood education in Taiwan, the pedagogy of learning through play is still not widely accepted by parents or adopted in early childhood programs (Chang 2003, p. 277).

It is important for early childhood educators to understand that how and why children play differs across cultural communities. It is also important to understand how parents and communities might perceive the role of play in children's learning. Children from communities where formal learning or learning by observation is considered important can be confused when offered open-ended play as the basis for the curriculum. Brooker (2005) clearly showed this in an important study conducted in the UK with Anglo-Saxon and Bangladeshi families. In this project, Brooker spent a year in the kindergarten attended by the children and also spent time with their families. Brooker found that the perspectives of the two communities diverged around the idea of play. In the Bangladeshi families direct instruction and observation were seen as important and children spent a great deal of time with other family members and siblings. In the Anglo-Saxon families opportunities for free play were valued and parental interaction during such play was also seen as important.

These family approaches to learning created different beliefs amongst the parents about the characteristics of a 'good' learner. For the Anglo-Saxon parents, a child who was doing well in kindergarten would be 'always busy, always doing something, and coming up and telling you about it, showing you what they're doing' (Brooker 2005, p. 123); the Bangladeshi parents described a good learner as a child who was able to 'listen intently, rather than speak up' in the classroom (p. 123). When Brooker observed the children learning in the kindergarten she noticed that the Anglo-Saxon children were more prepared to learn through play because the curriculum matched their home and community experiences of a 'good' learner. This meant the curriculum disadvantaged the Bangladeshi children because it failed to build on their strengths and capacity as learners skilled in observation and listening, rather than active play. Brooker (2005) provided a description of two children arriving at the centre which outlined in telling detail how the open-ended play experience failed to engage these learners:

> The outer door opened and Amadur and Mohiuddin were shepherded in by their mothers. As it closed behind them, all four stood stiffly just inside the room, staring ahead. Mrs Goode approached them with a welcoming smile: 'Hi there, come on in, lovely to see you! Mums, you can go, these two will be fine. Come on boys.' She took the hands of the 4-year-olds and led them cheerfully towards the sandbox, leaving their mothers to exchange glances and then exit, backwards through the door. Amadur and Mohiuddin stood beside the sandbox looking blank and bewildered. Mrs Goode collected shovels, gave one to each of them and dug industriously herself. After a few moments both boys dutifully squatted on the floor and began to dig, in imitation. They continued this way for some time, and Mrs Goode, after praising their efforts, moved off to another activity. The two boys, who were cousins, slowed their shovelling, stopped, and stared at each other (p. 115).

As a field, early childhood education is undergoing renewal and attempting to build new understandings of curriculum and play that are respectful of the many ways children learn and experience life (DEEWR 2009). Part of this process has involved researchers examining how children's existing cultural knowledge can be supported and extended within the early childhood curriculum. In Chapter 9 this idea is explored using Vygotsky's ideas around how children form concepts and acquire formal knowledge about their world. The chapter explains how children's learning is supported and extended when their everyday experiences are combined with formal knowledge. A cultural-historical approach to curriculum focuses on extending learning beyond the everyday to the development of mature concepts that help children build understandings about how and why their world works.

Extending learning within cultural-historical curriculum

Some teachers from the City of Casey in Victoria, Australia were interested in examining what the children in their kindergartens thought they were learning through play compared with what the teachers believed was being learned (Bruce, Davie, Notman, Kilpatrick, Stewart, Luxford, Hunt, Antoni, Battista, Wilson, Fames, Middleton & Keppick-Arnold 2008). This investigation was based on reading, reflection and professional learning the teachers had undertaken around cultural-historical approaches to curriculum. These teachers worked in small groups, and each group documented the children participating in a different learning experiences. They asked the children what they thought they were learning and reflected on the extent to which the children's responses met their own thoughts about the learning.

One group of teachers set up an open-ended play-based experience that involved the children washing and hanging out dolls' clothes. The teacher thought the children were learning sharing, teamwork and co-operative play skills. She also thought the children would use language and social skills and gain scientific knowledge about evaporation, balance (of the washing line, which tended to fall over when all the unwrung wet clothes were hung on one side of it), and why the clothes were wet. When this teacher talked about the learning with the children she found that they focused on describing the activity, not the concepts or skills she thought they would learn by participating in the play. The teacher wrote that the 'children had difficulty stating specifically what they had learnt, with most saying "I learnt" or "I learnt washing"'.

These children's responses are similar to those obtained in research conducted in two Victorian kindergartens. In this project, teachers set up open-ended play-based experiences for children and noted what they believed the children would learn when they participated in the activities. These children were video recorded whilst playing and later shown the footage of themselves playing with the materials. When invited to discuss what they were learning these children described the activity, rather than the concepts the teachers believed they would learn. For example, one group of children said they were trying to make dirty water clean (the activity), rather than talking about filtering the water (the concept) (Cutter Mackenzie, Edwards & Fleer 2009).

An example of the documentation associated with the teacher research from the City of Casey is presented in Boxes D and E. In these examples, one of the teachers recorded her thoughts about what the children would learn and noted some of the interactions between staff and children.

BOX D

Example 1 from the City of Casey teacher researcher 'Do children know they are learning?' (from Edwards 2009)

Child 1 is doing the washing. Later, Child 2 arrives.

Teacher:	What are you learning?
Child 1:	Nothing.
Teacher to Child 2:	What are you learning?
Child 2:	Hanging up washing.
Child 1:	I'm nearly finished, there's no more soap.
Assistant:	What happens when you mix it round and round?
Child 1:	Bubbles.

(Child 1 picks up a doll's dressing gown that is full of water.)

Child 1:	It's heavy.

continued »

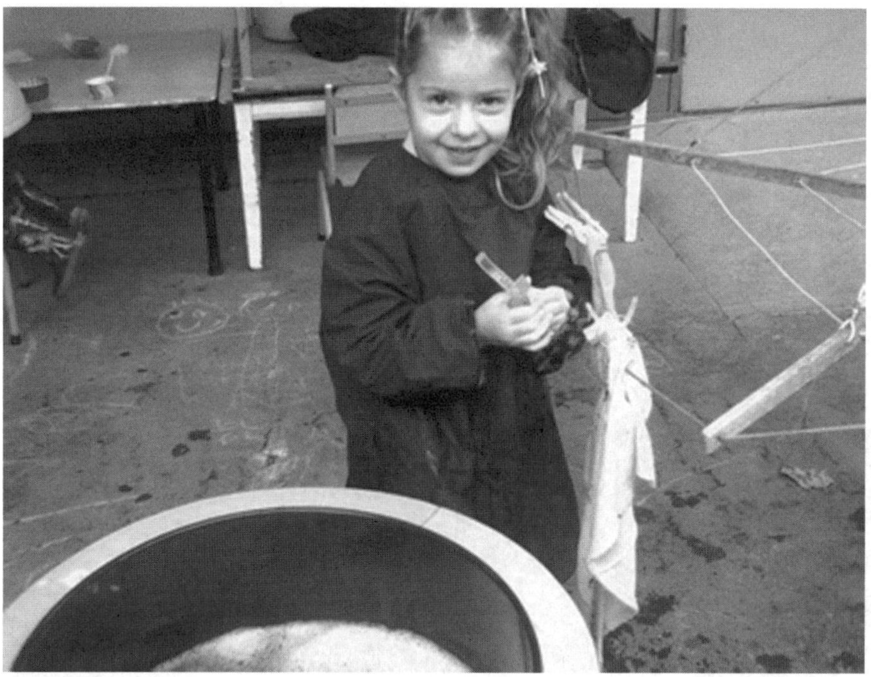

Figure 6.2 Example 1 from the City of Casey teacher researcher 'Do children know they are learning?' (from Edwards 2009)

Box D continued »

Teacher: Why is it heavy?
Child 1: 'Cause there's a lot of water in it.

(All the washing is hung up all on one side, and the clothes line falls over.)

Child 1: (Laughter)
Teacher: What made it tip over?
Child 1: It's too heavy.
Teacher: What can we do?
Child 1: Make it stand up.
Teacher: Come and stand over here and have a look at it. It's heavy on one side. What can we do?
Child 1: (Wearily) There's nothing really I can do.
Teacher: You could put some clothes on that side and see what happens.
Child 1: I should, but I'm not going to.

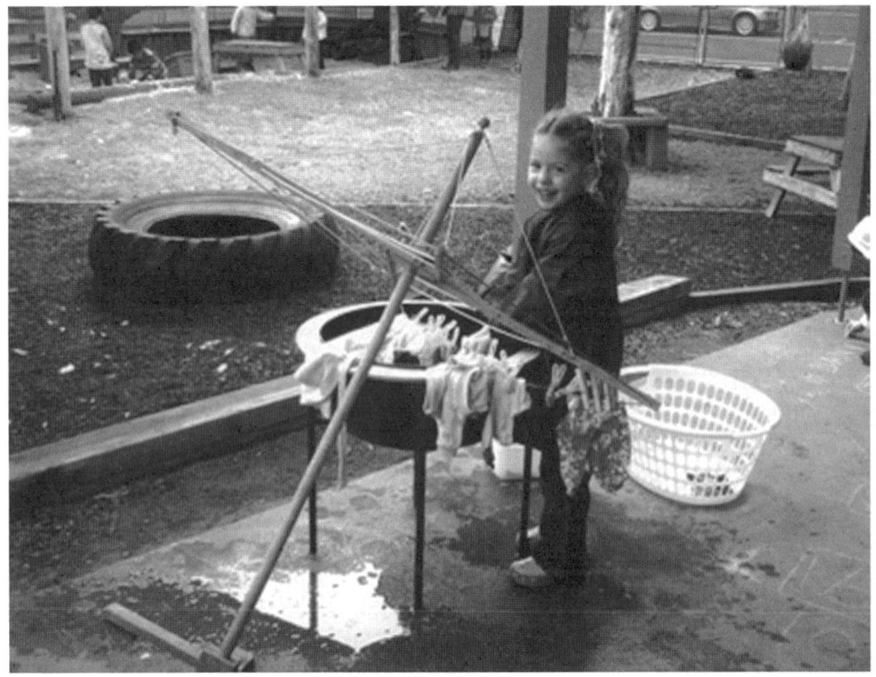

Figure 6.3 Example 2 from the City of Casey teacher researcher 'Do children know they are learning?' (from Edwards 2009)

BOX E

Example 2 from the City of Casey teacher researcher 'Do children know they are learning?' (from Edwards 2009)

A few days later Child 1 was shown some photographs of her at the experience.

Child: That's me, I'm doing the washing.
Teacher: What happened in this picture?
Child: I hung it all up to dry.
Teacher: Did it dry?
Child: It all fell over (laughter) and I picked it up and it just fell over again.
Teacher: What did you learn?
Child: It was too heavy.

It is interesting to note that the child in Box E was able to tell her teacher that the washing line fell over because it was 'too heavy'. However, it was not the washing line that was too heavy – it was the mass of washing on the line, combined with the concentration of clothes on one side of the line, that caused it to tip over. At the start of this play-based experience the teacher had noted that she thought the children would learn about the 'balance of clothes on the line to make it stable, the weight of water and why the clothes were heavy' (Bruce et al. 2008). The observation suggests that participating in the play provided a base for the child's learning, but that more discussion and a focus on the concepts was probably necessary to fully realise the learning.

The teachers involved in this project realised that there was a difference between what they thought children would learn through play and what the children thought they were actually learning. They reflected on their observations and concluded that 'a more active role by the teacher during conceptual development during play appears to be more satisfying for the teacher and valued by the child' (Bruce et al. 2008). These teachers discussed the importance of actively engaging with children during play to help them learn the conceptual knowledge the teachers believed was embedded in the experience.

Instead of focusing only on open-ended play, these teachers began to think about the importance of conceptually sustaining play (Fleer 2010) as a central feature of a cultural-historical approach to early childhood curriculum. In this way they could begin to focus on the concepts embedded in the children's play, and use discussion to support the learning. Siraj-Blatchford (2004) calls these discussions 'sustained shared thinking' (p. 147) and suggests that such thinking is necessary for children to learn from play. The importance of extending children's initial responses to play-based activity is discussed in detail in Chapter 9. In this chapter you can read in detail about using Vygotsky's theory to build a bridge between children's everyday understandings of the world and more academic or scientific explanations of how and why things work the way they do.

Summary

This chapter has examined the ways in which teachers can move beyond simplistic understandings of what it means to have culturally diverse learners in centres and classrooms: by engaging in conversations with children, parents, extended family and community about the approaches to teaching and learning adopted in different cultural groups and countries. It also addressed how teachers can bridge concept formation for children, so that they build on the knowledge they bring from home and merge it with conceptual or scientific knowledge in schools and centres. These ideas are developed further in Chapters 10 and 11 where we discuss how teachers, children and their families can form meaningful connections between learning in the home environment and in the educational setting, so that seamless transitions are achieved for children.

References

Brooker, L. (2005). Learning to be a child: cultural diversity and early years ideology. In N. Yelland (ed.), *Critical issues in early childhood education.* Maidenhead UK: Open University Press.

Bruce, J.U., Davie, T., Notman, L. Kilpatrick, H., Stewart, C., Luxford, K., Hunt, J., Antoni, T., Battista, M., Wilson, K., Fames, J., Middleton, K. & Keppick-Arnold, B. (2008). *Do children know they are learning?*, Poster presentation at the City of Casey Teacher Expo, Melbourne, Australia.

Chang, P. (2003). Contextual understanding of children's play in Taiwanese kindergartens. In D. Lytle (ed.), *Play and educational theory and practice.* Westport CT: Praeger, pp. 277–99.

Commonwealth Department of Education, Employment and Workplace Relations (2009). *Early Years Learning Framework Report: Belonging, Being & Becoming,* Canberra.

Cutter Mackenzie, A., Edwards, S. & Fleer, M. (2009). Investigating the environmental scientific concepts in children's play: How do children and teachers interpret play-based learning? *Australian Journal of Research in Early Childhood Education,* 16(1), pp. 49–63.

Dachyshyn, D. & Kirova, A. (2008). Understanding childhoods in-between: Sudanese refugee children's transition from home to preschool. *Research in Comparative and International Education,* 3(3), pp. 281–91.

Derman-Sparks, L. (1989). *Anti-bias curriculum: Tools for empowering young children.* Washington DC: NAEYC.

Edwards, S. (2006). 'Stop talking about culture as geography': Early childhood educators' conceptions of sociocultural theory as an informant to curriculum. *Contemporary Issues in Early Childhood,* 7(3), pp. 238–52.

Edwards, S. (2007). From developmental-constructivism to sociocultural theory and practice: An expansive analysis of teachers' professional learning and development in early childhood education. *Journal of Early Childhood Research,* 5(1), pp. 89–112.

Edwards, S. (2009). *Thinking through learning: Explorations in teaching and learning in the City of Casey*. Sydney: Pademelon Press.

Fleer, M. (2004). The cultural construction of family involvement in early childhood education: Some Indigenous Australian perspectives. *The Australian Educational Researcher*, 31(3), pp. 51–68.

Fleer, M. (2006). Potentive assessment in early childhood education. In M. Fleer, S. Edwards, M. Hammer, A. Kennedy, A. Ridgway, J. Robbins & L. Surman, *Early childhood learning communities: Sociocultural research in practice*. Sydney: Pearson.

Fleer, M. (2010). *Early Learning and Development: Cultural–historical concepts in play*. Melbourne: Cambridge University Press.

Fleer, M. & Williams-Kennedy, D. (2002). *Building bridges: Literacy development for young Indigenous Children*. Canberra: Australian Early Childhood Association.

Sadikeen, R. & Ritchie, J. (2009, forthcoming). Researching Tiriti-based practice: A teacher's journey. *Early Education*, 45, pp. 6–11.

Siraj-Blatchford, I. (2004). Quality teaching in the early years. In A. Anning, J. Cullen & M. Fleer (eds), *Early childhood education: Society and culture*. London: Sage Publications, pp. 137–48.

White, J., O'Malley, A., Toso, M., Rockel, J., Stover, S. & Ellis, F. (2007). A contemporary glimpse on play and learning in Aotearoa New Zealand. *International Journal of Early Childhood*, 39(1), pp. 93–105.

Chapter 7

Curriculum as a conceptual tool: Observation, content and programming

This chapter will outline the relationship between observation, planning and content in early childhood curriculum. The role of relationships, transitions, environments and play as informants to observations, planning and content selection will be examined. These constructs will be analysed in the context of international research about the role of relationships, transitions and play in children's learning and development and the implications for how they shape curriculum.

Linking observation to planning in the curriculum

REFLECTION 7.1

Kelly: I guess that's part of the curriculum design stuff, isn't it? That you work out what it is that you want children to be able to do and therefore you plan activities and work out in advance what you think they will achieve, so that you can assess whether or not it worked.

Kelly has articulated a particular model of assessment. Assessment is a way of finding out if what a teacher has organised for children to learn actually worked. She sees an important link between planning for teaching and what children do.

Graue and Walsh (1998) note that the process of 'finding it out' is particularly fraught with difficulty when it involves children:

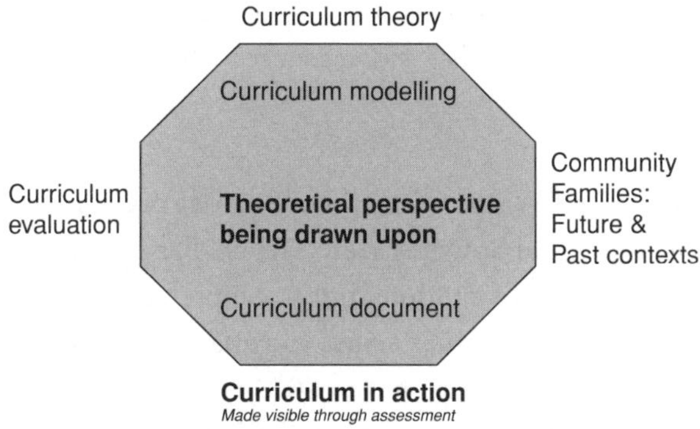

Figure 7.1 Curriculum development pathway – assessment

> Finding it out about children is exceptionally difficult – intellectually, physically, and emotionally. Physical, social, cognitive and political distances between the adult and the child make their relationship very different from the relationships among adults. In doing research with children, one never becomes a child. One remains a very definite and readily identifiable 'other' (p. xiv).

Warren (2000) considers it impossible to separate interpretation from observation: 'What is "seen" then, is not the real, in the sense of an experience distinct from interpretation.' He argues that 'reality is always a moving target, always in the process of becoming, always already interpreted' (p. 132). Vygotsky (1987) has made a similar point, arguing that in assessment, it is crucial to remember that development is always in a state of change – not static, ready to be captured – and as such it is very difficult to make judgments about children's learning and development. We find it useful to consider quantum physics when thinking about observing children. Heisenberg's uncertainty principle is useful: the act of observing something changes its nature. Apart from the effect of our observations on children's and adults' behaviour, we can never be certain that our interpretation of what we are seeing is 'real'.

As proposed in Chapter 2, despite the uncertainties when working with human beings, it is impossible to think about curriculum without having some guiding underpinning assumptions about what it is that you are trying to achieve and what the nature of children is. Usually these assumptions are based upon some theory about how children learn and the role of teachers in that learning:

> A good theory is a coherent narrative that allows one to see some part of the world in a new way. Theory is a map, a guide. It is a wise mentor who says, 'You know, if you shift how you are looking at it just a little

> bit – come try this new angle – you'll see it differently'. Theory allows one to see as connected what was unconnected before (Graue & Walsh 1998, p. 25).

However, as Graue and Walsh warn, theory can also act as a set of blinders, restricting what is seen and how it is seen. The challenge, then, is to use theory as a guide for observation of children, but to be prepared to think outside the square and sometimes apply other lenses to generate alternative explanations for what is being seen.

Espinosa (2005) argues that a robust assessment system is needed to support teachers and children working in culturally and linguistically diverse communities. Culturally and linguisticly diverse communities have become increasingly common in most centres and schools throughout many European-heritage communities as a result of changing immigration policies. Culturally loaded assessments and observation are usually not obvious. Take for example, the following situation:

> An early childhood teacher is sitting on a chair in front of a group of Indigenous and non-Indigenous children, reading a story. She sits upright, with her back straight, looking intently at the book she is holding, and then closely observing the children. The Indigenous children are looking away. The non-Indigenous children are looking at the teacher and the book.
>
> The teacher thinks, 'Those children who are not looking at me, are not paying attention, and therefore are not learning' (see Fleer 2010).

This vignette was videotaped and shown to some of the families of the children participating in the story-reading session. The families had quite a different response:

Mother: The teacher has a still body, and her posture indicates that she is cross, even though her voice is sweet and supportive. The children are looking away, so that they can concentrate upon what she is saying, rather than being distracted by her posturing of anger, as though she were scolding the children.

Indigenous Teacher: The teacher is thinking that the children are not learning. In Western education 'looking equates with learning' (Fleer 2010).

This is an example of one observation, but two quite different judgments (Fleer 2010).

Espinosa (2005) cautions against the use of standardised assessments, and draws on the National Association for the Education of Young Children (NAEYC) and National Association of Early Childhood Specialists in State Departments of Education (NAECS/SDE) position statement on assessment, which has the following key recommendation:

> To assess young children's strengths, progress, and needs, use assessment methods that are developmentally appropriate, culturally and linguistically responsive, tied to children's daily activities, supported by professional development, inclusive of families and connected to specific, beneficial purposes: (1) making sound decisions about teaching and learning, (2) identifying significant concerns that may require focussed intervention for individual children, and (3) helping programs improve their educational and developmental interventions (2003, p. 10).

Edwards (2009, p. 39) states that many traditional models of observation used in early childhood education are based on deficit notions (what children can and can't do), and these are often based on constructivist notions of child development, in which teachers are making constant comparisons of individual children against universal stage theories of child development. As Edwards (2009) says:

> The alternative argument posed by sociocultural theory emphasises the idea that children's development is determined by the contexts in which they live and by their cultural experiences (Robbins 2005). Sociocultural theory does not mean that teachers no longer value progress in key developmental abilities such as language and physical, cognitive, social and emotional development. It does however mean recognising that the processes by which these abilities develop and the age at which they occur are not the same for all children. Children's development is determined by their experiences, the interactions they have with people and the expectations held of them by their communities (p. 35).

Cultural-historical theory thus avoids determinism (e.g. all poor children will fail school) by emphasising that children's life experiences may be different from those they have in the educational setting and that it is the role of the teacher to build on the strengths and interests that the child brings to the classroom, to identify key areas in which they need support to learn and develop, and to provide relevant and meaningful curriculum opportunities. This might include thinking about how the classroom is set up, the expected relationships within that classroom and the predominant expected approaches to learning, such as free play. As Fleer (2002) has persuasively argued, some Indigenous Australian children will be unfamiliar with the notion of active engagement with play materials and may be more familiar with learning through observation. This is also important for teachers of Māori and Pacific Island children (for useful discussions see Hohepa & McNaughton 2007; Hanlen 2007) as they observe children's learning and development in a number of different domains. It is important that teachers do not make assumptions about the value placed on play in the home environment or the types of play that children may have experienced (Edwards 2009), as this can lead to misunderstandings about children's behaviour and to mistaken pedagogical assumptions about how to support children's learning – as was noted by the Indigenous teacher above.

In addition to thinking about the assumptions that teachers have about children's learning, teachers also need to think about any ethical conflicts or power relationships raised by undertaking observation (Cohen, Manion & Morrison 2000). An obvious example would be if you observe ethnic or Indigenous groups of which you have little prior knowledge, and you do not negotiate someone to act as your guide in that setting.

Crotty (1998) proposes that in order to do any kind of research, such as observing children's learning and development, we need to be thinking about four core principles:

Methods: the techniques or processes used to gather and analyse data related to some research question or hypothesis.

Methodology: the strategy, plan of action, process or design lying behind the choice and use of particular methods and linking the choice and use of methods to desired outcomes.

Theoretical perspective: the philosophical stance informing the methodology and thus providing a context for the process and grounding its logic and criteria.

Epistemology: the theory of knowledge embedded in the theoretical perspective and thereby its methodology (p. 3).

If we put this into the context of different approaches to curriculum, we might derive these sorts of answers to our questions about how we observe children.

Obviously these definitions of philosophical approaches to children's learning and their implications for observation are debatable (and we urge you to do that!); the intention is to help you to think through the implicit relationship between your theoretical world view, the approach to curriculum that is adopted and the implications for what and how you observe young children and their learning and development.

Table 7.1 A comparison of three curriculum models

	A constructivist curriculum	A cultural-historical curriculum	A behaviourist curriculum
Epistemology	Children learn through their senses and trial and error in stimulating environments, according to an innate schedule of development.	Children learn through interactions with more competent adults or peers in local, social and historical contexts.	Children learn through imitation, modelling, reinforcement and conditioning within social contexts.
Theoretical perspective	e.g. Piaget, Montessori	e.g. Vygotsky, Bruner, Rogoff, Hedegaard	e.g. Skinner, Watson, Thorndike, Bandura
Example of curriculum based on theory	High/Scope, Montessori preschools	*Golden Key Schools* in Russia; *Tools of the Mind* in the US; *Te Whāriki* in New Zealand; *Developmental Education* in the Netherlands (see Fleer 2010)	Distar, Bank Street
Methodology	To observe children's progress against predetermined ages and stages of development	To observe children's learning and development on their own, with the help of others and within the context of the particular setting	To observe if children have achieved predetermined learning outcomes or behaviours
Methods	Non-participant observation of children's play, looking at physical, cognitive and socio-emotional development	Participant and non-participant observation of children in all areas of the curriculum using a range of lenses: interpersonal, intrapersonal, institutional	Non-participant observation of children's demonstrated skills, competencies, behaviours and difficulties

What is observation and why is it important?

Denscombe (2007) proposes that there are essentially only two types of observation research used in the social sciences, including education. These are:

1. **Systematic observation**: This method has its origins in social psychology and in particular the study of interactions in settings such as school classrooms. Methods that fall into this category typically gather quantitative data and involve the use of statistical analysis.
2. **Participant observation**: This approach is more closely associated with anthropology and sociology and is used by researchers to infiltrate situations, sometimes undercover, to understand the culture and the processes of the group being investigated. Typically, methods used produce qualitative data, and in education, they usually involve teachers observing children as they work with them.

Denscombe argues that regardless of which type of observation is used, there are certain characteristics that any approach to observation entails:

1. **Direct observation**. Unlike other data collection methods, these methods rely directly on what the observer can see.
2. **Fieldwork**. Data is collected directly in the field of inquiry (i.e. the early childhood centre). It relies on the ability of the researcher – in this case, the teacher – to go directly in search of information rather than relying on secondary sources.
3. **Natural settings**. This method relies on gathering data as it happens, rather than by stimulating behaviour or simulating real-life conditions (such as what is done in laboratory research). Not disrupting the normal behaviour that would occur is a major concern, so in most observational methods, minimising the input of the observer is emphasised.
4. **The issue of perception**. Both systematic and participant observations recognise that the process of observing can never be neutral: the observer's perceptions of situations can be influenced by personal factors and thus the data collected can be unreliable. There are ways to reduce this unreliability, but it is always a problem that has to be addressed.

Perception of any situation or event is shaped by several factors, including memory, past experience and the current situation. In terms of memory, we essentially forget most of what we see, but there is a pattern to what we recall – what we recall is not random. This is called *selective recall*. Also, the mind filters information coming in, allowing some and putting up barriers to some, thus enabling a *selective perception* of 'what happened'. Finally, our perceptions are shaped by our emotional and physical state and the baggage that we carry around with us, so what we experience is shaped by our emotions of the moment. So being hungry, tired, angry, frustrated or prejudiced produces *accentuated perception*.

These perceptual filters mean that any observation will be shaped by mechanisms which accept, reject or highlight some information. Denscombe (2007) states that we also use the following sorting devices to determine what it is we are observing:

- **Familiarity**. We tend to see what we are used to seeing. If the situation is ambiguous we interpret it in terms of our past experiences.
- **Past experience**. Past experience teaches us to filter out certain 'nasty' stimuli and to exaggerate desirable things.
- **Current state**. Physical and emotional states and current priorities can also alter our perceptions.

The implications of the difficulties surrounding our own perceptions are quite evident and they mean that we need to constantly monitor ourselves as we carry out observation, and to find ways to crosscheck that our interpretation of an event or situation is shared by others. A cultural-historical framework can involve different lenses for observation and is therefore a useful approach to overcoming some of the difficulties and inherent perceptual blind spots associated with observation. Barbara Rogoff (1998, 2003), for example, has shown how observations and their interpretations can be framed through these three lenses:

- Personal;
- Interpersonal; and
- Contextual and institutional.

The personal focus directs the analysis to what the individual is doing, thinking, feeling and how they are behaving. The focus is on the individual child (see Figure 7.2, below).

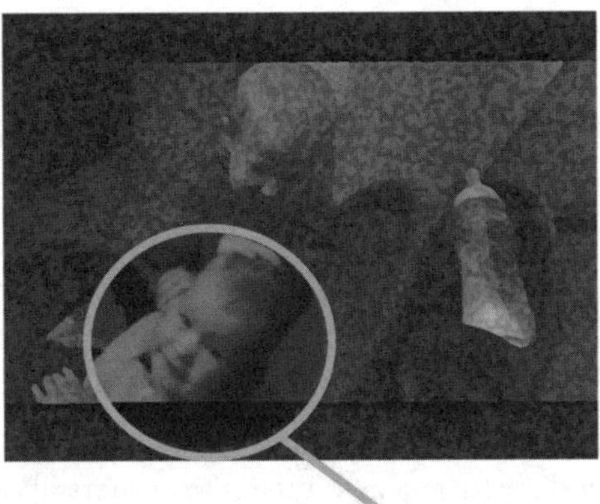

Figure 7.2 Rogoff's Individual focus for analysis

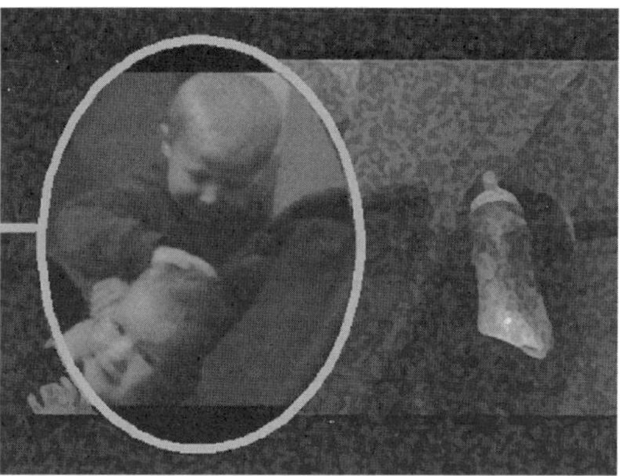

Figure 7.3 Rogoff's Interpersonal focus for analysis

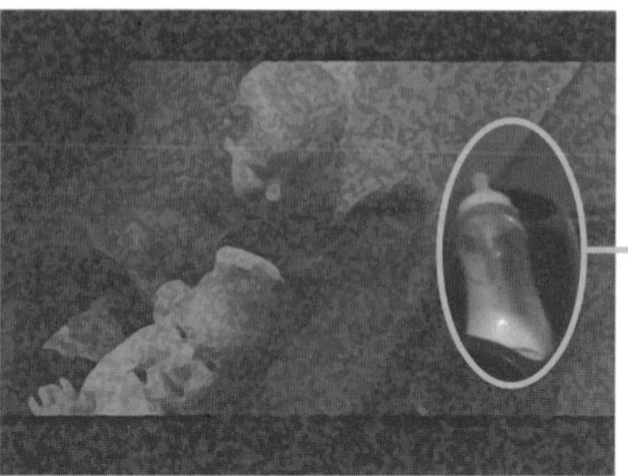

Figure 7.4 Rogoff's Contextual and institutional focus for analysis

The interpersonal focus is directed towards the conversations, the interactions, and the variety of ways that an individual is interacting with another individual or is located within the collective. Figure 7.3 shows this type of analysis.

Finally, the third focus for analysing an observation is centred on cultural, contextual or institutional factors which are impacting upon what might be possible for the child to do. For example, in the vignette given earlier, the Indigenous children were being asked to pay attention to the teacher reading the book. A deeper analysis (the third focus of analysis) of this observation would show that in many cultural communities families quite easily pay attention to a range of things simultaneously – hearing a story being read whilst using a computer game and gesturing 'a comment' to others about something that may be happening in the room, for instance (see Rogoff 2003 for a review of a large body of research being undertaken in her lab). Rogoff has shown that in many European-heritage communities, families tend to focus on one thing at a time, and do not promote this high level of simultaneous attention. Many early childhood centres work in this way also. In these centres, group time is about paying close attention to the teacher, and not having anything that may distract you in your hands. Using this kind of analysis, observers will recognise that this practice and expectation comes from a particular cultural perspective, which in turn has produced particular childrearing practices.

The role of environments: Observations in the early childhood setting

There are several common types of observations that teachers regularly engage in. Cohen, Manion and Morrison (2000) suggest that teachers act either as participants (observing while involved with the children) or non-participants (observing while not interacting with them). This either/or approach has been disputed in recent times (see Hedegaard & Fleer 2008) because it assumes a dichotomy that is not helpful for documenting children's learning. Other readings of the role of the teacher as an observer have been noted in cultural-historical research (see Hedegaard & Fleer 2008). The teacher forms part of the observation, and therefore an assessment of the child(ren) is only possible in relation to what the teacher is doing or has organised. However, the teacher is 'not a child' and therefore is not assessed, even though they are an important part of the context and thus have a bearing on what might be possible. The philosophy of the teacher and belief system – such as looking equates with learning – also influence what might be possible. So observations are a three-dimensional aspect of assessing children's learning.

Cohen, Manion and Morrison (2000, p. 305) have shown the dimensions of the role of environment. It is important in a cultural-historical view of assessment, that they too are considered in a multi-dimensional way:

- The physical setting – the environment and organisation.
- The human setting – the people being observed and their organisation and make up.
- The interactional setting – the types of interaction taking place.
- The program setting – the resources, organisation, pedagogic styles, curriculum.

There are many manuals written on approaches to observing children. McMurray, Pace and Scott (2004), for instance, have identified 11 steps involved in any observation:

1. **Decide the purpose of your observations**. In order to avoid information overload, it is helpful to focus your observation and think about the following:
   - Who do I want to observe?
   - What am I observing?
   - Why am I observing?
   - When should I be observing?
   - How am I going to go about observing?
   - Where should I be observing?
2. **Select a location**. You need to consider issues of comfort, a clear view and whether you will be able to adequately observe the focus of your observation.
3. **Select an observational vantage point**. Test out the usefulness of various vantage points before you begin your observation. Wear clothing that enables you to blend into the setting. The only exception to this rule is when children are very familiar with you and are used to seeing you in a range of clothing types.
4. **Select an appropriate time frame**. You need to be well acquainted with the routines of the setting, so that you can gauge when will be the best time and day on which to gather your observations.
5. **Do continuous counts or spot counts**. Continuous observation is also referred to as *continuous count* and sampling observation is referred to as *spot count*. Decide which method will work best for the data you want to gather.
6. **Decide how many observations to make**. Generally, you would record more at the beginning of a study, to establish trends, but this might reduce over time.
7. **Decide how long to observe**. Usually, observations are continued until you reach *saturation point*, where the observations become repetitive, but there may be a predetermined length of time for observations too.
8. **Decide what to observe**. Remain focused on the purpose of your observation and try not to record interesting but non-relevant incidents.
9. **Divide large areas into smaller parts**. Large areas are more readily observed if broken into smaller areas. Alternatively, use another person to do some of the observations, using the same criteria. There may still

be differences in recording and interpretation of observations but this can be overcome by agreeing on what and who will be observed and keeping identical record-keeping sheets.

10. **Devise a record sheet**. A simple record sheet for vital information is of great value. Things to record include: time, location, date, observer, area, behaviours or events, gender, and so forth, depending on the context and purpose of the observation.
11. **Complete observations**. If a clear structure has been used, engaging in observations should be straightforward. To maintain interest, McMurray, Pace and Scott recommend varying your vantage point and alternating between continuous observation and a sampling approach.

In addition to the focus of observation, there are several types of observation method that are commonly used by teachers and researchers. These include:

- **Structured observations** – where a predetermined checklist of things to observe is used (e.g. Can Annie hop? Can Annie do activities that require her to cross her midline? Can Annie catch a ball?).
- **Anecdotal or instantaneous sampling** – where teachers observe something as they are working with children that they think should be documented (e.g. Annie walks for the first time today or says her first word in the centre).
- **Event sampling** – where a particular event is observed (e.g. Is Joshua interacting with other children in the sandpit?).
- **Critical incident sampling** – observations of the setting and context of a particular regular occurrence to work out what is causing it (e.g. What was the context of the interaction in which Joshua bit another child this morning in the sandpit?).
- **Time sampling or interval recording** – where an observation is taken at a predetermined time interval (e.g. an observation is taken every five minutes about who is using the newly organised family play area in the centre and what types of play are occurring with the new resources available), or where observations are made at a regular intervals (e.g. observations are taken of a particular child once a day during a one month period to observe how they are settling into the centre).
- **Rating scales** – where an environment is rated against a set of criteria on a scale which ranks from best to worst. There are several published rating scales which are used for evaluating the effectiveness of early childhood environment. The Early Childhood Environmental Rating Scale (ECERS) (Harms, Clifford & Cryer 1998) is probably the most well known.

Whilst these approaches to observing have been developed using theoretical frameworks quite different from cultural-historical theory, they do show the types of assessment approaches and tools that are available for early childhood teachers. What is important is to decide upon what value they have and when they might be used.

REFLECTION 7.2

Examine the assessment tools in your centre. What types of approaches/tools are being used? How is the observer positioned? Inside the observation or outside it? Or do the observations look like those shown in Figures 7.2–7.4? What do you notice?

How the tools are used within the system of gathering information about children is important. A cultural-historical system of assessment can be thought about in relation to one of the ideas directly attributed to Vygotsky: the Zone of Proximal Development. The next section discusses this concept, as it provides a productive framework within which the tools McMurray, Pace and Scott (2004) could be applied.

Zone of Proximal Development and Zone of Actual Development as a framework for assessment

Daniels (2001) states that there are four versions of the Zone of Proximal Development: assessment; scaffolding; cultural; and collectivist. They will be briefly discussed in relation to the focus of this chapter, and followed by an elaboration of Vygotsky's work by Elena Kravtsova, his granddaughter.

1. Assessment

Normally assessment compares a child's performance with that of their peers, or identifies their competence to complete the assessment task based on factors of ability, understanding and contextual influences. In Vygotsky's version, assessment focuses on the development of the child and what they can do with expert guidance. It thus focuses on what the child will be able to achieve on their own in the future, rather than what they can currently do unaided. In this version, instruction and assessment are integrally linked.

Vygotsky's theory of the Zone of Proximal Development can be shown as a diagram (see Figure 7.5).

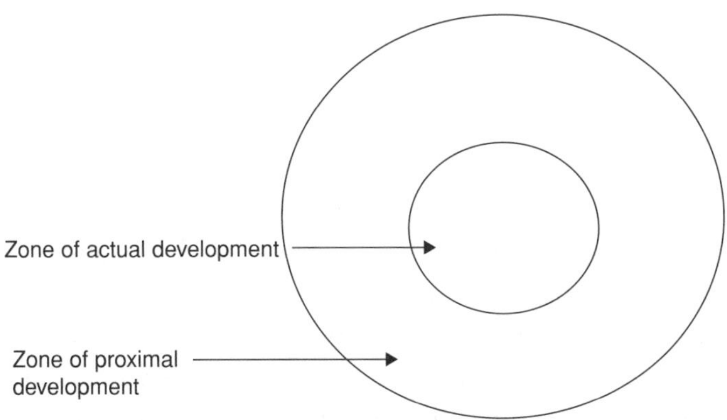

Figure 7.5 Vygotsky's theory of the Zone of Proximal Development (Kravtsova 2008)

2. Scaffolding

In this version, the expert constructs a scaffold or pathway for the child to acquire new knowledge and presents it to the child. The child follows the guidance of the expert and engages with the expert to solve a problem or carry out a task. Moll (1990) argues that Vygotsky was unclear about what forms scaffolding might take and whether or not the learner might be involved in negotiating how the scaffolding might take place. Many authors have since attempted to further define this concept (for example, Wood, Bruner & Ross 1976; Berk & Winsler 1995). One useful definition of scaffolding comes from Gallimore and Tharp (1990), who propose that it involves the following:

- Modelling – offering behaviour for imitation
- Contingency management – rewards/punishments to follow behaviour
- Feeding back – to assist performance
- Instructing – explicit guidance
- Questioning – checking understanding
- Cognitive or task structuring – chunking, segregating, sequencing or otherwise structuring a task into or from components, so that the task is modified for the learner.

Furthermore, Gallimore and Tharp (1990) state that there are stages in the Zone of Proximal Development, which children cycle through as they gain mastery of a task:

- Performance is assisted by more competent peers.
- Less dependence, and performance begins to internalise. Children use directed speech – self-regulation/guidance.

- Performance is developed, automated and fossilised – smooth and integrated.
- Deautomatisation – performance is forgotten or rusty. Re-enter ZPD.

It should be noted that the term 'scaffolding' has been contentious amongst neo-Vygotskians, with the mechanical nature of a scaffold being critiqued by Stone (1993) and the implied expert–novice control issues highlighted by Rogoff (1990). The term 'co-construction' is preferred by many recent theorists, including Rogoff, as it portrays the child as more powerful, and actively engaged with others in their own learning. Chapters 4 and 5 give some useful examples of how teachers in a range of settings have grappled with co-constructing knowledge with children and what cultural-historical theory means in terms of their everyday teaching practice.

In the context of assessment, the concept of scaffolding is important because it makes visible what the teacher is consciously seeking to do in collaboration with the child – as an interpersonal focus for analysis (see Figure 7.3 above). Assessing the child in relation to the supports or scaffolds provided by the teacher gives valuable information about the child, and about how effective the scaffolds are in relation to the particular child(ren).

3. Cultural

In this version, the ZPD refers to the distance between the child's everyday experiences and the body of cultural knowledge that is typically embodied in a formal curriculum. Scaffolding by the teacher supports the merging of these two types of knowledge so that informal knowledge is integrated into more formal or abstract versions of knowledge. This aspect of cultural-historical theory is discussed Chapters 9, 10 and 11 in particular, where a model of how to merge children's everyday knowledge with what Vygotsky called 'schooled knowledge' is explained and illustrated.

4. Collectivist

This version involves a more active role for the learner. The ZPD is defined as the distance between informal knowledge of the learner and new forms of understanding which are collectively constructed, often during a teaching and learning encounter. For instance, this view strongly supports the argument that children never learn by themselves, and that knowledge is never held within the head of one person – it is collectively constructed, enacted, and given meaning in a social context. For example, in a paper by Fleer and Richardson (2004) a group of young children of different ages and abilities are sitting together at a drawing and writing table. The older children are writing their names, some of the younger children are reproducing some of the letters that form the

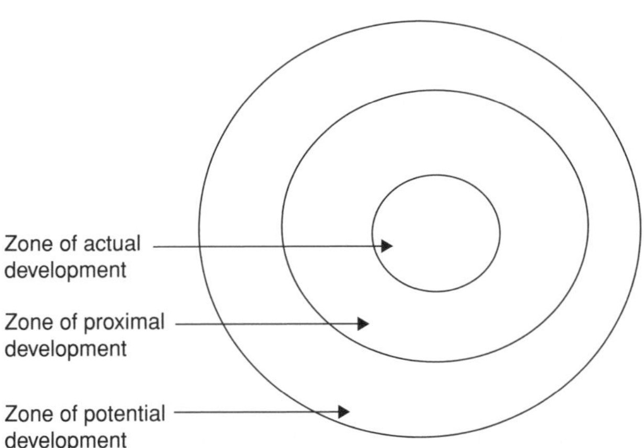

Figure 7.6 Zone of Potential Development (Kravtsova 2008)

first letter in their names, and a two-and-a-half-year-old watches on, and then makes marks on the paper. What happens next is what illustrates how this community of writers (Wenger 1998) turns into a collective that is conscious of the concept of writing. The older child writes a letter onto another child's page, the younger child adds some letters she is familiar with, and the two children form a story. The teacher notices what is going on and asks the children to talk about their story. The younger child tells her what the words say, and what they mean in her story and the older child adds to this by reading the words. The older child leaves and the younger child says, 'I can't tell you any more, but I can tell you more when my friend is here with me' (Fleer & Richardson 2004).

Kravtsova (2008) has added to the concept of the ZPD. She has conceptualised the zone of potential development. This is shown in Figure 7.6.

The community of learners illustrates nicely the zones introduced by Vygotsky and elaborated by Kravtsova (2008). The youngest child makes marks on paper. This child is not 'actually' writing, but there is the 'potential for writing' evident because this child is in a context where the others are drawing the child's attention to this possibility – it is the future, for tomorrow, it is the education that lies ahead of development, as Vygotsky (1987) argued.

The two children who are writing together, demonstrate nicely the ZPD, as the younger and older child are writing, and the younger child is supported by the older child. The older child keeps the 'story' writing going by contributing actual words to the text being produced. The child is unable to write her letters with the same level of coherence, without the older child completing the writing process for her. Together, the younger child can work above her actual level of development.

This kind of framework invites teachers to assess children's potential, and this has been termed by Fleer (2006) 'Potentive Assessment'. All the assessment techniques and considerations discussed above, when framed through these zones, can be used for a cultural-historical approach to assessment.

In the next section, the specific play-based context of early childhood education is foregrounded, and assessment is discussed – focusing specifically on observations during play. As you read this section, think about how the zones discussed here can be used to frame the observations made during play.

The role of play: Observing the child in action

For many of these types of observations, there is a range of things that can be recorded. Often our observations of children are taking place when they are at play, and capturing the observation is the greatest challenge, as things happen so fast!

While observation of children is a fantastic way to find out an enormous range of things about them, we also need to be careful about what it is we are observing. Long, Volk and Gregory (2007), in their study of children negotiating play in three different cultural contexts, argue that 'observations of children engaged in sociodramatic play can lead to insights about their knowledge and learning processes in ways that are not always possible in other contexts' (p. 242). Teachers who are observing children carefully can identify information that can help to shape culturally responsive curricula, curricula that is not based entirely on western conceptions of what constitutes play and learning:

> It is important to mention that a growing body of work critically examines accepted norms about children's play as being based on Western expectations. Although some universals are observed across cultural groups, differences are noted (Haight et al. 1999) as play takes 'distinctly different forms in different communities' (Rogoff 2003, p. 149) (Long, Volk & Gregory 2007, p. 242).

Rogers and Evans (2007), in their research on the role of play in reception classes in England, note that observation is a wonderful tool for assessing children's responses to role-play provision and relationships with other children, but it is dependent on children having time and space to play and assumes that teachers are available and have time to observe, rather than getting involved in the play or teaching somewhere else. Making time for observation is obviously something that needs to be budgeted into most teachers' daily lives if it is to be used as a tool for curriculum planning. Rogers and Evans (2007) also note that teachers need to think seriously about their role in children's play and how much time they spend structuring, stopping and interfering with play. They suggest a model of co-constructing play that would probably enable greater diversity of play, which may itself empower children to feel that they have some control over the nature and shape of their play:

> With this in mind, we suggest here that a critical pedagogy of play hinges on adults relinquishing some of their power and control of the play environment (without relegating it altogether to the margins). Drawing play into the heart of pedagogical practice, so that it becomes a space for negotiating cultural values and interests and evaluates questions of voice and power (Giroux 1994, p. 131) and in so doing, makes visible the less palatable aspects of children's interests in popular culture (Marsh 2000), gender stereotypical behaviour (Browne 2004) and peers could, within a critical perspective, provide a powerful context for exploring identities, social justice and cultural diversity. Sharing of power between children and adults seem to be particularly apt in the context of role play. Thus we argue here that a co-constructed pedagogy of play may facilitate children's participation further in how their play manifests itself in the classroom (Rogers & Evans 2007, p. 165).

Capturing aspects of children's play requires a range of 'data-gathering' strategies (Fleer & Richardson 2004). McMurray, Pace and Scott (2004, p. 192) recommend the following things to take note of, supplemented by photos, audio recordings and documents, if video recording can't be used, so that the scene can be revisited. We have taken these ideas and categorised them in relation to the three foci for analysis discussed by Rogoff (2003) above (see Table 7.2).

The ways that the observations will be written up depend on the individual, although there are some helpful things that it is useful to record, to aid your memory of the event. It is obviously helpful to write these up as soon as possible

Table 7.2 Using three planes for analysis

Personal	Interpersonal	Contextual/Institutional/Cultural
• What is happening?	• Who is it happening to? • What is being said? • Who is saying it? • Who was it said to?	• When did it happen? • What changes are occurring in the physical surroundings? • Record emotional reactions of individuals and personal impressions. • How long the event lasted, if this event has occurred before and your impressions of outcomes, issues arising and so on.

after the event, so that your memory is still fresh. Some of these things, loosely based on suggestions by Gray (2004, p. 247), include the following:

- Key quotes, preferably verbatim.
- Details about the children involved in the observation – ages, physical build, ethnicity, clothing, appearance.
- Verbal interaction – the characteristics of speech and the speaker (use of slang, technical language, etc); who does most of the talking; whose suggestions are followed and whose are ignored; who interrupts and who doesn't; the tone of the conversation (hostile, bored, indifferent, enthusiastic, etc).
- Non-verbal behaviours such as body language, facial expressions, body posture, how children move (e.g. confident or diffident), length and frequency of eye contact.
- The time of events and activities, and the sequence.
- The observer's feelings and views of the situation at the time.

Another approach to increasing the validity of your observations is to include the child's commentary or observations of the play. Warren (2000), reflecting on the inadequacies of his own doctoral research on finding out about boys' success in school, has this to say about how he would now do observational research differently:

REFLECTION 7.3

I would need to start with a different set of questions, which might look something like this: How are the boundaries of maleness and femaleness defined through action in the classroom? How do some modes of maleness come to dominate over others? How does this dominant mode of maleness regulate, subordinate or alternate ways of being male? I would be seeking to engage the children, and the particularly the boys, in reflecting on how they construct meaningful self identities and why some appear to be more possible than others. Let us say I gave each child a disposable camera and asked the children to photograph places, people, objects and activities that were important to their sense of self. These could be used in a variety of ways. Collages could be produced, story lines sketched, relationships between images explained, personal diaries written. Whatever holding frame is chosen, the aim would be to encourage the children to reflect on why they had chosen those images over others, what processes of choosing they had involved themselves in, what other images could have been chosen, how the meanings of the images change over time and in

continued »

Reflection 7.3 continued »

the context of doing the research. There would be a degree of challenge to these dialogues necessary for any reflective action. While the collage and the story line would always have the danger of suggesting fixed identities, the images are always understood as partial and temporary. They become gateways into the meaning-making practices of self-making. They constantly beg further questions, and possibly further images, constantly making reference to worlds outside of the classroom. The activity is engaging rather than distancing, yet also contains reflection and critique (Warren 2000, p. 133).

The principles in this excerpt are clear. Involving children in the collection of data around an event brings in a perspective which may confirm or deny your interpretation, but helps to bridge the 'insider-outsider' phenomenon of observing children and interpreting meaning. Additionally, using a cultural-historical approach, you would include observations and reflections from children's families, as further ways of validating your observations and interpretations.

The role of transitions: The importance of observation, documentation and reflection

Children experience many transitions in their early years: major vertical transitions between centres, classrooms and schools, as well as a number of horizontal transitions within each day in their educational setting. Observing how children cope with the more minor horizontal transitions can give clues as to how they might cope with the more major vertical transitions between settings.

BOX A

Jeremy in the under 2s: Claire's experience of the usefulness of observation

My younger son Jeremy always intensely disliked making transitions. As a little boy, he did not settle well in strange beds and he used to cry loudly whenever I left him

continued »

Box A continued »

in child care each morning, although I was assured by the teacher that he was quite happy during the day. I found this very distressing and was at my wit's end as to whether he would ever make the adjustment to being away from me during the day and if child care was a viable option for him. One particularly helpful teacher that he had when he was about 18 months old suggested to me that she would videotape my son when he was making transitions throughout the day, as part of our investigations into why Jeremy was so distressed when I left each day and to identify ways in which we could support him to make transitions. She videotaped his arrival with me in the morning, his transitions to morning tea, mat times, lunch, nap times and home time in the afternoon. Once she had collected this over a few days, she asked me to come in and we reviewed the videotape of her observations. What we witnessed astounded me: Jeremy gave an extraordinary performance of clinging and crying while I was in sight and the moment I left, he ran off quite cheerfully to ride bikes and play with his friends. During the day, he was often reluctant to make transitions unless it suited what he was doing at the time, but coped better if he was given some responsibility for organisation of whatever the event was. Following these observations, I realised I was part of the problem with Jeremy's settling behaviours in the morning – I became much swifter in my departures when I left Jeremy each day so that he could get on with his play and the teachers gave him many more things to do at each transition throughout the day in the centre. Once we did this, Jeremy ceased to cry at my departure and became much more settled and happy about being asked to change activities during the day. In this case, the videotapes gave me a window into Jeremy's world that I otherwise wouldn't have had. What's more, the teacher engaged me in this exploration and we collaboratively came up with a plan for helping my child settle more readily into the child care centre. Some of the lessons learned in that early study of my young child have been invaluable throughout the various moves that my family and I have had to make between countries and cities for our careers . . . and with surviving his adolescence!

What this small example illustrates is the need for observation of children in the various transitions they make, including before, during and after school entry. The nature of the data gathered could be negotiated between centres and local schools prior to school entry, as part of what Mutch (2002) describes as a 'democratic learning community', in which all interested stakeholders, including the children, make decisions about what is documented. It is important to have a robust evidential base on which to make decisions around children's learning.

The relationship between the early childhood centre, family and the primary school is particularly important during a child's transition to school. Tayler (2006) reports on three case studies of partnerships, with parents and families in Western Australia, Queensland and New South Wales, during children's transition years. In all the studies the key factor for successful partnerships was the stance of the school principal. Leaders who fostered collaborative networks and respect for all players were found to be most effective, especially if the relevance, style and manner in which learning outcomes would be achieved was negotiated. The extensive studies on transition to school by Dockett, Perry and others in Sydney has clearly indicated that successful transition for children involves layers of relationships between teachers in both settings, children and parents, and that the issues for each group may differ. One of the important things that Dockett and Perry (2005, 2006) found – their research was based on a community of practice model – was that giving children the opportunity to observe the new setting and document its important features by taking photographs helped them make a successful transition. For children as well as for adults, observation and documentation of the unfamiliar is a valuable tool for gaining insight.

The 'Picking up the Pace' project (Phillips, McNaughton & McDonald 2001) suggested that greater collaboration and negotiation between early childhood centres and primary schools can support continuity in learning, particularly in language and literacy development. Research by Tagoilelagi-Leota, McNaughton, MacDonald and Ferry (2005) with Samoan and Tongan children from six months before school entry until a year after school entry indicates that children who were incipient bilinguals at the beginning of the study were supported to gain language and literacy skills in both their home language and English when teachers in both early childhood and primary schools shared information about children and made regular and specific observations and assessments of children's learning, so that they could monitor the development of both the children's first language and their knowledge and use of English. Hohepa and McNaughton (2007) argue that teachers need effective strategies to add to the experiences that children bring from home and also to add to their classroom practices to enable children who are linguistically and culturally diverse to learn. Encouraging parents to become partners in observation and 'data gathering' of their children is clearly a strategy that will yield dividends in both settings.

The role of relationships: Documenting observations in the early childhood setting

Observation in the early childhood context is rarely an individual event, even if you don't involve the children. It is more likely that your observations of children will be confirmed or denied by other teachers, who either share or do not share your interpretation of what you have observed. In some ways, the collaborative team-based setting of most early childhood centres and junior schools is ideal for doing observational research, as you have readymade opportunities for establishing validity, reliability and triangulation of any data that you generate about young children.

Edwards (2009) proposes a model of observation, based on sociocultural theory, which incorporates the layers of relationships which surround children's learning. She cites Fleer and Richardson (2004), who consider sociocultural observation a form of 'data gathering' with no set methods, and which is more fluid than conventional methods and may include interactions between people, ideas and materials. Edwards reports a group of teachers in the City of Casey trialling sociocultural approaches to curriculum planning and assessment, including using a 'ZPD targeted approach' (see Figure 7.7) in which teachers documented what the children were doing on their own and with peer and adult assistance when working in groups.

They also trialled Rogoff's (1995) three planes of analysis for interpreting their observations of children's learning, so that their observations included examples of the intrapersonal, interpersonal and institutional issues surrounding the child's play. What is useful in this methodology, which is particularly pertinent to this book, is that the teachers made the effort to name the learning that was happening.

The approach advocated by Edwards and her teachers involves teachers' perceptions, children's reflections on their learning and potentially parents' reflections or observations. Riley's clock is a lovely example of how teachers have named the concept knowledge that they think a child has gained, as well as documenting the child's reflections on what he had learnt.

Another method of observation, assessment and documentation that is becoming more commonly used in early childhood in New Zealand is the 'learning story', made much more visible and accessible to teachers by the publication of *Kei tua o te pae*, the early childhood assessment exemplars (Ministry of Education 2005). In New Zealand, the notion of 'noticing, recognising

Future intentions

- Encourage correct hand grasp/grip on brush resting between index and thumb
- Prompting
- Verbal interactions if necessary
- Modelling/praise

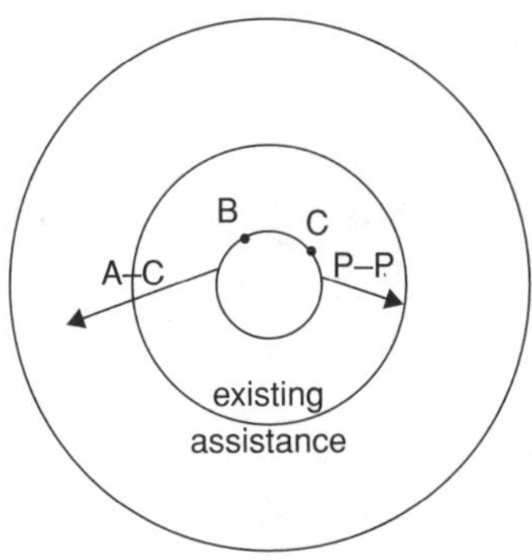

Adult–child

- Prompting ideas for person
- Assisting repositioning hand grasp
- Verbal interactions

Peer–peer

- Checking/observing what C was painting

Figure 7.7 ZPD targeted approach (Edwards 2009, p. 55)

and responding' underpins *Kei tua o te pae,* which is promoted as a way of assessing children's learning from a sociocultural perspective. It is argued that as teachers work with children they notice a great deal, recognise what they notice as learning, and respond to some of what they recognise. Drummond's (1993) definition of assessment is used:

> [Assessment is all the] ways in which, in our everyday practice, we (children, families, teachers, and others) observe children's learning (notice), strive to understand it (recognise) and then put our understanding to good use (respond) (cited in Ministry of Education 2005, p. 6).

There is also instruction in the *Revised Statement of Desirable Objectives and Practices* (DOPS) (Ministry of Education 1998) for chartered services:

> Educators should implement curriculum and assessment practices which: (a) reflect the holistic way that children learn; (b) reflect the reciprocal relationships between the child, people and learning environment;

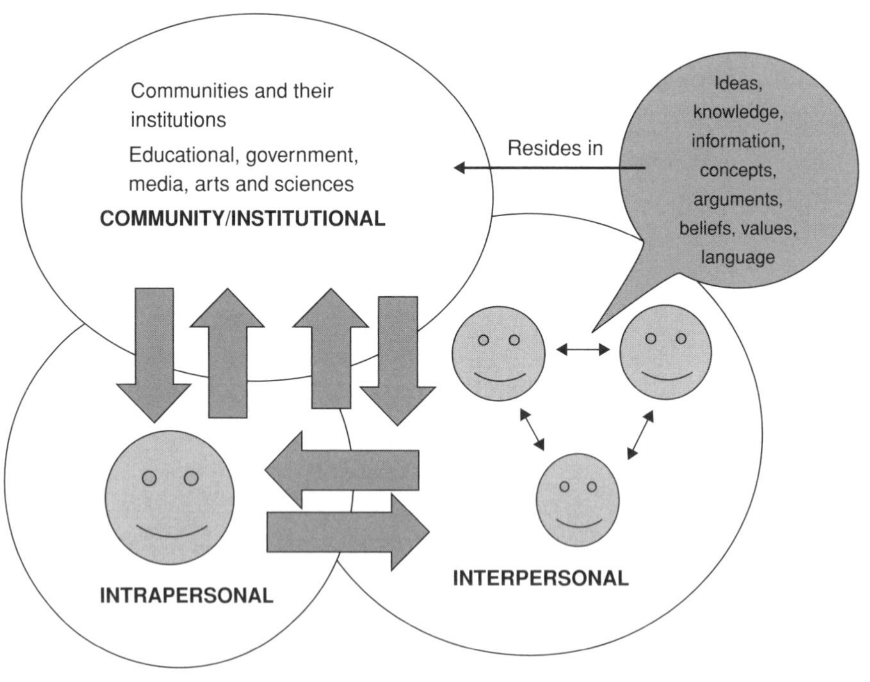

Figure 7.8 Three planes of analysis example (Edwards 2009, p. 18)

> (c) involve parents/guardians, and where appropriate, whānau; and (d) enhance children's sense of themselves as capable people and competent learners.

These four points relate to the principles of *Te Whāriki* (Ministry of Education 1996): family and community, empowerment, relationships and holistic development. *Kei tua o te pae* also stresses that 'assessment for learning implies that we have some clear aims or goals for children's learning' (Ministry of Education 2005, Book 1, p. 9) and states that *Te Whāriki* provides the framework for defining learning and for what is to be learned. The goals and indicative learning outcomes in *Te Whāriki* of wellbeing, belonging, contribution and communication provide further guidance.

Following the release of *Te Whāriki*, the need for better alignment of assessment and observation procedures with the curriculum document became apparent (Carr 2001; Nuttall 2003). Carr's (2001) project provided the concept and the methodology – which has since evolved into the foundation for *Kei tua o te pae*. Fifty early childhood centres participated in a two-year pilot project,

Riley's Clock

What the teaching team thought Riley learnt:

- The difference between numbers and letters
- How to write numbers he could not write previously
- Problem solving – using the wall clock to copy from
- Identifying the numbers on a clock typically go up to 12
- Concentration
- Fine Motor Skills

What Riley thought he had learnt:

'Time'

'How many numbers there is'

'Learn how to write numbers; I already knew 4 and 7'

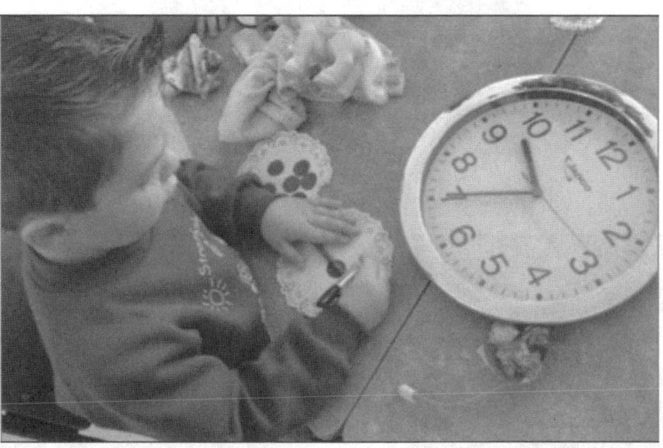

Figure 7.9 Riley's clock, 8 April 2008 (Edwards 2009, pp. 88–89)

Riley's Clock

Riley approached Heidi and asked her to write the letters in his name that he couldn't write. When Heidi started to recite the letters in Riley's name, because it looked like he had already written a 'little r', Riley stated, 'No not those letters, I can write them, I mean the number letters'.

Heidi realised Riley was making a clock and needed assistance to write the numbers so Heidi got the wall clock down for Riley to copy. When Riley went to write the '3' he stated 'I can write that, it's like a "C"'. To the 4 he said, 'I can write that, 'cause that's how old I was'. Before writing the 7, Riley declared 'I can write that, 'cause that's my house number'.

After writing the numbers up to twelve and counting them on the wall clock and his clock, Riley realised he had more room, so he said he could write the number 13. As the number 13 was not on the wall clock, Riley asked Heidi how to write it: '13 is made up of two numbers, a 1 and a 3'. Riley accurately wrote 13.

He then proceeded to write the numbers up to 16 because they could fit on his clock. Each time, he asked how to write the number; Heidi would verbally explain each number to him and he would write it correctly. After completing his clock, Riley smiled and said he could make more clocks to fill the room.

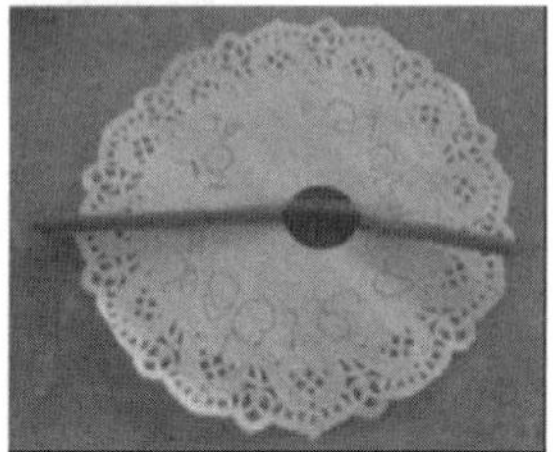

Figure 7.10 Riley's clock, 8 April 2008 (Edwards 2009, pp. 88–89)

which ran alongside the National Exemplar project in schools. *Kei tua o te pae* also advises teachers to monitor children's learning dispositions, drawing on Carr's (2001) work in this area, as a further tool for assessment, and urges teachers to make sure that 'assessment notes what children can do when they are "at their best"' (Ministry of Education 2005, p. 18). Carr (2001, p. 23) outlines five domains of learning dispositions:

- taking an interest;
- being involved;
- persisting with difficulty or uncertainty;
- communicating with others; and
- taking responsibility.

The notion of dispositions for learning is also evident in some Australian curriculum documents, such as the *Essential Learnings Framework of Tasmania* (Department of Education, Tasmania 2002) and the *South Australian Curriculum, Standards and Accountability Framework* (Department of Education, Training and Employment, South Australia 2001).

One of the strengths of the 'learning story' framework for documenting children's learning (see Figure 7.11) is that it is based on a sociocultural framework and builds in opportunity for the voices and perceptions of children and parents, as well as the teacher(s), to be heard. Carr (2001) argues that using a learning story can help draw families into discussions about their child's learning and development, enable families to contribute to planning for the child's curriculum and future learning and maintain continuity in the child's learning over time. It also enables children to be part of the discussion and decision making around their own learning. Carr believes that learning stories serve multiple purposes in an early childhood setting, including:

- describing what learning is happening;
- talking about the child's learning with other staff;
- documenting what the child is observed to be doing in the centre over time; and
- making decisions about 'where to next' for the child.

Although learning stories are becomingly increasingly popular in New Zealand and elsewhere, if the numbers of hits on a Google search is anything to go by, there is also a growing level of critique about whether the learning story framework, as it is being implemented by teachers, is sufficiently robust for capturing evidence of concept formation. Nuttall argues that *Kei tua o te pae* does

Sofia the reader

8 August

Pamela has told me about how much Sofia loves her books. They go to the library on a regular basis and Pamela reads to Sofia often.

Today when I went to visit Pamela and Sofia, I was able to see this for myself.

Sofia was sitting near her basket of toys and began to take some out. She chose books and there were quite a few in there. She didn't just take the first book though. She looked through each one until she came to the one that she wanted, which was *Thomas the Tank Engine*. She then proceeded to open the book in the correct way, the right way up, and to turn the pages from left to right! She also pointed to some of the pictures and made some sounds.

When she had finished that book, she did the same thing again and chose another story, *Brown Bear, Brown Bear*. It wasn't the first book she saw either.

It was great to watch Sofia reading her stories and revisiting experiences that she has had. It is wonderful for such a young child to be so interested in books and show such an understanding of the way that they work.

We know children are learning when we see them practise old things and take an interest.

Sofia enjoys returning to her favourite books and the enjoyment that they bring.

(*Te Whāriki*, Communication/Mana Reo.)

What's happening here?

Pamela is a home-based provider who has recognised Sofia's love of books. The home-based co-ordinator wrote this story after visiting Sofia and Pamela in the home-based setting.

What does this assessment tell us about the learning (using a Communication/ Mana Reo lens)?

This exemplar is about Sofia, an infant, being a reader. The co-ordinator records in detail the skills of knowing about books, and loving books, that Sofia demonstrates. This inclination and the skills associated with it include: choosing books rather than other toys; choosing specific books rather than any book; opening the book in the correct way, the right way up; turning the pages from left to right; and pointing to some of the pictures and making accompanying sounds. The commentary also points out that Pamela and Sofia go to the library on a regular basis and Pamela reads to Sofia often.

How might this documented assessment contribute to Communication/Mana Reo?

The audience for this assessment will include Pamela, Sofia's family, and Sofia. The assessment is an affirmation of Pamela's practice (it is implied that the What next? will be more of the same), and for Pamela and Sofia's family, the assessment gives specific information about the characteristics of an emergent reader and about Sofia's achievements and interests. In the future, Sofia will be able to revisit this assessment and "read" the photographs of herself reading *Thomas the Tank Engine*. The assessment demonstrates for her (as observer and the one observed) that this is something she does, even though she will not yet understand the words "being a reader".

What other strands of *Te Whāriki* are exemplified here?

This documented assessment has highlighted some of the routines followed in this home-based setting – there are regular trips to the library, and Sofia and Pamela often read books together. In this sense, the assessment also demonstrates elements of Belonging/Mana Whenua.

Figure 7.11 Example of a learning story

not provide enough guidance on what should be assessed and how teachers can make sense of children's learning, and states that although the exemplars are based on sociocultural theorising that the development of higher mental functions depends on fostering engagement with more knowledgeable members of the culture, this is not borne out in the teachers' interpretations. The problem, according to Nuttall, is that teachers do not appear to be recognising the children's funds of knowledge, skills or understandings in their observations: 'Many of the exemplars, for example, show children engaged in sophisticated literacy practices, yet these appear to be overlooked in the teachers' interpretations. Instead the teachers tend to emphasise dispositions such as collaboration and exploration' (Nuttall 2005, p. 21). Blaiklock (2008) similarly argues that there are a number of issues for teachers who rely on learning stories as their only method of documenting observations. These issues include difficulty with establishing the validity or accountability of learning stories, problems with making subjective evaluations based on short observations, lack of guidance on where, when and how often to make learning stories, problems with defining and assessing learning dispositions and difficulties in using learning stories to show changes in children's learning over time.

None of these critiques is insurmountable, but all require thought. Perhaps the issue that stands out more than any, which is very evident in *Kei tua o te pae*, is that all too often, the learning stories focus on children's dispositions and do not capture when children have gained new concepts or understandings. There are few examples in which the learning that is happening is clearly identified. Used well, the narrative forms of assessment discussed here can provide rich and meaningful accounts of children's learning, but teachers need to avoid just taking pictures and writing descriptive stories and instead focus on using their observations to document learning that is happening and to inform their curricula decision making.

Shaping curriculum around key informants

The next chapter provides you with some examples of how teachers plan, enact, assess and evaluate curriculum based on their observations of children and their learning. Teachers who are reflecting on the best approaches to their own practice are what many researchers would call *practitioner researchers* or *teacher researchers*. They are insiders in their organisation and are therefore in an ideal situation to understanding the history, culture, community relationships, strengths and weaknesses of the educational setting. They are also likely to have good access to institutional information that might not be readily available to an outsider. However, as Gray (2004, p. 243) states, 'one of the limitations of using practitioner-researchers is the fact that they may be imbued with the organization's ethos and attitudes and so have difficulty in adopting fresh approaches'. Gray suggests that action research offers most teachers the opportunity to work with others to identify alternative perspectives and insights into their own practice.

It is also productive to use the basic framework of action research methodology for thinking about how to use your observations of children in your early childhood setting to shape curriculum. Fraenkel and Wallen (2006, p. 570) argue that there are four crucial steps in action research methodology:

1. Identify the research problem or question.
2. Obtain the necessary information to answer the question(s).
3. Analyse and interpret the information that has been gathered.
4. Develop a plan of action.

Using the observations you have gathered by one method or another, when you come to shaping curriculum, your planning is based on all of these steps. Often this process is referred to as a PDSA cycle: PLAN>DO>STUDY>ACT. This idea is also clearly articulated in New Zealand in *Quality in action* (Ministry of Education 1998) as the program planning cycle; there is some slightly different terminology, but the principle of a cycle of observation, planning, acting and reflecting draws on PDSA ideas.

So if you were interested in how children's literacy abilities were developing, for example, you would set about observing specific aspects of children's literacy, such as writing or recognising their own name, taking part in singing of rhymes and songs at mat time, or using 'book language' (vocabulary that clearly come from books children have had read to them) or language that has clearly come from oral storytelling in their play. For example, one recent observation revealed a child mixing mud pies in a bucket in a muddy patch of ground outside, singing 'Wombat stew, wombat stew, icky sticky, gooey wooey, wombat stew'. This child has clearly made the link between stories read to him (in this case the delightful book, *Wombat stew*) and his own mud play, and that is clearly reflected in his language.

However, following a period of careful observation, you might decide that children do not have enough opportunities to gain any of these useful literacy skills. Then you plan ways to enhance this knowledge: you plan it, you do it, you then study it and reflect on the success or failure of your plans, and then you then act on those reflections.

SUMMARY

This chapter has introduced you to some of the fundamental skills that many early childhood educators use for observing children during play, interpreting what they see and planning for future learning. We have taken these basic techniques and approaches and have framed them using cultural-historical theory. In particular, we have used Rogoff's (2003) seminal writings on personal, interpersonal and cultural/institutional/cultural lenses, and we have used Vygotsky's (1987) and Kravtsova's (2008) zones of devlopment for our framing. We have used these because they speak directly to early childhood education, and their framing captures the dynamic nature of child observations in play-based programs. Although the methods described here may seem somewhat mechanical, over time they are internalised and become an automatic part of a teacher's repertoire of teaching skills.

It is useful, though, to be able to articulate which approach to observing children's learning and development you are taking and how it fits with your philosophical world view of education. The trick is to find a good match, so that the realities of your use of observation in the educational setting are congruent with your personal, centre or school's philosophy, and ensure that culturally and linguistically diverse communities are not 'othered' in the analysis process. The next chapter will give you some useful examples of what this looks like in practice, within the context of school or centre evaluations.

REFERENCES

Berk, L. & Winsler, A. (1995). *Scaffolding children's learning: Vygotsky and early childhood education*. Washington DC: NAEYC.

Blaiklock, K. (2008). A critique of the use of learning stories to assess the learning disposition of young children. *New Zealand Research in Early Childhood Education*, 11, pp. 77–88.

Carr, M. (2001). *Assessment in early childhood settings: Learning stories*. London: Paul Chapman.

Cohen, L., Manion, L. & Morrison, K. (2000). *Research methods in education*. 5th edn. London: Routledge Falmer.

Crotty, M. (1998). *The foundations of social research: Meaning and perspective in the research process*. Sydney: Allen & Unwin.

Daniels, H. (2001). *Vygotsky and pedagogy*. London: Routledge Falmer.

Denscombe, M. (2007). *The good research guide for small-scale social research projects*. 3rd edn. Maidenhead UK: Open University Press.

Department of Education, Tasmania (2002). *Essential Learning: Essential learnings framework*. Hobart.

Department of Education, Training and Employment, South Australia (2001). *South Australian Curriculum, Standards and Accountability Framework*. Adelaide. Available at http://www.sacsa.edu.au.

Dockett, S. & Perry, B. (2005). 'You need to know how to play safe': Children's experiences of starting school. *Contemporary Issues in Early Childhood*, 6(1), pp. 4–18.

Dockett, S. & Perry, B. (2006). *Transitions to school: Perceptions, expectations, experiences*. Sydney: University of Western Sydney Press.

Drummond, M.J. (1993). *Assessing children's learning*. London: David Fulton.

Edwards, S. (2009). *Early childhood education and care: A sociocultural approach*. Sydney: Pademelon Press.

Espinosa, L.M. (2005). Curriculum and assessment considerations for young children from culturally, linguistically and economically diverse backgrounds. *Psychology in the Schools*, 42(8), pp. 837–53.

Fleer, M. (2002). Sociocultural theory: Rebuilding the theoretical foundations of early childhood education. *Policy and practice in education. Early Education: Policy, curriculum and discourse*, 54(1 & 2), pp. 105–21.

Fleer, M. (2006). Potentive assessment in early childhood education. In M. Fleer, S. Edwards, M. Hammer, A. Kennedy, A. Ridgway, J. Robbins & L. Surman, *Early childhood learning communities. Sociocultural research in practice*. Sydney: Pearson Education, pp. 161–73.

Fleer, M. (2010). *Early Learning and Development: Cultural–historical concepts in play*. Melbourne: Cambridge University Press.

Fleer, M. & Richardson, C. (2004). *Observing and planning in early childhood settings: Using a sociocultural approach*. Canberra: Early Childhood Australia.

Fraenkel, J.R. & Wallen, N.E. (2006). *How to design and evaluate research in education*. 6th edn. Boston: McGraw Hill.

Gallimore, R. & Tharp, R. (1990). Teaching mind in society: Teaching, schooling and literate discourse. In L.C. Moll (ed.), *Vygotsky and education: Instructional implications and applications of sociohistorical psychology*. Cambridge: Cambridge University Press, pp. 175–205.

Graue, M.E. & Walsh, D.J. (1998). *Studying children in context: Theories, methods and ethics*. Thousand Oaks CA: Sage.

Gray, D.E. (2004). *Doing research in the real world*. London: Sage.

Hanlen, W. (2007). Indigenous literacies: Moving from social construction towards social justice. In L. Makin, C. Jones Diaz & C. McLachlan (eds), *Literacies in childhood: Changing views, challenging practices*. Sydney: MacLennan & Petty, pp. 230–42.

Hedegaard, M. & Fleer, M. (eds) (2008). *Studying children: A cultural-historical approach*. Maidhead UK: Open University Press.

Hohepa, M. & McNaughton, S. (2007). Doing it 'proper': The case of Māori literacy. In L. Makin, C. Jones Diaz & C. McLachlan (eds), *Literacies in childhood: Changing views, challenging practices*. Sydney: MacLennan & Petty, pp. 217–29.

Kravtsova, E.E. (2008). *Zone of potential development and subject positioning*. Paper presented at Monash University, Peninsula campus, 15 December.

Long, S., Volk, D. & Gregory, E. (2007). Intentionality and expertise: Learning from observation of children at play in multilingual and multicultural contexts. *Anthropology and Education Quarterly*, 38(3), pp. 239–59.

McMurray, A.J., Pace, R.W. & Scott, D. (2004). *Research: A common sense approach*. Melbourne: Thomson.

Ministry of Education (1996). *Te Whāriki: Early childhood curriculum*. Wellington: Learning Media.

Ministry of Education (1998). *Quality in action: Implementing the Revised Statement of Desirable Objectives and Practices in New Zealand Early Childhood Services*. Wellington: Learning Media.

Ministry of Education (2005). *Kei tua o te pae. Assessment for learning: Early childhood exemplars*. Wellington: Learning Media.

Moll, L.C. (ed.) (1990). *Vygotsky and education: Instructional implications and applications of sociohistorical psychology*. Cambridge: Cambridge University Press.

Mutch, C. (2002). *Border crossing: Early childhood and primary teachers constructing an education for citizenship*. Paper presented at the Collaborative Approaches in the Early Years Conference, 4–7 April.

NAEYC (2003). *A position statement of the National Association for the Education of Young Children Early Childhood Curriculum, Assessment, and Program Evaluation*. http://www.naeyc.org/about/positions/cape.asp, accessed 17 October 2008.

Nuttall, J. (2003). Exploring the role of the teacher within *Te Whāriki*: Some possibilities and constraints. In J. Nuttall (ed.), *Weaving* Te Whariki*: Aotearoa New Zealand's early childhood curriculum in theory and practice*. Wellington: NZCER, pp. 161–86.

Nuttall, J. (2005). Looking back, looking forward: Three decades of early childhood curriculum development in New Zealand. *Curriculum Matters*, 1, pp. 12–28.

Phillips, G., McNaughton, S. & MacDonald, S. (2001). *Picking up the pace: Effective literacy interventions for accelerated progress over the transition into decile 1 schools*. Auckland: The Child Literacy Foundation and Woolf Fisher Research.

Rogers, S. & Evans, J. (2007). Rethinking role play in the reception class. *Educational research*, 49(2), pp. 153–67.

Rogoff, B. (1990). *Apprenticeship in thinking: Cognitive development in social context*. Oxford: Oxford University Press.

Rogoff, B. (1995). Cognition as a collaborative process. In W. Damon (ed.), *Handbook of child psychology*, Vol. 2: Cognition, perception and language. New York: John Wiley & Sons, pp. 678–744.

Rogoff, B. (1998). Cognition as a collaborative process. In D. Kuhn and R.S. Siegler (eds), *Handbook of child psychology*, Vol. 2, 5th edn. New York: John Wiley, pp. 679–744.

Rogoff, B. (2003). *The cultural nature of human development*. Oxford: Oxford University Press.

Tagoilelagi-Leota, F., McNaughton, S., MacDonald, S. & Ferry, S. (2005). Bilingual and biliteracy development over the transition to school. *International Journal of Bilingual Education and Bilingualism*, 8(5), pp. 455–79.

Tayler, C. (2006). Challenging partnerships in Australian early childhood education. *Early Years*, 26(3), pp. 249–65.

Vygotsky, L.S. (1987). Thinking and speech. In L.S. Vygotsky, *The collected works of L.S. Vygotsky*, Vol. 1. R.W. Rieber & A.S. Carton (eds), N. Minick (trans.). New York: Plenum Press, pp. 39–285.

Warren, S. (2000). Let's do it properly: Inviting children to be researchers. In A. Lewis & G. Lindsay (eds), *Researching children's perspectives*. Buckingham UK: Open University Press, pp. 122–34.

Wood, D., Bruner, J. & Ross, G. (1976). The role of tutoring in problem solving. *British Journal of Psychology*, 17, pp. 89–100.

CHAPTER 8

ASSESSING CHILDREN AND EVALUATING CURRICULUM: SHIFTING LENSES

This chapter will examine the relationship between observation, assessment and evaluation. The interrelated nature of assessment and evaluation is explored, along with the implications of that for the roles of teachers, children, families and communities. We will examine how one curriculum leader in one school generates a school-based curriculum and works with state and federal education systems to assess children and evaluate curriculum. We will explore how a school can combine school and community needs with departmental curriculum evaluation and assessment imperatives. In the first part of this chapter, the concept of assessment is further elaborated (building on Chapter 7), in order to build a context for discussing the relationships between assessment and curriculum evaluation.

WHAT DO WE MEAN BY ASSESSMENT?

In the previous chapter, we discussed how teachers in Australia, New Zealand and internationally are using observation and narrative methodologies as a way of documenting their observations of children learning. We also made the point that observation has been a primary means of assessment in many early childhood settings for many years. In primary schools, a wider range of assessment methods have typically been used, but there continues to be enormous debate around which methods should be used with younger children (see, for example, Brassard & Boehm 2007).

In his seminal paper on assessment, Crooks (1988) defined the reasons why we assess:

- Selection and placement: for working out which children or adults should progress or in which groups they should be placed.

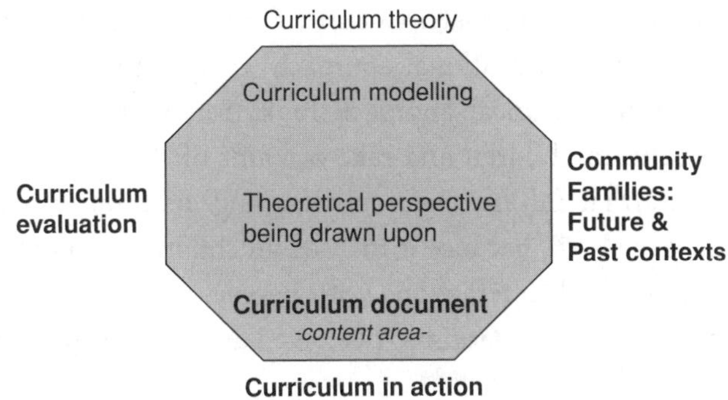

Figure 8.1 Curriculum development pathway – evaluation

- Motivation: it can help or hinder motivation.
- Focusing learning – the hidden curriculum: what is assessed sends a message to all stakeholders about what is important, regardless of all other rhetoric.
- Consolidating and structuring learning: it can be used to reinforce learning or to provide a structure to what is learnt.
- Guiding and correcting learning: used formatively, assessment can provide guidance to learners.
- Determining readiness to proceed: it can be used to determine readiness to proceed – this is a more common practice in the US with young children.
- Certifying or grading achievement: it is often used to recognise level of achievement.
- Evaluating teaching: it can be used for evaluating how effectively teachers have been teaching.

Crooks (1988) made the point that not all the reasons why we assess are particularly good reasons, but they do form the basis of much decision making. He also argues that there has been a paradigm shift in assessment from psychometric to educational models of assessment in recent years:

- **Psychometric approach:** this approach focuses on being objective about learning. According to this model of assessment, individual ability can be reliably measured, and it is claimed that such ability is unaffected by context or the testing situation.
- **Educational approach:** this model rejects psychometric criteria of reliability, validity and generalisability and does not claim to be objective. This approach focuses on authenticity and trustworthiness in assessing children's learning.

With a cultural-historical approach to curriculum, assessment is more likely to be aligned with the 'educational approach' than with the 'psychometric approach'. A cultural-historical approach looks for methods of assessment that are meaningful to children and take account of the social, cultural and historical contexts that inform children's learning. It differs from the ideas outlined by Crooks (1998) because it focuses on children's potential development, as enacted through interactions with people, rather than on children's individual achievements in relation to perceived age or class 'progression'. For example:

> Western approaches to assessment are less likely to examine what children do when supported by others, and therefore are unlikely to map the potential capabilities of children. The assessment for tomorrow (the ZPD) examines the children's strengths rather than their weaknesses. Measuring children's potential level of development allows early childhood teachers to plan more thoughtfully. Sociocultural or cultural-historical assessment moves the focus from a deficit view of assessment to a much more powerful and useful assessment practice for informing teaching and learning practices (Fleer & Richardson 2008, p. 131).

Box A outlines five criteria (adapted from Absolum 2006) for thinking about assessment approaches. In this chapter, we will use these criteria to think about the ways in which a cultural-historical perspective on assessment can be used so that it is valid, reliable, manageable and trustworthy for both children and teachers.

BOX A

Five criteria for thinking about the usefulness of assessment approaches

1. **Validity** – Does the assessment measure what it purports to measure? Is the assessment appropriate for the age of the child, their cultural and linguistic background and the learning context?
2. **Reliability** – Can the assessment be relied upon to give accurate information? Does it give a consistent result over time and with a similar sample?
3. **Manageability** – Does the assessment need to be one to one, or can groups do it at the same time? Is a quiet space needed? Does the teacher need classroom release time?

continued »

Box A continued »

4. **Trustworthiness** – Is the assessment trustworthy according to the following categories
   a. Credibility – e.g. is it based on prolonged classroom assessment, dialogue or observation?
   b. Transferability – is the context of achievement specified? Can others also judge the likelihood of the skill transferring across contexts?
   c. Dependability – are the process and the judgments made open to scrutiny? Have audit processes such as moderation taken place?
5. **Authenticity** – To what extent have relevant stakeholders' constructs been fairly and adequately covered? Have children and their families had the opportunity to be involved in the assessment?

Fleet and Torr (2007) apply these ideas when they consider appropriate ways of assessing young children's literacy. For example, they ask:

- Is the assessment reliable? Will it reflect accurately what this child knows about literacy?
- Is it appropriate? Is this assessment embedded in the literacy practices of the child's social and cultural context?
- Is it relevant? Will this assessment provide information relating specifically to the child's ongoing literacy development?

Whilst these questions consider the appropriateness and relevance of assessment they do not necessarily deal with the idea of assessing for future development that is encompassed in a cultural-historical perspective. However, the questions are important because they concern the appropriateness and relevance of assessment. From a cultural-historical perspective, additional questions might include: What is the child's potential level of development? And in what social and cultural contexts is the child most effectively able to show evidence of their potential development? This allows us to begin to think about assessment as providing information for teachers and children that helps to build learning, rather than assessing what children have learned. For example, Absolum (2006) argues that we should think about assessment as assessment *for* learning instead assessment *of* learning. He further argues that assessment should be integrally embedded in teaching and learning so that it helps teachers support children in growing their ideas and capacities.

One approach that is used in this way is formative assessment. Black and William (1998) describe formative assessment as 'the process used by teacher and students to recognise and respond to student learning in order to enhance that learning, during the learning' (in Absolum 2006, p. 20). An example of this in practice is when teachers provide feedback to children when they are engaged in an activity that helps the children learn. For example, a child learning to write his name said he didn't how to write the first letter (letter N). The adult asked him if he knew how to draw straight lines. The child said yes. The adult then asked the child to draw a straight line. Then the adult positioned the pen on the top point of the line and helped the child draw a diagonal line down. Together they repositioned the pen and the adult said 'now draw a line straight up'. The child did so and exclaimed, 'An N – I can draw Ns!' From this point on the boy always wrote his own N at the beginning of his name. This is an example of formative assessment in that it helped the child move forward his literacy development during the moment of teaching and learning. It also illustrates aspects of cultural-historical assessment, because the focus on assessment was on the child's potential achievement within the writing context as he engaged with the adult. In this example, the assessment was valid, reliable, manageable and trustworthy for both the child and the adult.

This example echoes Mary Jane Drummond's (1993) definition of assessment, which suggests that it includes 'the ways in which, in our everyday practice, we observe children's learning, strive to understand it, and then put our understanding to good use' (p. 13). This underpins approaches to assessment used in New Zealand's *Kei tua o te pae* (Ministry of Education 2005). In addition, the Education Review Office in New Zealand states that:

> good assessment practice recognizes the child as a competent and confident learner, takes into account the whole child, and involves parents, whānau and educators. This sociocultural approach to teaching and learning recognizes the influence of the society in which the child lives and of its cultural values on children's learning and development (2007, p. 4).

One way in which some researchers are building on these ideas is by arguing that assessment can also be designed to allow family participation (Carr, Cowie, Gerrity, Jones, Lee & Pohio 2001, p. 29). Absolum (2006) highlights the many factors of which teachers need to be aware when thinking about assessment:

- Strong understandings of curriculum and informal assessment;
- How to observe learning;

- How to form professional learning communities and let others help with assessment;
- How to collaborate with children and use children's self and peer assessment in meaningful ways;
- How to maintain quality in assessment methods used;
- To learn new technical skills to cope with diverse assessment methods;
- How to keep an eye on all these aspects of assessment; and
- How to keep the big picture of why they are doing assessment firmly in mind.

The following case study provides an example of how one teacher has been able to frame her approach to assessment within a cultural-historical perspective.

Curriculum context at Wooranna Park

Esme Capp is the deputy principal and curriculum leader of Wooranna Park Primary School. Her school is situated in a culturally diverse community, and the school looks like any other school in that region. Figure 8.2 shows the school and its grounds. We need to ask, 'Is the learning, the assessment and the evaluation of the curriculum at Wooranna Park Primary School like that of any other school?'

Figure 8.2 Just looks like any other school

If we step inside this school, we soon see that the spaces we would normally expect to find – classrooms, with walls separating one room from the next – have all been removed. Figure 8.3 shows part of the learning space within

Figure 8.3 When the classroom walls come down, new spaces and places for learning and evaluation are created

the preparatory grade to the second year level area (subsequent photos in this chapter give more detail of the interesting spaces within the learning spaces).

The school has specially designed spaces for multi-age groups. The children do not work with one teacher; the space which would traditionally have been 3 classrooms side by side has now become a space for a multi-age group of children with a team of teachers. Children's learning is organised across a larger space, with special areas for focused or specialised work to occur – such as a film and sound studio, a quiet study area, puzzle and games spaces, a theatre, reading areas, a lecture hall, workshopping spaces, interactive whiteboard areas, writing areas, etc.

You may be wondering what this has to do with assessment and evaluation. How learning is organised is directly related to how assessment can or should occur. Your beliefs about learning should be reflected in your beliefs about assessment. Evaluation is based upon the assessment of learning in relation to the intended learning goals. Assessment, learning and evaluation are interdependent concepts.

REFLECTION 8.1

On your next field placement, seek out the statements that are made by the centre or school in relation to learning, assessment and evaluation. Record the links you see between these statements and the types of learning areas used in the school. What do you notice?

Assessment, learning and evaluation are interdependent concepts

Assessment as learning

When we enter the preparatory to second year level area at Wooranna Park school, we are greeted with planning documents for specific groups (see Figure 8.4), and with an ongoing record or portfolio of children's work, directly below the planning documents (Figure 8.5). The assessment materials are conceptually and physically linked in this school. This material is displayed in an inviting manner, encouraging children, staff and families to read and use the

Figure 8.4 'Assessment as learning'

Figure 8.5 'Learning as assessment'

documents. They are not filed away or placed in an office area away from children and families, but are there for all to engage with, and for all to use – as living documents reflecting learning at the school.

REFLECTION 8.2

Look for the assessment and evaluation documents in your local school or centre. Where are they? Who has access to them? What format do they take? Can children view them?

In this school, assessment and learning support each other. Considering the relationship between assessment and learning is useful, because the intersection between them suggests where most can be learned about how a school is performing and/or how well a particular program is going. Esme discusses this idea:

> Assessment must be totally embedded in the learning process; collecting evidence of the learning that is taking place, and teachers having an understanding about what experiences and understandings that they want those children to develop. When they can do this, they can successfully evaluate their own programmes.
>
> We have the concept of 'Assessment as learning'. How do I collect evidence about these children, and what do I do with it? The evidence that is collected becomes a tool for reflecting. The children are embedded in that process and they are encouraged to reflect upon their own learning, and to think about what challenges lay ahead for them. The teacher is thinking 'Where do I take them now?' This is an important programme evaluation question.

What we notice about the philosophy for learning, assessment and evaluation in this school is that these interdependent concepts are in constant motion. They are not static – that is, the teachers do not simply assess the children independent of the children's own self-reflection on their learning. This represents a cultural-historical approach to assessment that is valid, reliable, manageable and trustworthy, as teachers and children are involved in assessing their own learning in ways that help them understand their potential development and draw on the social context of the teachers and learners. The children and the teachers work cooperatively in relation to both assessment of children, and

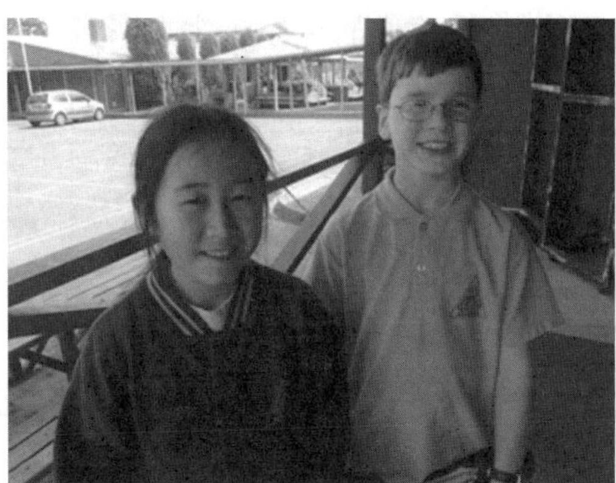

Figure 8.6 Amanda and Thomas

evaluation of the teaching program. If we ask the children about their learning and about the assessment, we can see how assessment and learning are a part of the evaluation process. Amanda and Thomas, two children from this classroom, share their thoughts (see Figure 8.6):

Thomas: The school is different. It has lots of different cultures. Lots of people new to Australia. Every country is here. The school has more room to walk around than in most other schools. We have Learning Agreements. We get to choose what to do – if it is all right with the teacher.

Amanda: We negotiate with the teacher. We write down in our learning journeys what we will do in the Learning Agreement time.

Amanda: In the learning journeys [see Figure 8.7] you write what you want to do; which learning area it is in; and you negotiate with the teacher, get their signature. It has to be educational.

Thomas: You can create your own project. They are called Passion projects – it is not what you know a lot about, it is about something you don't know and you want to find out a heap more about.

Amanda: What we need to know and what we want to know.

Thomas: We also have a Discovery forum – that is where we get together and talk about what we have done during the week.

Amanda: You show them your work and you ask the others to give their opinion on it, and how to improve it. On this [scale drawing of 'My ideal festival', see Figure 8.8], I asked them how I could measure this, and she said try using the graph paper.

In Wooranna Park school, 'assessment as learning' is supported through five key strategies. These align with the criteria for thinking about the effectiveness of assessment and with key ideas associated with a cultural-historical perspective on assessment (see Table 8.1).

Learning Journey Term 3

Name: Amanda Thai	Date: 07/08/08

Class Aim: To reach the goals of our class pledge and communicate effectively.

Learning Agreement Possibilities: Reader's Response, maths investigations, science investigations, passion projects, descriptive writing, story writing, complete a reading or maths challenge, persistence log.

34CD CLASS PLEDGE

I will be kind, trustworthy, respectful, honest, generous and appreciative.
I promise to take responsibility of my behaviour, my work, my belongings and my classroom too.
I will do my best at all I do at school, the community and at home too.
I will respect the guidance of my teachers.
I pledge to communicate and work as a team, to learn at my best and reach my dreams.

DATE	LEARNING AREA	ACTIVITY	NEGOTIATED WITH
7-8-08	Visual Art	Planet Poster for Mini Monsters Project	[signature]
7-8-08	Numeracy	Mathletics - I want to get a Silver Certificate	[signature]
7-8-08	Literacy	Reading Response to Jessica Juniper	[signature]
11-8-08		Persistence Log ???	
21/8/08	Visual Art Literacy	I will work on my Beanie Kid Passion Project	[signature]
21/8/08	Literacy	I will work on my third draft of my Written Writing	[signature]
3/9/08	Literacy	Reading "Fairy Dust" by Gwyneth Rees	

Figure 8.7 Amanda's learning journey

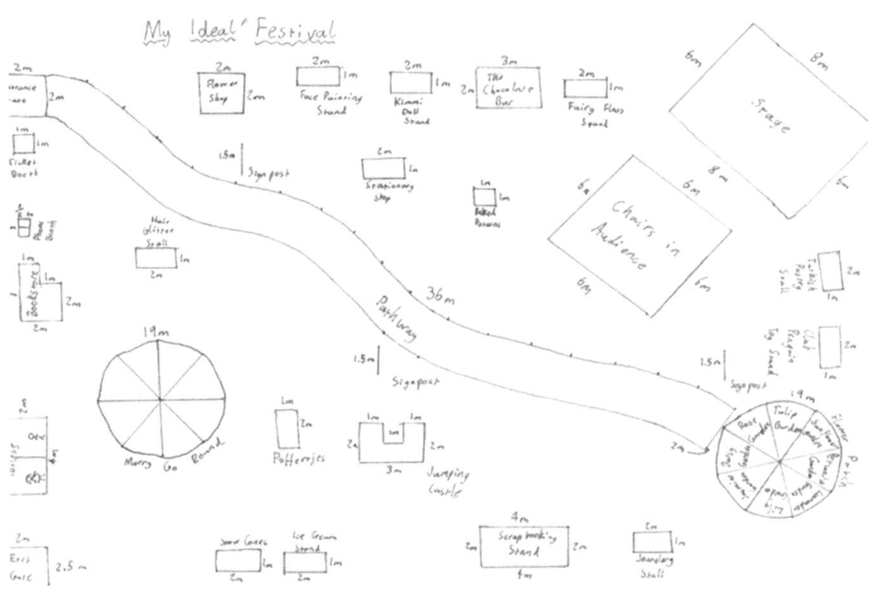

Figure 8.8 Amanda's ideal festival

Table 8.1 Aligning assessment strategies, assessment criteria and ideas from cultural-historical theory

Woorana Park Primary School assessment strategies	Type of criteria about useful assessment reflected	Idea from cultural-historical theory reflected
Learning agreements that children co-construct with their teachers	Meaningful Valid	Socially situated Strengths-focused
Learning journey that children write to plan out how they will go about their learning project	Manageable Reliable	Aware of potential development Contextually relevant
Passion projects which focus on the children's interests, but in areas they have not previously studied before	Meaningful Valid	Awareness of potential development Strengths-focused
Learning portfolios which include a collection of the children's work which reflects their current understandings	Trustworthy Reliable	Contextually relevant Strengths-focused
Learning spaces which afford the kinds of interactions which allow all of the above assessment and learning tools to be utilised	Meaningful Manageable	Socially situated Contextually relevant

These strategies support the learning that is organised in the school and provide evidence for staff about how the school is going in relation to its intended outcomes and stated goals.

Evaluation and assessment: Why evaluation matters

Teachers need to evaluate how they approach the relationship between assessment and learning. This is important across a range of educational settings, including early childhood settings and school. The process of evaluation helps teachers and the early childhood/school communities examine the extent to which they are achieving their goals. Evaluation can be formally or informally conducted and can be at the system, school and/or teacher program level. More recent analyses of curriculum in the early childhood sector also illustrate this definition of evaluation (see Brock 2008).

Michael Scriven, a recognised world leader in assessment and evaluation, states that evaluation is the process of determining the merit or worth or value of 'something' (Scriven 1977). That 'something' is what a particular school community decides is important, or 'something' that a state education system decides is important. Similarly, it can be what an individual teacher decides is significant for learning for their particular group of children. At Wooranna Park Primary School the 'something' is the children's capacity to drive their own learning and to work in collaborative ways to achieve learning goals they have created for themselves.

Scriven states that evaluation can be either formative or summative. Formative evaluation is undertaken to provide feedback to people who are trying to improve something. It's often relatively informal and is designed to identify strengths and weaknesses of a program or intervention. For example, it might occur when a teacher invites a colleague into her classroom and asks them to provide feedback on how she is approaching and implementing learning and assessment. In contrast, summative evaluation aims to determine the overall effectiveness of a program and provide judgment on whether or not it should continue to run (Gray 2004). Summative evaluations are typically written as reports by an external body, such as the Education Review Office in New Zealand or the Office for Standards in Education (Ofsted) in the UK.

These types of evaluations look at how well particular schools or early learning programs are meeting a set of stated criteria. For example, the Ofsted reports list a series of indicators, including 'Overall effectiveness of the school; Achievement and Standards; and Personal Development and Well-being'. Schools are evaluated on how well they are achieving on each of these indicators, using a grading scale of 4 (inadequate) to 1 (outstanding). An example of how this evaluation can be used was when a graduate teacher from Australia went to the UK to look for work. He was offered a temporary position at a primary school and looked up the school's Ofsted report to learn more about the school. He forwarded copies of the report to his family and friends back home so that they could help him make his decision about this position.

Whilst evaluation can provide useful information to families, teachers and communities, it is important to consider whether or not the evaluation has been fairly and ethically conducted. Also, evaluation can sometimes work to put schools in positions that make it difficult for them to succeed or even to attract funding. This leads us to consider the ethical dimensions of evaluation.

ETHICAL FRAMEWORK FOR EVALUATION

Ballantine, Levy, Marton, Munro and Powell (2000) have constructed an ethical framework for evaluation. This framework is useful for making judgments about evaluation conducted in educational contexts, involving early learning centres and schools. They argue that the philosophy underlying an evaluation has a significant influence on how the evaluation is conducted, the tools used, the goals of the evaluation and the people contributing to the evaluation. Their framework involves six factors which, they argue, influence the choice of evaluation approach used: philosophy; power; culture; management style; the kind of evaluator; and resources available. Against each of these factors, the ethics related to the purpose of evaluation, the process of evaluation, and the people affected by the evaluation are measured. Table 8.2 provides an overview of what decision making around evaluation could involve from an ethical perspective.

Table 8.2 A framework for ethical evaluation (adapted from Ballantine et al. 2000)

Ethical attributes Evaluation influences	Purpose of evaluation	Process of evaluation	People affected by evaluation
Philosophy	Summative ↔ Formative	Positivist ↔ Interpretivist	Automata ↔ Human
Culture	Control ↔ Learning	Ritualistic ↔ Purposeful	Organisational ↔ Individual
Management style	Covert ↔ Overt	Implicit ↔ Explicit	Directive ↔ Consensual
Power	Manipulative ↔ Emancipate	Autocratic ↔ Democratic	Dictatorial ↔ Participative
Evaluator	Judgmental ↔ Assist	Investigate ↔ Collaborate	Control ↔ Facilitate
Resources	Minimalist ↔ Comprehensive	Limited ↔ Sufficient	Constrain ↔ Enable

Within the cultural-historical model of curriculum we have focused on in this book, evaluation would primarily fall on the right-hand side of the column for each factor, although constraints of time and resources may limit the extent of evaluation undertaken. For example, under the factor 'evaluator', a cultural-historical perspective on evaluation would seek to assist, collaborate and facilitate the purpose and process of evaluation in cooperation with the key stakeholders in the relevant learning community.

Fetterman and Wandersman (2005) express ideas similar to those outlined by Ballantine et al. (2008). They use an approach to evaluation known as 'empowerment evaluation'. Empowerment valuation is an:

> [a]pproach that aims to increase the probability of achieving program success by (1) providing program stakeholders with tools for assessing the planning, implementation and self-evaluation of their program, and (2) mainstreaming evaluation as part of the planning and management of the program/organization (Fetterman & Wandersman 2005, p. 28).

Fetterman and Wandersman believe that empowerment evaluation does not reduce the need for a range of approaches to be used; however, they consider the empowerment evaluation model particularly useful when the purpose of evaluation is the improvement or development of people and programs. From their perspective, effective evaluation includes all members of the community who have interest in the program being evaluated. They also believe that fair, transparent and equitable decision making by all the people involved is fundamental to the evaluation. In this model, the community has expert knowledge about their own context, which is used in relationship with the evidence gleaned from research and scholarship. One of the primary purposes of empowerment evaluation is to build capacity and further learning. Fetterman and Wandersman (2005, pp. 31–38) argue that empowerment evaluation should be based on the following 10 principles:

1. **Improvement** – improvement in people, programs, organisations and communities is valued.
2. **Community ownership** – the community has the right to make decisions about actions that affect their lives.
3. **Inclusion** – involves direct participation of key stakeholders wherever possible.
4. **Democratic participation** – assumes stakeholders have capacity for intelligent judgment and action when supplied with appropriate information and conditions. The importance of deliberation, collaboration, fairness and due process are fundamental.
5. **Social justice** – a fair, equitable allocation of resources, opportunities, obligations and bargaining power is integral to this approach, which strives to recognise and overcome social inequities.
6. **Community knowledge** – community-based knowledge and wisdom are valued and promoted.

7. **Evidenced-based strategies** – values the role of science and evidence-based strategies in designing and/or selecting a program to address a community need. Valuing knowledge from research evidence avoids re-inventing the wheel.
8. **Capacity building** – the changes in individual thinking and behaviour, and the program or organisational changes in procedures and culture that result from the learning that occurs during the evaluation process.
9. **Organisational learning** – the process of acquiring, applying and mastering new tools and methods to improve processes. Improvement is enhanced when there is a process that encourages learning (organisational learning) and an organisational structure that encourages learning (a learning organisation).
10. **Accountability** – provides an innovative vehicle for helping programs to be accountable to administrators and the public by generating process – and outcome – data within an evaluation framework that heightens an organisation's sensitivity to its responsibility to the public and to itself. The approach is results and process accountability oriented; a self-driven accountability model.

These 10 principles can underpin many types of evaluation, including those conducted at the classroom, school or district level. The important feature is who can, and should be, involved in the evaluation. Given that teachers are likely to be involved in evaluation of some type or another during their careers, it is useful to consider the different types of evaluation that might be encountered.

Planning for evaluation

There are many types of evaluations that are useful for providing information about how programs or schools might improve their current practices and outcomes. Most evaluations cover particular areas such as 'Outcome, 'Process, 'Input and 'Design:

- *Outcome evaluation* is based on a collective analysis of other interim outcomes or prerequisites. For example, student state tests results, parent satisfaction surveys, and levels of staff engagement in professional development. These combine to give a picture of whether or not a school is achieving the outcomes they strive for, or that might have been set by governing bodies.

- *Process evaluation* focuses on the degree to which a school has performed the activities as planned. For instance, process evaluation might include the degree or frequency of parent complaints, staff attendance at professional development sessions, or student involvement in committees.
- *Input evaluation* focuses on the availability of resources, particularly people, materials, and money that are being utilised within the program, classroom or school.
- *Design evaluation* focuses directly on program planning. This is where it is important to focus on how a school designs and delivers its educational programs, and how it designs the measurement tools to be used. It is also important to think about how the school decides upon the kinds of evidence that are needed for making judgments about its programs (see Madaus, Scriven & Stufflebeam 1983). These ideas can be represented in a table so that teachers, schools or system-level evaluators can use them as guide for framing the evaluation of programs, and for collecting evidence for the evaluation (see Table 8.3).

Table 8.3 An evaluation plan

Evaluation question posed	Design	Standard	Evidence	Tools	Date
What is important in this school community?	What planning documents, input, process, and outcome are being considered?	What standard is desired of the learning and the learning outcomes?	What collection strategy will be used to gather evidence about the design and standard?	What tools will be used to gather the evidence?	When is the evidence needed by?

REFLECTION 8.2

Examine the documentation that your centre or school has in relation to program evaluation or conducting school reviews. Are there features which relate to process, input, outcome and design? What headings have been used by the teachers in the school/centre you are reviewing?

Having an evaluation plan is important, but how it is constructed depends upon the school and early learning centre beliefs and practices in relation to learning, assessment and evaluation. The creation of an evaluation plan is something that is usually undertaken at the school level. Sometimes this will occur under the leadership of a Director or Principal, and at other times it might be a leadership group within the school or centre, such as a team of early childhood teachers working in the junior school or in a particular area of the early learning centre (such as the babies and toddlers teachers).

Leading evaluations: Outcomes, processes, inputs and design

When participating in evaluations the leader or leadership group will make decisions about what types of evaluation they will conduct. They can draw on the range of approaches considered above. We can see how these approaches have been used in Esme's school.

Staff at Wooranna Park Primary School have developed what Esme calls the 'Thinking Curriculum'. The Thinking Curriculum works so that creativity and discipline knowledge, such as mathematics and literacy, are linked. In a school where the focus is on teachers and children generating a Thinking Curriculum, evaluation must also examine whether or not the curriculum the teachers are providing is allowing for thinking to be generated by the children and staff as they engage in learning activities. Planning for evaluating a Thinking Curriculum can use process, input, design and outcome evaluation.

Process evaluation

Figures 8.9 to 8.13 show an audit of the learning spaces which was conducted in Wooranna Park school. This is a process evaluation because it looks at how well the school is working towards implementing its planned curriculum. The process evaluation is important because it provides information about how the Thinking Curriculum is being implemented. It also helps Esme in her role as the Principal to see if the learning spaces that were created are working to support the goals of the Thinking Curriculum. The interactive spaces demonstrated in these images are created to maximise collective problem solving and collective learning, which is one of the stated goals in the Thinking Curriculum. The examples are for mathematics and for technology and design, but the spaces could support any area of a curriculum oriented towards engaging children in thinking.

Figure 8.9 The table is set to invite specific forms of thinking and learning

Figure 8.10 Resources for children to use are readily available

Figure 8.11 A felt board, with felt pieces created by the children in a previous project, is being used as a stimulus for a further challenge – to 'Create and build a model of Wooranna Park Rainbow Garden'

Figure 8.12 Materials are displayed in an inviting manner

Figure 8.13 A role-play area within the prep–Year 2 area has been created

The children are greeted with a card which says 'How to play the addition game'. The children are also encouraged to create their own games, which they put onto cards and leave for other groups to use.

On the far wall of this space, we notice a challenge that has been placed on a wall in the form of a 'sign' to the children. The sign says: 'This kitchen has food all over the floor. You cannot eat at this restaurant. By order of Building Inspector.' The challenge put to the children by the teachers relates to their everyday learning situation, but moves the children forward in their discipline knowledge. Real texts are used: beginning readers are encouraged to read them, and then act on them. This provides evaluative evidence of the part of the Thinking Curriculum which aims to 'Connect with children's interests and life experiences'. The sign also helps develop the children's play because it introduces a new idea into the play theme for the children to develop further.

Figure 8.14 A theatre area and an adjacent sound and film studio

The Building Inspector must have visited. What happened? What do we do now? How can we get the sign removed? This is evaluative evidence of another of the curriculum goals – that children's play is developed and extended.

This space allows small groups of children to develop their learning projects through creative expression. Real equipment is made available, along with specialist teacher support, as projects are generated – children have authentic and useful resources available to them. This evaluative evidence meets another of the goals of the Thinking Curriculum, which is that children can create projects in ways that support professionalism and further inquiry.

Input evaluation

Examples of input evaluation are also evidenced in Figures 8.9 and 8.11. Input evaluation looks at the resources that are available and being used to support the goals of the Thinking Curriculum. These figures show the materials available to the children so that they can independently or collectively work on challenges they have co-constructed with their teachers.

Design evaluation

Design evaluation is considered in relation to how the curriculum goals are being delivered. Esme says that the design aspect of evaluation is reflected in questions that are often asked by visitors to the school. Visitors from other schools or educational institutions ask, 'How does your school make this curriculum work?' 'How is it possible to operationalise a Thinking Curriculum?' 'How do you evaluate this type of program?' Esme explains how they deliver the Thinking Curriculum. These factors would fall under a design evaluation:

- *Leading thinkers:* We bring in leading thinkers, such as mathematicians or mathematics educators, and invite them to listen to our ideas, to react to our planning and thinking, and to advise us about how to create and evaluate our curriculum.
- *Structure of the school:* The structure of our school allows us to release extra staff when experts come in or when we need curriculum planning time to innovate or touch base with how things are going. This allows for intense discussion. Sending staff off to ad hoc professional development is not as effective as doing it in-house or bringing in experts to work alongside teachers in our school.

Significantly, we see that the evaluation of the program occurs as a collective enterprise. It mirrors the curriculum development process. Leading thinkers support the concept of a Thinking Curriculum and provide input into the evaluation of the program that puts the Thinking Curriculum in place in the school.

This example shows that Esme is able to pinpoint the factors that contribute to the successful implementation of the Thinking Curriculum. In terms of design evaluation, Esme can use these factors to think about whether or not these measures are helping the school achieve its curriculum goals.

Outcome evaluation

Outcome evaluation involves thinking about how well the stated goals of the school are being achieved. Some measures that might be used to evaluate the outcomes are National or State student tests (for example the National Assessment Program – Literacy and Numeracy [NAPLAN] tests conducted across Australia). Other measures might include consideration of parent satisfaction with the school. For many schools, developing a strong parent–school community is highly valued. This means that family views on how the school is going in relation to the educational programs it delivers are important. In Esme's school, for example, family involvement goes beyond the traditional participation in tasks or activities of the school. When considering outcome evaluation Esme needs to think about how is she is achieving her goal of including and respecting families:

> We have developed a parent research group. That group surveys the parents. That is part of our review process of the school. It is a culturally diverse community. As such, we are always seeking to find out how to get parent involvement in a range of forums. We have different forums for parents to make them comfortable so that they can have their say.

> As a parent group, they ask how they can cater for the diverse group of families. As a result we have a range of ways of interacting with families. For instance, we have:
>
> - drop in for a coffee sessions;
> - a formal review process in the evenings (where we encourage debate); and
> - open nights.

In Wooranna Park Primary School, the teachers also put on exhibitions for families, where they share their own learning with the community. In this way, information and communication becomes a genuine two-way process. In this school, outcome evaluation uses a range of measures for obtaining feedback on how well the school is going, and suggestions for improvement.

The achievement of the children is also a very important aspect of program evaluation. Knowing how the children are performing as a collective is important for knowing if learning is occurring, and if the program is successful. All schools provide individual results to families about the learning of their children. In Wooranna Park Primary School, the reporting formats are followed, but in the context of gathering work samples from the children during and at the end of their projects. Esme explains:

> We need to meet Government requirements in terms of reporting – we use the approved report format. We have moderations of samples of work around the criteria. This allows us to develop sets of sample folders, which we use for making judgments about all the children in the classroom.
>
> As a staff we talked about the criteria for assessment. We decided to work out the key understandings that children need in the different areas. For example, in reading, 'What does a five year old understand and what do they need?' A portfolio then becomes the mechanism for collecting evidence of children's understandings. Observable behaviours that demonstrate this understanding, but in context. This gives the guidelines for assessment and for working from an informed or evidence-based way.

Curriculum, assessment and evaluation

The examples of assessment and types of evaluation from this school show the importance of developing curriculum, assessment and evaluation together.

When these things occur in a related way the curriculum will relate more strongly to the children's learning, and the evaluation of the learning and the children's outcomes will feed into further curriculum development and improvement. What we always need to ask are these sorts of questions: Do the resources and processes support the direction that the school wishes to go in? Does the input from experts in particular curriculum areas stimulate and support the teachers? Are the families satisfied with how the school is going in delivering the promises it has made in relation to their children? Does the school have ways of knowing about children's learning outcomes and successes as learners in the program? All these aspects of evaluation are related to each other, and together they create a holistic perspective on evaluation that feeds purposefully into curriculum development. Box B outlines some examples and provides further information about how evaluation can be implemented and organised in education settings.

BOX B

School evaluation or self-evaluation (the difference between internal and external evaluations)

At the school level, it is important to have some form of evaluation to see whether the stated goals or outcomes are being achieved and how they are being achieved. The 'how' question is important, as staff planning and professional development are important qualitative ingredients that must be factored into the overall evaluation of a teacher's program; the 'how' question also links with the overall evaluation of the particular school the teacher is in. Sometimes at the centre or school level, this type of evaluation is called 'self-evaluation' (Fetterman & Wandersman 2005) or 'self-review', which can be defined as:

A review that is undertaken from within an early childhood education service in order to evaluate practice. This may also be called internal review, quality review or centre review. Self-review is usually based on the priorities set by the service. Self-review is conducted within the early childhood education service by members of that same service (who are sometimes referred to as a 'learning community' (Ministry of Education 2006, p. 8). The Ministry of Education in New Zealand states that this type of review is distinct from an external review, in which an external body (such as the Education Review Office) evaluates the quality of an early childhood service

continued »

Box B continued »

against a set of external and local priorities. The review is conducted by people who are not members of the centre or school and who thus bring an outside perspective. The benefits of undertaking regular self-review are twofold: centres and schools can improve their practice to ensure that teaching practice supports children's learning, and they can ensure that they are meeting legal requirements, responsibilities and accountabilities. Typically, centres and schools would have a program of planned reviews over a 1 to 3-year cycle (Ministry of Education 2006).

Summary

In this chapter we examined how learning, assessment and evaluation can be thought about as interrelated concepts. We considered evaluation and assessment as dynamic (not static) processes that foreground the children's reflections on their own learning, the teacher reflections on the program and the families' beliefs about how well the school is achieving its aims. This is a cultural-historical view of evaluation because it focuses not just on the teacher's and children's reflections, but also involves a genuine family voice in how the school is going. In this model, questions about what and how to assess and evaluate are made by the learning community, which is made up of children, teachers, families, and the wider school and community. The following evaluative feedback from a parent of a child at Wooranna Park Primary School highlights the extent to which this school is effectively integrating curriculum, assessment and evaluation:

> As a parent you want your child to be happy, really wanting to go to school, to be contributing, and coming up to you and saying, 'I would like to do this', or, 'I would like to try that.' Your child should have an 'I can do it' attitude. When that happens, my child will get to be the best that she can possibly be! (Linda, Parent, Wooranna Park Primary School).

Acknowledgments

Thank you to Amanda and Thomas, who took Marilyn around their school and shared their learning, and to Esme Capp and Linda Sinadinos for kindly agreeing to be interviewed.

References

Absolum, M. (2006). *Clarity in the classroom: Using formative assessment, building learning focused relationships*. Auckland: Hodder Education.

Ballantine, J., Levy, M., Martin, A., Munro, I. & Powell, P. (2000). An ethical perspective on information systems evaluation. *International Journal of Agile Management Systems*, 2/3, pp. 233–41.

Brassard, M.R. & Boehm, A.E. (2007). *Preschool assessment: Principles and practices*. New York: The Guilford Press.

Brock, A. (2008). Curriculum and pedagogy of play: A multitude of perspectives? In A. Brock, S. Dodds, P. Javis & Y. Olusoga (eds), *Perspectives on play. Learning for life*. UK: Pearson Education Ltd, pp. 67–93.

Carr, M., Cowie, B., Gerrity, R., Jones, C., Lee, W. & Pohio, L. (2001). Democratic learning and teaching communities in early childhood: Can assessment play a role? In B. Webber & L. Mitchell (eds), *Early childhood education for a democratic society*. Wellington: NZCER, pp. 27–36.

Crooks, T. (1988). *Assessing student performance*. Sydney : HERDSA.

Dahlberg, G., Moss, P. & Pence, A. (1999). *Beyond quality in early childhood education and care: Postmodern perspectives*. London: Falmer Press.

Drummond, M.J. (1993). *Assessing children's learning*. London: David Fulton.

Education Review Office (2007). *The quality of assessment in early childhood education*. Wellington: ERO.

Espinosa, L.M. (2005). Curriculum and assessment considerations for young children from culturally, linguistically and economically diverse backgrounds. *Psychology in the Schools*, 42(8), pp. 837–53.

Fetterman, D. & Wandersman, A. (eds) (2005). *Empowerment evaluation principles in practice*. New York: The Guilford Press.

Fleer, M. & Richardson, C. (2008). Cultural-historical assessment: Mapping the transformation of understanding. In A. Anning, J. Cullen & M. Fleer. (eds), *Early childhood education: Society and culture*. 2nd edn. Los Angeles: Sage, pp. 130–44.

Fleet, A. & Torr, J. (2007). Literacy assessment: Understanding and recording meaningful data. In L. Makin, C. Jones Díaz & C. McLachlan (eds), *Literacies in childhood: Changing views, challenging practice*. 2nd edn. Sydney: MacLennan & Petty/Elsevier, pp. 183–200.

Gray, D.E. (2004). *Doing research in the real world*. London: Sage.

Madaus, G.F., Scriven, M. & Stufflebeam, D.L. (eds) (1983). *Evaluation models: Viewpoints on educational and human services evaluation*. Kluwer Academic Press.

Ministry of Education (2005). *Kei tua o te pae. Assessment for learning: Early childhood exemplars*. Wellington: Learning Media.

Ministry of Education (2006). *Ngā arohaehae whai hua: Self-review guidelines for early childhood education*. Wellington: Learning Media.

Scriven, M. (1977). *Evaluation thesaurus*. 3rd edn. Inverness CA: Edgepress.

Chapter 9

Content knowledge: The sciences, maths and numeracy

In this chapter the theory and the practice of Vygotsky's (1987) work on concept formation will be introduced. This work is important for framing approaches to building content knowledge in mathematics and science in the context of the environment. This is an important part of the early childhood curriculum that can sometimes get lost in play-based approaches. In this chapter, a model for understanding how concept formation occurs in relation to children's everyday experiences of the world and their acquisition of formal knowledge will be examined. The model is explained using examples from practice which show how children and teachers can work together to build conceptual knowledge within play-based approaches to curriculum.

Mathematical concept formation within everyday practice

It is 10.00 am and Jacinta and her teacher are wiping the tables in preparation for morning tea. Jacinta's teacher has recently attended a workshop on curriculum planning and has brought back a series of cards which give suggestions for how everyday practices can be used to promote mathematics education in young children. As she wipes the table she recalls the dialogue on the back of the cards (see Figure 9.3) and says:

Teacher: Jacinta, see if you can move the cloth all the way to the edge of the table.
Jacinta: Like this (moving the cloth across the table surface, running her hand along the edge).
Teacher: Yes, that's it. We are wiping the whole area of the table – right to the edge.
Jacinta: I have got every spot, haven't I?

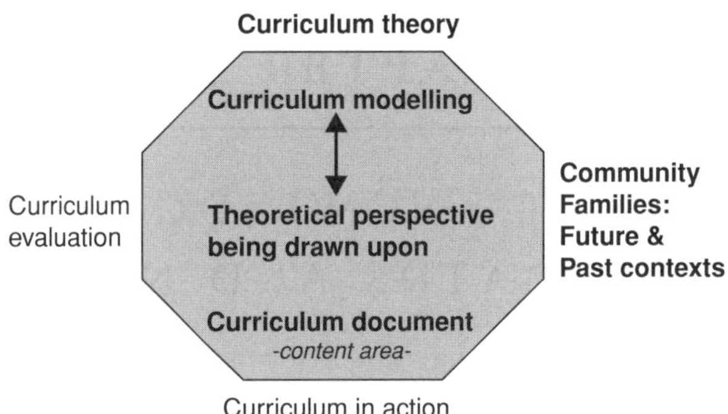

Figure 9.1 Curriculum development pathway – content knowledge

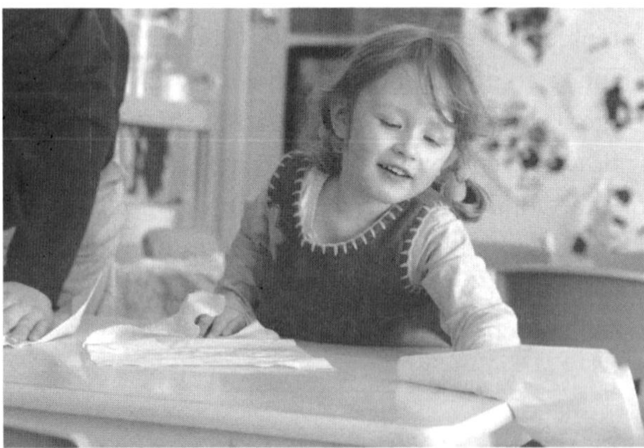

Figure 9.2 Mathematics in everyday life – in the home and in the centre (see Fleer & Raban 2007)

During the planning workshop Jacinta's teacher and her colleagues spent the afternoon learning about the importance of concepts that children learn through everyday practices such as wiping the table. She also learned about the significance of her role as teacher in identifying the mathematical concepts associated these everyday practices – such as the concept 'area' when wiping down a table. Importantly, Jacinta's teacher realised the significance of making conscious these mathematical concepts during everyday practice. Contrary to popular practice in her centre, she was asked to think more deliberately about her 'teaching role' when she was with the children and about being conscious of what concepts she was actually supporting children to learn during their everyday practices. Research in the UK has shown that teachers having conversations with children – 'shared sustained thinking' – supports better learning outcomes for children (Siraj-Blatchford 2004).

Dad: Let's wipe the table together.

Using paper towels, the children wipe the table.

Dad: Did you wipe to the edge? We cover the whole surface!

When we talk about 'edge', 'top' and 'bottom', we can help children learn about area. Children often don't think about area. Helping children pay attention to it helps them later on when they will measure these surfaces and make comparisons.

Figure 9.3 The information on the back of the card

REFLECTION 9.1

When you are working with children do you make the concepts conscious to children during your interactions? Do you believe that participating in 'experiences' is enough for supporting children's learning? What do you see as your role in relation to introducing mathematical and scientific concepts to children? Do you believe that maths and science are part of the early childhood curriculum?

A CULTURAL-HISTORICAL READING OF CONCEPT FORMATION

Research has increasingly shown that the content of early childhood curriculum is as important for children's learning as the process of implementing curriculum (Gibbons 2007; Hedges & Cullen 2005). Traditionally, early childhood education has focused on thinking about how children learn through play, and suggested that the curriculum should focus on providing children with opportunities to play in ways that will let them construct their own knowledge about certain topics. This idea has been challenged, and now researchers are arguing that teachers need to be more aware about 'what' they are actually teaching children through play, and how their deliberate interactions in children's play can be used to help children acquire content knowledge in areas of learning such as maths and science (Grieshaber 2008; Thorpe et al. 2004). Vygotsky's (1987) work provides a helpful way of thinking about how to bring together children's everyday experiences with the development of conceptual knowledge in particular content areas.

Vygotsky (1987) introduced to educators and psychologists the important idea that concept formation in children should be thought about as occurring at two interrelated levels: the everyday level and the scientific or 'schooled' level. In curriculum development and planning in early childhood settings, it is important to know how these two levels relate to each other because this will help teachers build the learning of content into play-based learning. The ideas in this chapter provide the theoretical framework for thinking about curriculum content for Chapters 10 and 11, which also discuss curriculum content knowledge.

At the everyday level, concepts are learned as a result of interacting directly with the world – developing intuitive understandings of how to do things. For example, Jacinta was directly experiencing her world by the wiping the table. She was learning that the best way to effectively wipe the table was by moving the cloth over the whole surface. Vygotsky (1987) argued that the concepts children learned through their everyday activities lay the foundations for learning scientific (or 'academic' or 'schooled') concepts. Developing concepts in the context of children's everyday worlds is important for successfully participating in the family and community.

Everyday concepts can be introduced in verbal and non-verbal ways (or both ways) between children and adults. For example, when a young boy and his mother go shopping to buy yoghurt they go straight to the dairy section of the supermarket. This is an example of non-verbal learning about how objects in the supermarket are categorised according to product type. Cultural and family differences affect the balance between verbal and non-verbal language in families (Rogoff 2003). Many everyday concepts cannot be easily transferred to other contexts unless children are helped to understand the scientific knowledge behind them. For example, in Jacinta's experience, wiping the table was an everyday practice. Knowing how to wipe a table will not help her in other everyday contexts, such as hanging out the washing. However, if Jacinta's everyday knowledge about table wiping is used to help her build conceptual knowledge about area, she can apply her conceptual knowledge about area to other tasks, such as painting a letterbox: it will help her understand that she needs to paint the entire area of the box. The same idea would apply with the boy buying yoghurt. Knowing how and where to buy yoghurt will not necessarily help him buy fruit to go with his yoghurt. However, knowing about categorisation as a concept will help him know that he needs to look for the part of the supermarket where all the fruit is. If children only ever know about everyday concepts, their thinking is predominantly embedded in the here and now (the wiping of the table or looking for yoghurt), and this can reduce their opportunities to apply concepts in new situations.

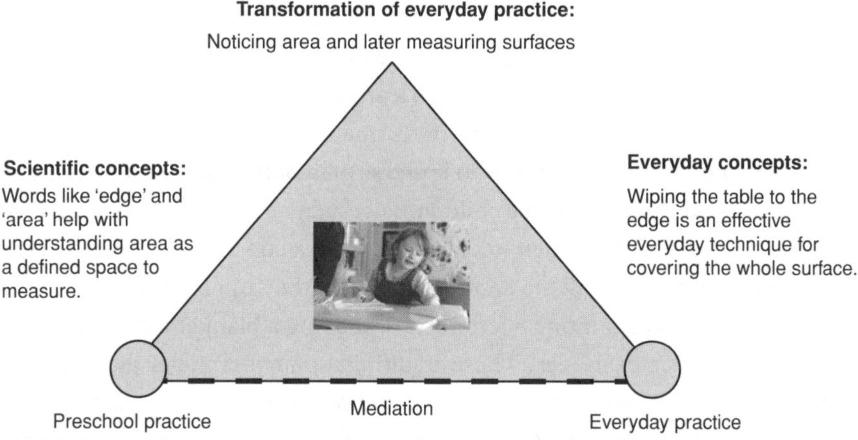
Transformation of everyday practice:
Noticing area and later measuring surfaces
Scientific concepts:
Words like 'edge' and 'area' help with understanding area as a defined space to measure.
Everyday concepts:
Wiping the table to the edge is an effective everyday technique for covering the whole surface.
Preschool practice
Mediation
Everyday practice

Figure 9.4 A model to show the mediated relationship between the everyday concepts of 'wiping the table' and scientific concepts of 'area' (adapted from Fleer & Raban 2007)

THINKING CONSCIOUSLY ABOUT CONCEPTS

Thinking consciously about the surface area when wiping the table, cleaning a window or painting a letterbox helps children build the concept of covering a surface area. Thinking consciously about concepts is an important skill. For example, considering surface area matters when you are making a blanket for a doll's bed and you need to make sure it fits. Thinking about area in this way is an abstract idea, and is the beginning of understanding the concept of area measurement. To think about the edge of the table (the everyday concept) and then to think about the boundary of the area you wish to measure (the scientific concept) requires linking these two concepts through experience, and through someone helping to make the concepts conscious during meaningful practice. Building a curriculum that explicitly relates everyday and scientific concepts as a way of building concept formation in young children is clearly worth doing.

Figure 9.4 illustrates how curriculum can develop content knowledge in mathematics. When teachers engage in conversation that helps the children become aware of a concept, the child has experienced 'mediation' between their everyday and scientific concepts. This means that an explicit relationship now exists between the everyday practice and the scientific concept. The teacher's role here is to find ways to mediate this conceptual development.

Vygotsky (1987) argued that when children simply learn scientific or academic concepts at school away from the everyday context in which they have meaning, the scientific concepts are disembedded from children's experiences and are not helpful for everyday living. For example, a traditional practice in education which is meant to help children learn about area involves asking them to cover the surface area of a square with small measuring squares, and then count the number of small squares to find the 'area of the square'. This activity does not necessarily relate to the children's everyday life experiences, and thus makes it more difficult for them to easily develop a conceptual understanding of area they can apply in all the contexts in which they might encounter area – when wiping a table, painting a letterbox or making a blanket for a doll's bed, to use our previous examples. These traditional practices mean that children may not use these school-learned mathematical concepts when trying to solve a problem in their everyday life. This was observed in one classroom where some children were making curtains for their doll's house: they guessed the size of the fabric they needed, and simply cut out a square shape to attach to their window.

Vygotsky did not see everyday concepts and scientific concepts as separate ideas. Instead, he saw them as very much related to each other – like the two sides of the same coin. Everyday concepts are grounded in children's day-to-day life experiences, and these experiences create the potential for the development of scientific concepts in the context of school experiences. There is an abundance of research evidence which supports the view that engaging with real situations is important for fostering learning (see National Research Council 2001). However, what we now know is that providing the experience alone is not enough to lead to concept formation. Vygotsky's (1987) research has shown that scientific concepts prepare the structural formations necessary for the strengthening of everyday concepts. That is, the scientific concepts help children to make better sense of what they are experiencing in their everyday worlds. Rather than Jacinta simply wiping the table, she now thinks more purposefully about going to the 'edge' and covering the 'whole area' that she is wiping. This conscious action came about because Jacinta's teacher drew her attention to the importance of covering the whole area of the table. Jacinta was receptive to thinking consciously about doing this, because her teacher introduced the concept of 'area' and 'edge' (boundary of the surface) to her during a daily activity Jacinta was participating in. That is, the concept of area was introduced to Jacinta in the context of an everyday activity – wiping the table. For Vygotsky, mediating the relationship between everyday concepts and scientific concepts constituted the basis of concept formation.

A curriculum model for working with everyday concepts and scientific concepts

Understanding the relationship between everyday and scientific concepts helps focus our attention on the teacher's role in building an early childhood curriculum that brings together these concepts. Figure 9.5 presents a curriculum model based on cultural-historical theory that supports concept formation for young children.

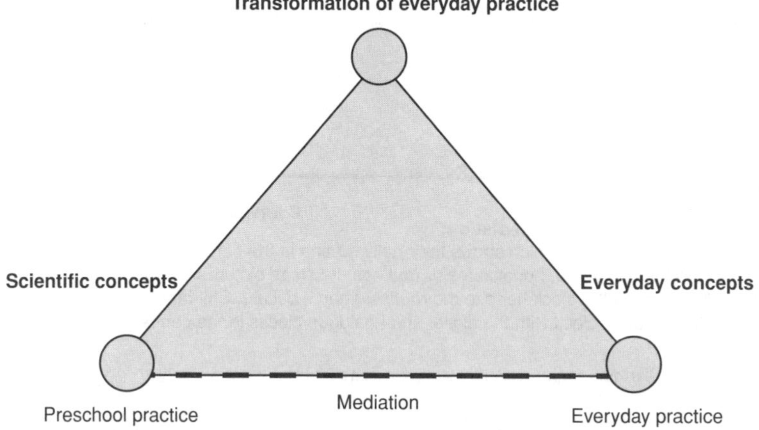

Figure 9.5 A curriculum model to show the relationship between everyday concepts and scientific concepts (Fleer & Raban 2007)

Reflection 9.2

Using the model shown in Figure 9.5, take one of the following mathematical concepts and identify an everyday context in which the concept would arise:

Sharing is about division.
Full and empty are about measurement.
Upside down is about position and direction.
Sorting things is about classifying.
Time is about measurement.

After you have selected one of these mathematical concepts, generate an example of the type of conversation and interactions that would occur between the child and adult (i.e. the process of mediation) so that the child's everyday practice is transformed (i.e. the child thinks consciously about the concept in practice). Once you have done this, look at the working example provided in Figure 9.6 to see how well you are working towards understanding how to mediate children's everyday and scientific knowledge.

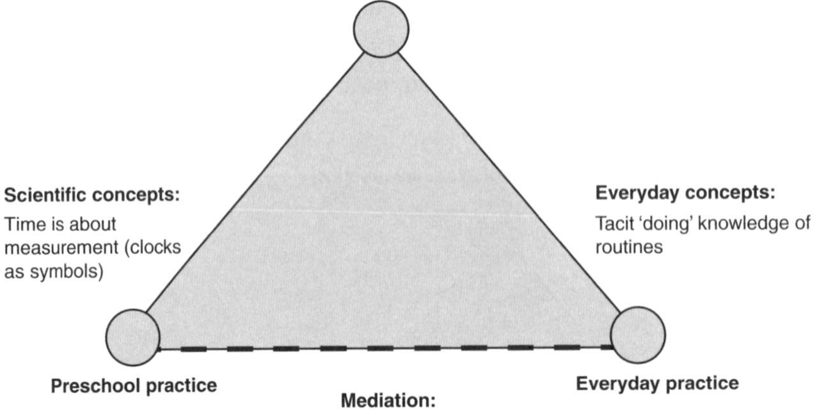
Transformation of everyday practice:
The child can operate more effectively in the world when they can plan to view a favourite programme on television
Scientific concepts:
Time is about measurement (clocks as symbols)
Everyday concepts:
Tacit 'doing' knowledge of routines
Preschool practice
Everyday practice
Mediation:
Children and staff create a 'clock' which shows their daily routine in the centre. The clock has a face with times marked, but also major routines drawn as pictures on the clock face. Children move the clock hand to the routine when it occurs. Children regularly compare their routine clock with the digital and analogue clocks in the centre

Figure 9.6 Planning for concepts in context: 'Time is about measurement'

Thinking about the working example (Figure 9.6)

Figure 9.6 is an example of how time can be made conscious to children. This example shows how experiencing routines (everyday concrete experiences) can be better understood when children's attention is drawn to the measurement of time: connecting routines to time periods, then to clocks as symbols of time/routines. As children bring their working everyday knowledge ('tacit' doing knowledge) of routines together with their scientific knowledge (measurement of time using clocks), they transform their everyday practice and realise how time works and clocks are read. Having a concept of time helps children (and adults!) operate more effectively in the world because they can plan for future activities: dinnertime or breakfast or walking the dog, for example.

The examples provided in this section of the chapter have focused on daily routines (9.5) and daily tasks (9.3) as the context for mediate conceptual development. Play is another important activity that often occurs in early childhood centres, and it can also be reconsidered in relation to curriculum development from a cultural-historical perspective using the two levels of concept development. In the next section, we explore concept formation in the area of science during a children's play activity.

CURRICULUM IN PRACTICE: BUILDING SCIENTIFIC CONCEPTUAL KNOWLEDGE

This section introduces the work of a preschool teacher, Jacqui, who works with Christian's interest in insects, and develops a conceptual program to support his and the other children's learning in this area (see Fleer 2010 for a full analysis of this example). As you read this case study of Jacqui's teaching, try to identify the elements of the curriculum model presented in Figure 9.5 that underpin and frame the curriculum Jacqui is using. Make notes about the relationship between the curriculum model and what Jacqui does to support the children's concept formation in this science area.

Case example: A treasure hunt

Christian finds an ant in the outdoor area of a preschool. The preschool is in a bush suburb close by a rural city of 150,000 people. Christian's family work in science-related fields and have encouraged a keen interest in science in their children. Christian gathers up the ant and takes it to his teacher, Jacqui. Jacqui is aware of Christian's interest and uses this opportunity to support concept formation. She gives Christian a special container where the lid acts as a magnifying glass. This inspires Christian and he returns to the outdoor area to explore. Christian's interest in living things stimulates the other children, who gather around Christian to examine his finds. Jacqui provides the interested children with a range of magnifying tools and suggest they consider creating a map of what they have found. They name their activity a 'treasure hunt'.

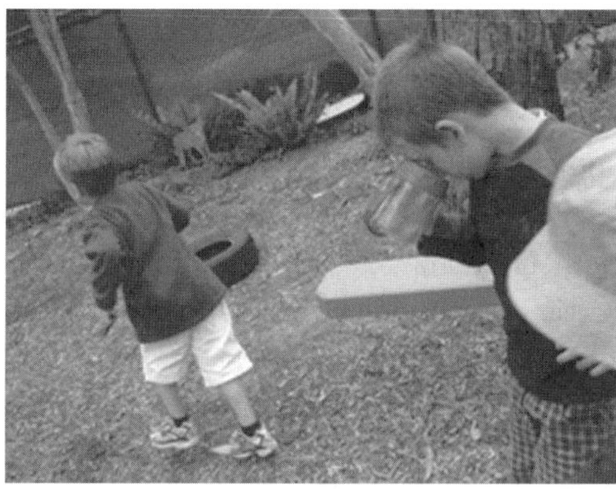

Figure 9.7 A treasure hunt – X marks the spot where the insects were found

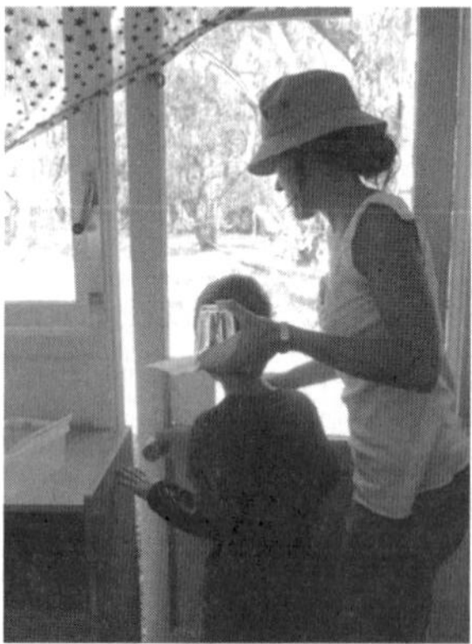

Figure 9.8 A treasure hunt – X marks the spot where the insects were found

Jacqui works together with Christian to develop a working knowledge of what Christian understands about insects. She is actively identifying his everyday concepts and is determining the contexts which can be used to support scientific concept formation.

On a later day, Christian takes the 'treasure map' he has created and invites his teacher to go with him to hunt for bugs.

Jacqui: Should we go and find the path?
Christian: Yes . . . [can we find it] without the map?
Grace: I gave something to Christian. (Grace hands Christian a magnifying glass to encourage his treasure hunt search in the environment)

A group of children follow Christian and the teacher. They explore the outdoor area in order to better understand the nature and place of small creatures living in it. Using the treasure map, the children played with the idea of finding and documenting the creatures in their environment. This activity makes conscious for children the important idea of understanding whole ecosystems rather than simply finding an individual creature. In Table 9.1, we can see how Christian is supported to actively build conceptual understanding in science. What emerges from this understanding is a new question which allows Christian to continue building his conceptual knowledge – what do the creatures eat?

The interactions between the teachers and Christian are around expressing what is known about the digestion of insects in the context of a close relationship between creatures and their environment. The teacher has asked questions which promote these conversations and focus Christian and other children's attention more closely on what the creatures eat. It is clear that some of the children think about the concept of 'eating' in terms of the mechanics of the process. Some make an association between the concepts of eating and digestion, and place this in the context of the environment. In this example, Christian appears to be developing quite a sophisticated knowledge of organisms and their environment. Other children pay attention to these ideas.

Concept formation is also supported through some activities introduced by the teacher. For example, Jacqui sets up painting materials, encouraging the children to paint or draw their finds. An example of the conversations between the teacher and Christian indicate the way in which concept formation is developing. Christian is clearly playing with some of the ideas (see Table 9.2).

Christian's probing in relation to the function of 'eating' is extended further when the nature of the interface between the structure of the creature (the mechanics of eating) and the environment in which the creature is located is examined. In particular, we note that Christian's sense of environment and human care comes together to ensure that the creatures are safe. He actively seeks to ensure that the bull-ants are moved for his own and other's safety, too.

The active exploration of small creatures by many of the children was partnered with teacher–child interactions where scientific concepts were introduced, as is shown in the next example.

Naming bugs

Jacqui has charts and insect identity sheets as resources for children who want to name the bugs they find. Christian has found a 'bug' and believes it to

Table 9.1 Tools, talk and thinking

Conceptual tools	Observations	Transcripts
The children use a range of conceptual tools to support investigations, such as magnifying glasses, binoculars, a camera, containers with lids, a bug catcher with a magnifying lid, an overhead projector, local environment photographs in a book, micro-life book, insect identity charts, a poster of bushland creatures, pens, chalks (six-legged creature) (huh?), paint brushes and dye, collage materials and pencils, playdough (butterfly and eggs) and animal figures (especially dinosaurs, crocodiles).	Observation 21.2 Christian's fascination with ecosystems extends and associations occur. He regularly lifts logs, collecting the slaters and millipedes under them and putting them in his bug catcher. In this encounter with the assistant teacher (Jessy) he seems to understand that bugs digest differently from humans. When the research assistant showed this conversation to his mother she believed that Christian's father had read him a book about this at home (field notes).	*Jessy:* What do slaters eat? *Christian:* Wood, leaves, everything. *Jessy:* If I ate wood, I'd get a tummy ache. Why doesn't the slater get one? *Christian:* It has germs in its tummy and they kick the tummy ache away. We don't have germs in our tummy.
	Why won't it eat? Christian often carries a bug catcher with him and on this day he is observed talking to the bug as if it is a person. He seems concerned (hm. The first thing he says is 'naughty boy', which is hardly concern) about the bug not eating the grass he has put in to sustain it (field notes).	*Christian:* Naughty boy (referring to bug not eating). *Researcher:* What have you put in there to help him? *Christian:* Grass, and he's not going to eat it. *Researcher:* He doesn't seem to like grass. *Christian:* He does eat grass. *Researcher:* Does he? *Christian:* He's supposed to eat it. *Researcher:* What else does he possibly eat? *Christian:* Grass, trees . . . leaves, but not trees. *Researcher:* I suppose the things that are around him. *Christian:* Grass, leaves, branch, trees leaves, grass, leaves, trees, grass, trees, leaves . . . (he repeats these names over and over).

Table 9.2 Exploring the form and function of insects

Observations	Transcript	Field notes
Bug machine Christian is at a table with food dye and brushes and spontaneously paints and explains a machine he has represented on paper that can suck up bull ants.		The day before, Christian had found a large bull-ant near the sandpit and called for his teacher to come and get it. She had carefully removed it (using a glass and cardboard) to the adjacent bushland whilst he watched and told her about how bull-ants have jaws and teeth to bite.
The machine he painted represented a functional solution to managing stray bull ants that might bite and offered thought as to what might happen should they get sick (field notes).	*Christian*: It goes up there and it gets the ants and this is when they go to the dentist. *Jessy:* Go to the dentist? *Christian:* Yeah that's when they get sick and then they go here.	
Pacman person chomping Rowan continues to represent his earlier idea about digestion and has chosen the collage table to create an imaginary bug-like pacman from a round piece of paper. He wants the character to function with a mouth that opens so it can 'burp, eat, bite and chomp'. With encouragement from assistant Jessy, he cuts a design that allows the character to do this. Later Jacqui role plays with Christian's creation and he jumps with excitement when it is animated in front of his peer, Colin. Christian often converses with the creatures he finds and is delighted when Jacqui brings this imaginary creature 'to life' with comic voices.	*Jacqui*: Oh wow . . . what fun . . . (she plays with the pacman person opening its mouth) *Colin:* Excuse me . . . *Jessy:* He got a circle right and he got two dots for eyes and he cut cut cut for the mouth . . . look, Christian.	Later in the day, when Christian's peer, Colin, stamps on a beetle, he cries out loud in anguish. Christian has strongly expressed concerns about preservation of life. JP (Jacqui?) empathises and begins a new search with a group of children to find a new beetle/bug in the yard.

Figure 9.9 Studying insects

be a centipede. He brings it indoors for clarification of identification. Christian looks closely at the chart and points to – and names – the centipede, mosquito, praying mantis and lacewing.

Christian: I think that's a centipede.
Jacqui: I think that's a centipede. Yep. I'll read the word centipede; yep, that one's a centipede. That one's a millipede. They're the ones we find around the kinder all the time.
Colin: We found one. Sticks on. I think it will go through those holes.
Christian: Mosquito.
Jacqui: That one's called a scorpion fly.
Christian: Praying mantis.
Jacqui: Special names.
Colin: Praying mantis.
Jacqui: Yep.
Christian: Lacewing.

The naming of small creatures represents a bringing together of scientific knowledge and observational knowledge of the creatures that the children have actively sought (as Christian shares his understandings), uncovered, cared for and played with. This is an example of how everyday concepts and scientific concepts can be brought together and supported. The teachers actively brought the scientific concepts to the children's attention, but did so in the everyday context that the children were exploring. This example shows how the teachers mediated the everyday and scientific concepts with the children.

The teacher introduced activities that were framed in relation to the structure and function of organisms. Each of the 'activities' was clearly linked to a 'meta-plan' of investigation of small creatures in this environment (i.e. bugs). Collectively, the 'play activity' about relations between the environment and the organisms, contributed to the children's formation of scientific concepts.

The learning context, which included the program planned and implemented by the teacher, allowed for the interlacing of everyday concepts that the child was exploring with scientific concepts gained at home and in the centre. For example, the teacher encouraged the representation of the environment the children were exploring by creating maps, providing tools for orienteering and exploration (e.g. binoculars, treasure maps), and reading scientific books and charts (introduced by the research assistant).

What is significant in this case is that the playful context provided in the centre supported this interlacing of the everyday and the scientific.

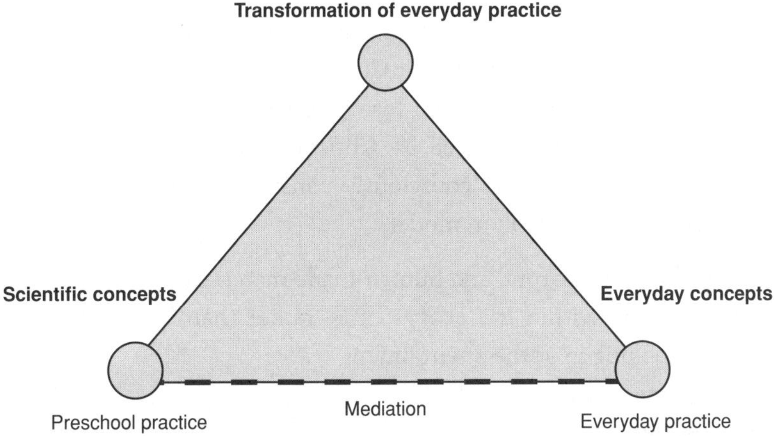

Figure 9.10 A curriculum model for investigating ecosystems in free play settings

Using the curriculum model (Figure 9.10), extract from this example about the insects the everyday and the scientific concepts the children and teachers mediated, and map them onto the model. As you do so, think about the following questions, which will help you identify the everyday and scientific concepts and the strategies the teachers used.

- What do you notice about how the teacher worked?
- What were the contexts in which concepts were introduced?
- At what point were the concepts made conscious to the children?

- How does this curriculum model differ from those models talked about in Chapters 10 and 11?

REFLECTION 9.3

Generating an environmental education curriculum model

In order to gain a working knowledge of this model, we invite you to take the case example of Christian and Jacqui, and prepare a curriculum model for environmental education. You can draw on Christian's everyday knowledge of the insects found in the outdoor area of the centre, and then consider what might be the environmental education concepts that you could introduce to him.

We suggest that you use the concept of an ecosystem as a starting point for your planning. What other concepts might Christian need to develop in order to gain an environmental perspective on his everyday world? Would any of the following concepts be experienced by Christian? Should we determine the essence of these concepts and consciously consider any of these in our environmental education curriculum model?

- Relationships between natural and human-made materials
- Positioning humans within the ecosystem – rather than humans seeing themselves as looking in at the environment
- Indigenous perspectives
- Global perspectives
- Thinking about the future
- Thinking about the past
- Intergenerational learning
- Poverty
- Energy and alternative sources of energy
- Making a difference
- Sustainability
- Consumerism.

In many parts of the world, early childhood teachers organise special excursions into the forest or bush so that children can have some rich environmental experiences – experiences they can build on in situ but also later, back in the centres. The Forest Schools (Knight 2009) are a case in point. Originating in the Scandinavian countries, they can now also be found in England. Knight (2009) suggests that the Forest School experience is designed:

- within settings that are not the usual place of learning;
- to occur in safe environments where children are encouraged to take risks;
- to happen over time;
- with the philosophy that there is 'no such thing as bad weather, only bad clothing';
- with trust as central;
- to position learning as play based, and child initiated and child led;
- with blocks of sessions, where there are beginnings and ends; and
- to be operated by staff who are trained.

Children experience the natural environment, and are encouraged to explore all elements of it, without boundaries. These special places are highly valued, and teachers seek to build a close relationship between the children and the environment, and to develop children's emotional wellbeing. This context is different from the one that Christian experiences. Christian uses his natural environment in the early childhood setting – something that is valued by Christian, the teachers and the all the other children. The two types of curriculum – the one for Christian, and the Forest Schools one – are different models of learning and curriculum development, but they both focus on environmental education.

The curriculum model introduced in this chapter will also be used in Chapters 10 and 11. Specifically, we use this model to show how ideas about everyday and scientific concept formation can be used to support children in other content areas, including literacy, health education, and the arts. As you read through these chapters you will begin to see how the model can be used to frame curriculum in ways that help children and teachers mediate everyday and academic learning so that children continue to build and acquire conceptual knowledge.

Summary

In this chapter we have examined how concept formation occurs in early childhood settings when teachers pay careful attention to children's everyday knowledge and the scientific knowledge that relates to those everyday experiences. Routines, daily tasks and carefully supported play can be used to identify important everyday concepts that can be mediated with scientific concepts. The curriculum model used in this chapter for demonstrating how content knowledge can be integrated into early childhood settings draws upon cultural-historical theory to explain the relationship between children's lived experiences and concept formation. This chapter focused on the content areas of mathematics and science.

Acknowledgments

Australian Research Council (Discovery) funding provided the resources for the study reported in this chapter. Avis Ridgway made an enormous contribution to the project through acting as the main field officer for this study.

References

Fleer, M. (2010). *Early Learning and Development: Cultural–historical concepts in play*. Melbourne: Cambridge University Press.

Fleer, M. & Raban, B. (2007). *Early childhood literacy and numeracy: Building good practice*. Canberra: Department of Education, Science and Training.

Gibbons, A. (2007). The politics of processes and products in education: An early childhood meta-narrative in crisis? *Educational Philosophy and Theory*, 39(3), pp. 300–11.

Grieshaber, S. (2008). Interrupting stereotypes: Teaching and the education of young children. *Early Childhood Education and Development*, 19(3), pp. 505–18.

Hedges, H. & Cullen, J. (2005). Subject knowledge in early childhood curriculum and pedagogy: Beliefs and practices. *Contemporary Issues in Early Childhood*, 6(1), pp. 66–79.

Knight, S. (2009). *Forest Schools and outdoor learning in the early years*. Los Angeles: Sage.

National Research Council (2001). Eager to learn: Educating our preschoolers. Committee on Early Childhood Pedagogy. In B.T. Bowman, M.S. Donovan & M.S. Burns (eds), *Commission on Behavioral and Social Sciences and Education*. Washington DC: National Academy Press.

Rogoff, B. (2003). *Cultural nature of human development*. Oxford: Oxford University Press.

Siraj-Blatchford, I. (2004). Quality teaching in the early years. In A. Anning, J. Cullen & M. Fleer (eds), *Early childhood education: Society and culture*. London: Sage, pp. 137–49.

Thorpe, K., Tayler, C., Bridgstock, R., Grieshaber, S., Skoien, P., Danby, S. et al. (2004). *Preparing for school*. Brisbane: GOPRINT & Queensland Department of Education Training and the Arts.

Vygotsky, L.S. (1987) Thinking and speech. In L.S. Vygotsky, *The collected works of L.S. Vygotsky*, Vol. 1. R.W. Rieber & A.S. Carton (eds), N. Minick (trans.). New York: Plenum Press, pp. 39–285.

Chapter 10

Content knowledge: Language, literacy and ICT

This chapter will examine the role of content knowledge in early childhood education across the key areas of language and literacy and information and communication technologies (ICT). Issues associated with how content knowledge is related to and evidenced in the early childhood curriculum will be theorised using Fleer's work on concept formation in early childhood contexts.

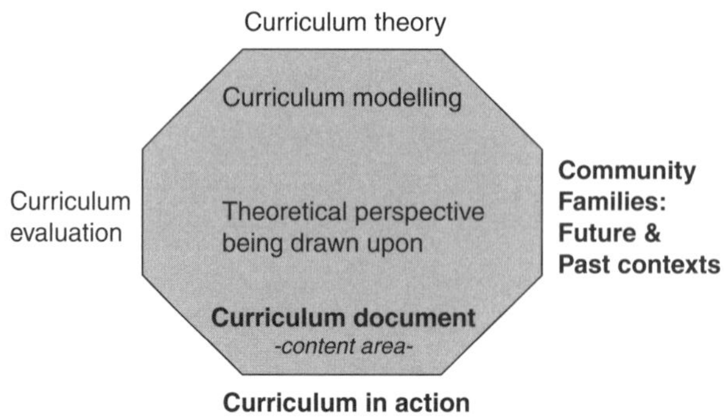

Figure 10.1 Curriculum development pathway – content knowledge

Language and literacy

We will first return to the questions asked of you in Chapter 3 in relation to the curriculum you use in your teaching and reflect on these questions specifically in relation to language and literacy in your early childhood setting:

- *How are children viewed?* How is children's language and literacy development viewed in this setting?
- *What content is valued?* What types of language and literacy knowledge and skills are valued for children?

- *How is knowledge framed?* Whose language and literacy knowledge is prioritised and organised in this setting?
- *How is progression organised (or not)?* How is language and literacy progression viewed and used for structuring curriculum?
- *Who decides on the content?* Who has decided on the language and literacy content that is offered to children in this setting?

As Chapter 3 argued, all these questions shape the ways in which teachers make choices about curriculum content and how to interact with children's developing literacy knowledge and skills. Recent research into children's literacy reinforces Vygotsky's notion that development is a dialogical, interactive process in which children learn through engagement with their families and communities (Makin, Jones Díaz & McLachlan 2007). Although there are definite patterns of literacy acquisition in different countries in terms of the speed with which children acquire language and literacy – these are related to the linguistic difficulty of the sounds in the language: the phonemic sounds in German or Italian are easier to learn than the phonemic sounds in English – the acquisition of literacy for most children is a continuum, reflecting the interaction of biological capacity, cultural and community experiences and mediation of their learning in home and school environments.

Much of the research around children's developing literacy falls into two camps: emergent literacy and literacy as a social practice. Neither theory is useful without the other. Vygotsky's (1987) writing on speech and language illustrates this well. The term 'emergent literacy' refers to the idea that the acquisition of literacy is conceptualised as:

> a continuum, with its origins early in the life of a child, rather than an all or nothing phenomenon that begins when children start school. This conceptualisation departs from other perspectives in reading acquisition in suggesting there is no clear demarcation between reading and pre-reading (Whitehurst & Lonigan 1998, p. 848).

The example of the group of early childhood children who were writing as a collective community in Chapter 6 shows how this may be possible. This body of work, which primarily comes from cognitive, psycholinguistic and neuroscience research, suggests that children go through a period of growth from infancy to middle childhood (until the start of adolescence) in which they develop reading, writing and oral language concurrently and interdependently, as a result of their exposure to social contexts in which literacy is a component, and often in the absence of formal instruction (Whitehurst & Lonigan 1998). As discussed in Chapter 3, Vygotsky (1987) introduced to educators and psychologists the idea that concept formation in children should be thought about at two levels – the everyday level and the scientific or schooled level.

In terms of literacy, children develop fundamental understandings at an everyday level, which are then built upon in schools as part of formal instruction. Their everyday knowledge falls into specific concept areas which predict later literacy achievement in English (Nicholson 2005):

- knowledge of alphabet letters and sounds;
- phonological awareness or sensitivity;
- grammatical sensitivity;
- concepts and conventions of print;
- receptive vocabulary;
- ability to use 'book' or decontextualised language;
- ability to produce narratives;
- ability to produce pre-conventional spellings; and
- an extensive vocabulary of unusual words.

Letter name knowledge is one of the strongest predictors of literacy achievement because it acts as a bridge to the alphabetic principle (the understanding that each letter represents a sound) and in turn to phonological awareness (being able to hear and separate phonemes in words) (Foulin 2005). Along with letter–sound knowledge, phoneme awareness is generally considered an important component of decoding skill. The teaching of these skills and knowledge are considered essential for children most at risk of reading difficulties, who have less emergent literacy knowledge, particularly in phonological awareness and alphabet knowledge (Tunmer, Chapman & Prochnow 2006). So it is imperative that teachers have a solid understanding of the concepts associated with children's language and literacy development and how to support the development of these concepts in infants, toddlers and young children.

Cunningham, Perry, Stanovich and Stanovich (2004) state that, 'There are strong theoretical reasons to suspect linkages between teacher knowledge and the ability to teach reading effectively (e.g. being able to teach phonemic awareness and choose good literature)' (p. 160). They found that a lack of conceptual knowledge about literacy severely impeded teachers' ability to make good choices about content and resources to support children's learning. As Anthony and Francis (2005) state, teachers' understanding of the progression of alphabetic knowledge and phonological awareness allows them to tailor their teaching for individual children and for groups, as was shown in Chapter 6, where the teacher supported group writing and reading, despite the fact that each child was at quite a different level of literacy acquisition.

A CASE STUDY

One of our Bachelor of Education students had been placed in a mid-sized urban town for her teaching placement in year 2 of her degree. At that time, she had had nearly two years of courses about language and literacy as part of her pre-service teacher education, which had a strong emphasis on supporting the concept areas of literacy described by Nicholson (2005).

When asked to run the mat session one morning in the kindergarten, the student teacher chose the big book, *What's in the Shed?*, which was on a topic that many of the children were interested in, demonstrated by their involvement in play during the morning session. In addition to matching children's demonstrated interests and therefore being relevant and meaningful to the children, the book also used a strong repetitive rhythm and rhyme, which provided many opportunities to enhance phonological awareness, and clear grammatical structure; something that the student teacher had been told many times were strong predictors of literacy achievement.

The children enjoyed the story and chanted along with the rhymes, happily emphasising phonemes that were highlighted as part of the story reading. Flushed with her apparently successful story reading session, our student teacher asked her Associate Teacher how the mat session had gone, only to be met with a stony frown and the statement that, 'We don't do that school stuff here.' Our student teacher was puzzled and a bit distraught that she had been doing something wrong.

On discussion back at the university, it appeared that her Associate Teacher had trained some time ago and had quite strong age/stage understandings of literacy, and believed that all teaching of the sounds of the language should be left to her primary school colleagues. On debriefing, it was made clear to the student that although her Associate Teacher did not approve of her approach to literacy, her decision making was sound from a cultural-historical perspective. She had chosen literature based on children's interests and current area of play, as well as on her understanding of what conceptual knowledge children at kindergarten could legitimately engage with. Her role in supporting children's concepts of literacy in a playful but meaningful way was to be applauded, not discouraged.

This was a clear example of where the student's knowledge exceeded the teacher's! This example also illustrates how teacher beliefs about 'development', as discussed in Chapter 3, influence teacher judgments about when 'curriculum content' should be taught – in this case the teacher based the decision on the 'age' of the child, rather than on what would be culturally and socially relevant and meaningful at a particular moment. This latter point is taken up in the next section.

Table 10.1 Literacy and language-rich environments

Literacy and language-rich environments	Resources available
Books How many? Where are they? Do they have a particular focus? Do they reflect the cultures, ethnicities, values and interests of the children in this setting?	
Communications E.g. songs, rhymes, language games, messages, greetings, children's stories, artwork with writing on Do they reflect the languages of the children in this setting?	
Lists E.g. sign up lists, alphabet charts, number charts, locker lists	
Directions E.g. 'wash your hands', 'process cooking charts'	
Schedules E.g. Notice boards, curriculum plans, weekly plans	
Labels E.g. children's name tags, labels on activities	
ICT E.g. computers, printers, digital cameras, video cameras, smart boards	
Writing materials E.g. plastic letters, pens, crayons, paints	
Other E.g. environmental print, such as collage materials	

How to encourage language and literacy in the early years

There is a great deal of literature which emphasises the importance of children having access to a literacy-rich environment, so that they have opportunity to try out and play with a range of literacy tools (Neuman 2004; Tafa 2008). Much of this research is based upon Vygotsky's twin notions of access and mediation (Vygotsky 1978). In other words, children need both access to the literacy tools of a culture and mediation by more capable adults or peers, so that they understand the functions of the various literacy tools available. There is now growing evidence that children who have had opportunities for dramatic play in enriched literacy environments are more likely to develop the knowledge and skills required for literacy (Snow, Burns & Griffin 1998; Neuman 2004).

In Table 10.1, identify the literacy tools and resources that you have in your centre or classroom for enriching children's literacy experiences. Note whether the resources are for children or for adults.

REFLECTION 10.1

1. How many of the spaces could you fill?
2. What areas are you missing?
3. Does your centre or classroom reflect the interests of the children who are present at this time, or is the environment unchanging from term to term?
4. Does the environment reflect the diverse cultures of the children who attend?
5. Is it clear how different languages and literacies are represented in this setting?

Resources themselves will not teach literacy concepts. That requires an adult or another more capable child (or group of children, as shown in Chapter 6), to draw their attention to them, model their use, or orient them to literacy practices within a meaningful social context. However, it is still very important to have literacy opportunities in the environment, as Kravtsova (2008) has illustrated through her concept of the Zone of Potential Development (see Chapter 3).

ASSESSING CHILDREN'S INTERESTS IN AND EXPERIENCES WITH LITERACY

If we work from the principle that our role as teachers is to provide a language and literacy-rich environment and to work with children to ensure that they are able to access and try out the opportunities offered by that environment, then there are a number of questions that can be asked about the language and literacy opportunities each centre provides. Overleaf are some of the questions that we often ask ourselves as we look around centres and consider the possibilities that each classroom or centre provides.

Storybook reading

- Are children listening to stories? How often?
- What sorts of questions do they ask – pictures, characters, names of letters, sounds of letters, written form of words, meanings of words, content of stories, other?
- Do they ask the same questions over and over again?
- Does the same question ever occur in the same place in a story?
- Do children have favourite books?
- Do children ask to be read to? How often?
- Do you think that children know that you are reading the words on the page?

Writing and drawing

- Do children write their own name or any other words?
- Do they attempt to spell words, even if the spelling is unconventional?
- Do children ever copy or trace titles of books?
- Do children ever draw pictures related to stories they have read?
- Do children ever draw pictures related to stories they have made up themselves?
- Do children ever attempt to write stories on the computer?
- Do they use computer software such as PowerPoint or Paint to write and illustrate their stories?

Language and phonemic awareness

- Have you heard children sing nursery rhymes?
- Have you heard children sing songs?
- Do children use a wide vocabulary of interesting words?
- Have you ever heard children use words they have heard in a book?
- Have you heard children use language in play that sounds as if it came from a book or from oral stories that have been told?
- Can children recognise words that rhyme?
- Can children recognise the beginning sound in a word?
- Are children able to recognise the onset and rime in a word – can they break initial beginning sound (the onset) away from the rest of the word (the rime) e.g. c/at?
- Are children able to complete blending tasks – to blend sounds together e.g. m/ a/ p/ = map?

- Can children complete oddity tasks – are they able to pick the words which don't match on the beginning, middle or end sounds?

Letter name/Alphabet awareness

- Do children know the letters of the alphabet?
- Can they recognise their own name in print?
- Can they recite the alphabet?
- Can they recognise individual letters of the alphabet?
- Do children use plastic letters? What do they use them for?

Environmental print

- Do children read environmental print? (e.g. newspapers, magazines, cereal boxes, etc)
- Do children read signs and labels?
- Do children display a functional knowledge of literacy – do they know what a cookbook, newspaper, grocery list is for?
- Are there areas of the classroom or common activities of which literacy is a component part? (e.g. book corners, writing areas, computer stations, sign up lists, sign in lists, etc)

Logical and analytical abilities

- Are children able to group, classify, seriate (being able to line things up from small to big, etc) or conserve quantity?
- Do children know how to count and use counting as part of daily activities?
- Do children attempt puzzles?
- Do children attempt problem-solving tasks?

Narrating stories

- Do children make up stories?
- Do they use these stories in symbolic play?
- Do they share these with friends and teachers?
- Do children ever write the story down or draw a picture related to the story?

Although this list is obviously not exhaustive, it provides a beginning framework for thinking about the opportunities for language and literacy that the curriculum can offer.

A social practice perspective on literacy

A literacy as social practice perspective suggests that literacy is a social construction, shaped by social, cultural and historical factors, and with connections between literacy, power and inequality (Jones Díaz 2007). Within this framework, it is imperative that teachers have in-depth knowledge of what languages and literacies are used in children's homes, so that these can be recognised and valued in the early childhood settings. Gee (2004) argues that literacy is always a sociocultural (cultural-historical) practice, integrally linked to ways of talking, thinking, believing, acting, knowing, interacting, valuing and feeling. Knobel and Lankshear (2003) state that there are both 'in school' and 'out of school' literacies and often the 'out of school' literacies are not recognised as valid by teachers in centres and schools, and children who may be perfectly competent in their everyday home and community 'out of school' practices may fail in the 'in school' literacies that they are less familiar with. They cite the classic ethnographies of 'out of school' literacy behaviours documented by Shirley Brice Heath (1983) in the Piedmont Carolinas, Volk and Acosta's (2001) ethnography of Puerto Rican children in a midwestern US state, Pahl's (2002) study of children's text production at home and Hicks' (2002) study of two working class boys in a large US city, all of which demonstrated that children who were literacy failures at school all experienced literacy at home deeply embedded in familial, community and school relationships. McNaughton (2002) in New Zealand has argued that the stronger the pedagogical match between the home and the school, the more likely it is that the child will successfully acquire literacy. This means that teachers need to understand not only 'what' children need to develop in order to develop language and literacy, but also 'how' these concepts are introduced to children in their homes and communities, so that they can build on this conceptual knowledge in the centre or school setting.

How to incorporate out of school literacies in the early years setting

Any discussion of 'out of school' literacies can be readily situated in a discussion of the advantages and disadvantages of bilingualism and biliteracy.

Recent research suggests that bilingual children can have certain linguistic and cognitive advantages, given the right set of conditions (Gregory & Kenner 2003). Vygotsky was one of the few early researchers to propose that being bilingual enabled a child 'to see his language as one particular system among many, to view its phenomena under more general categories . . . [which] leads to awareness of his linguistic operations' (1962, p. 110). Vygotsky argued that by gaining control over two lexical, syntactic and semantic systems, and possibly two different written scripts, the child gained added analytical abilities and a more conscious understanding of the linguistic patterns of both languages. Children who are bilingual understand that each language enables different ways of saying the same thing.

Recent research provides evidence that if a child acquires a degree of competency in language and literacy in the home and community environment, a second language can be successfully added on (Gregory & Kenner 2003; Tabors & Snow 2001). This is called the 'linguistic interdependence principle' (John-Steiner 1985 in Gregory & Kenner 2003): the first language and second language skills are interdependent, so the acquisition of one affects the acquisition of the other.

Teachers need to find out about children's language and literacy abilities if they have a first language, the one used at home, and a second language will be 'added on' to this in the early childhood centre or school. Second language learners need to be closely monitored in New Zealand and Australia and other countries with large immigrant populations, as we have such multicultural societies, which include Māori, Aboriginal and Pasifika children who have attended total immersion language nests, the children of recent immigrants and refugee children. Although these children bring a wealth of literacy experiences with them into early childhood and primary settings, they are in danger of losing their language and literacy skills when they enter mainstream educational settings, unless their first language is supported. When children start to acquire a high-prestige language (such as English in European communities or Mandarin in Chinese communities), there is real threat that they will, at the same time, suspend development in, or even lose, use of their first language (Tabors & Snow 2001). Tabors and Snow's research indicates that children who are put into monolingual early childhood centres are at risk of losing their first language or becoming 'at-risk bilinguals' – not stable users of either the home language or English.

Research by Tagoilelagi-Leota, McNaughton, MacDonald and Ferry (2005) with Samoan and Tongan children in Auckland (New Zealand), from six months before school entry until a year after school entry, demonstrated that children who were potentially bilingual at the beginning of the study gained language and literacy skills in both their home language and English when they experienced programs that focused on the quality of teaching in reading to children, guided reading and telling, and retelling of stories. However, the variability in children's achievement across two languages meant that ongoing assessment by the teacher was crucial and that it was very important that the teacher understood the child's development in both languages. Harris (2007) argues that teachers need to focus on difference rather than deficiency when helping children develop emergent literacy in English. Although children may be gaining emergent literacy in their own language, they may be completely unfamiliar with the sounds and conventions of the English language, such as directionality, the alphabet, grammar and so forth. Tunmer, Chapman and Prochnow (2006) argue for 'differential instruction', rather than deficiency, so that children's differing skill needs are met. This may mean that teachers adopt quite different strategies for developing literacy with children from different cultures.

Gregory and Kenner (2003) argue that 'out of school' literacies may use patterns of instruction which are quite unfamiliar in mainstream European settings. They cite the example of the Samoan community church in Los Angeles, California, where children are taught to recite and master the letter, sound, number and word chart that is taught in pastors' schools in the Samoan Islands. Word by word repetition is used to help children learn the songs and chants used in traditional religious ceremonies; this is complemented by using peer support to help children learn. Thus children coming into centres and schools may have experienced completely different pedagogies in their everyday lives, making the learning of a new language through other methods a more complex proposition.

Meeting the learning needs of second language learners is a complex issue. Some centres and schools will have teachers who are bilingual or support personnel who can help children in the early days of 'adding on' another language. For others, teachers may have to first work out which aspects of language and literacy in the dominant language of the classroom the child already has and which they are going to need support to learn. For children who already use an alphabetic language, 'adding on' may be a matter of learning the English equivalent of words, so repetition of the names of objects and showing the child the word in print would be a helpful strategy. Asian children, who are familiar with an orthographic script, are going to need to be introduced to both the word and the alphabetic script.

The following extract from *Kei tua o te pae* (2005), the assessment exemplars used in New Zealand for assessing using *Te Whāriki*, provides a nice example of how teachers might support second language learners in the classroom. Many readers of this book may have similar approaches to supporting communication in their own curriculum documents.

Rahmat and the snakes

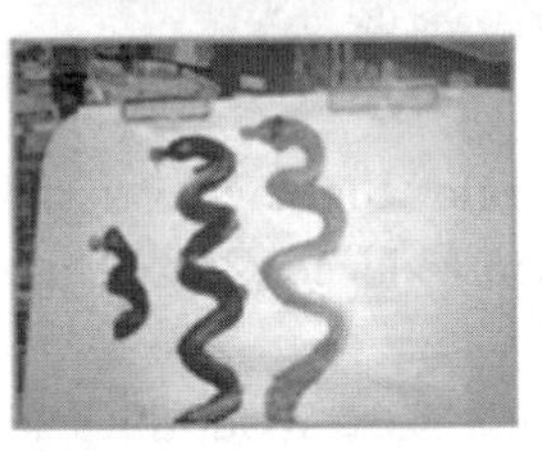

I noticed Rahmat was calling to me and gesturing for me to come over to his easel. He was painting on the far side of the easel and I couldn't see his creation from where I was.

I went over. "WOW! Snakes." "All have tongues and eyes," he said.

"Beautiful snakes," I said. "Do you have snakes in Afghanistan?" I asked. "Yes, and in Pakistan too." I began to write about his snakes on the painting – my version.

Rahmat listened respectfully to me. I could sense he was not satisfied with my ideas. He called to Sadia. Sadia is a teacher from Afghanistan who speaks Dari, the same Afghani language as Rahmat. He had some discussion with her. She listened. She began to write his story in Dari as Rahmat dictated.

He asked her to explain to me. She then explained that Rahmat's story goes like this:

The little snake ate lots of food and grew bigger, and then he ate lots and lots more food and he grew bigger still, and then he ate lots and lots and lots more food and he grew huge.

It is so fortunate that Rahmat can access Sadia and through her clarify his thinking for me. He wants me to know what he is thinking. He is not prepared to accept a watered-down version of his thoughts and he knows there is a way in this centre for that not to happen. I definitely had it wrong. Sorry, Rahmat. But you know how to teach me and graciously remind me that we are friends and that I am a learner. We belong to a community of learners.

Robyn. June.

What's happening here?

Rahmat is painting, and the teacher begins to write an accompanying commentary. He is not satisfied with the teacher's interpretation of his work and calls to another teacher who speaks his home language. This second teacher translates Rahmat's commentary for him, revealing that his painting tells a story.

What does this assessment tell us about the learning (using a Communication/Mana Reo lens)?

For Rahmat, English is an additional language. He can communicate in English, but a complex story, like this one about snakes, can be told only in his home language. As the teacher comments, "It is so fortunate that Rahmat can access Sadia [the translator] and through her clarify his thinking for me." Robyn, the teacher, is aware that without this assistance to overcome language barriers, teachers run the risk of documenting "watered-down" versions of children's communications.

How might this documented assessment contribute to Communication/Mana Reo?

This assessment sends out a reminder to teachers to listen carefully and, where possible, to elicit interpretations or translations from speakers of the children's home languages.

However, there are practice and policy implications about the availability of home-language speakers in early childhood centres where there are families for whom English is an additional language. There can be no straightforward solution to this issue, since the communities of some early childhood centres include fifteen or more different home languages.

What other strands of *Te Whāriki* are exemplified here?

This exemplar is also about a child's sense of *well-being* and *belonging*. In this early childhood centre, Rahmat can tell stories to the teacher in his home language – an opportunity that makes it clear that home culture and cultural identity are valued, respected, and connected to this place.

13

Figure 10.2 Rahmat and the snakes

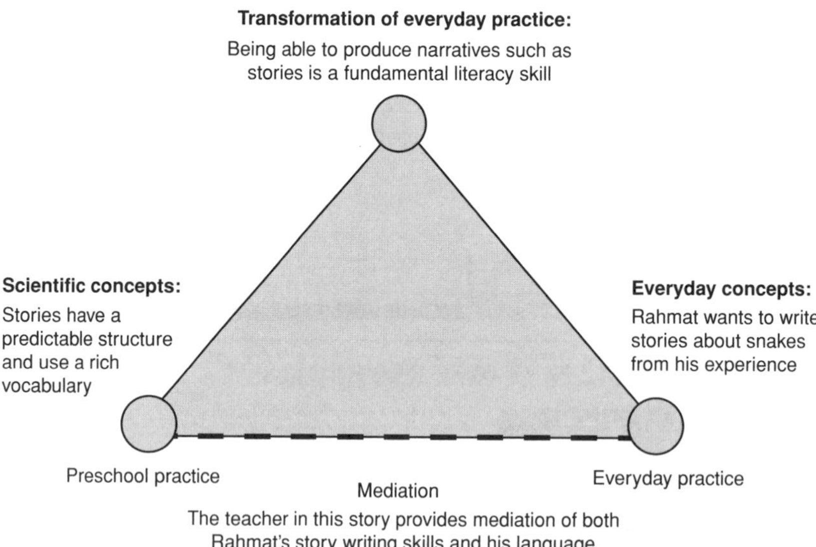
Transformation of everyday practice:
Being able to produce narratives such as stories is a fundamental literacy skill
Scientific concepts:
Stories have a predictable structure and use a rich vocabulary
Everyday concepts:
Rahmat wants to write stories about snakes from his experience
Preschool practice
Mediation
Everyday practice
The teacher in this story provides mediation of both Rahmat's story writing skills and his language development in English.

Figure 10.3 Transformation of practice: Rahmat and the snakes

In Chapter 9, a curriculum model for bringing together everyday concepts and scientific or mathematical concepts was introduced. We will use this same model in relation to literacy.

Thinking back on the example of Rahmat's story about the snake, we can see that the child's knowledge and understanding of snakes clearly outstripped the teacher's. With the help of a teacher who could speak his language, Rahmat was able to bring his home knowledge of snakes to the school setting, and with teacher assistance he was able to achieve conceptual knowledge around story writing (or schema for stories), as well as increasing his vocabulary in English.

Information and communication technologies (ICT)

Discussion around the use of ICT is relatively recent in early childhood, although it has been debated in the wider school sector for the last two decades (Oldridge 2007). Yelland (2006) argues that there has been a 'moral panic' around the use of technology and computers in particular in the early childhood setting, often framed around the notion that children will spend so much time on a computer that they will not experience traditional play materials, although this has not been reinforced by research. In fact, Yelland cites a study by Shields and Behrman (2000) that demonstrated that children of between 2 and 7 years spend on average 34 minutes per day using computers at home, with use increasing with age, and that computer use at home is associated with slightly better school achievement: these children score better on literacy, maths, computer knowledge and following instructions than children who have not experienced computers (Blanton, Moorman, Hayes & Warner 2000). Yelland argues that the computer and other digital technology should be considered as just another resource in the early years setting, like blocks or puzzles, but says that the 'moral panic' position has raised questions about what children will get out of using technology, questions that are not usually asked in relation to traditional play materials such as books, puzzles, blocks and playdough.

It's useful to return to our questions around curriculum again, and to think about them from the perspective of ICT in the curriculum:

- *How are children viewed?* How is children's knowledge and use of ICT viewed in this setting?
- *What content is valued?* What types of ICT knowledge and skills are valued for children?
- *How is knowledge framed?* Whose ICT knowledge is prioritised and organised in this setting?
- *How is progression organised (or not)?* How is progression in use of ICT viewed and used for structuring curriculum?
- *Who decides on the content?* Who has decided on the ICT content that is offered to children in this setting?

Marsh (2005) states that children are immersed in digital technologies in their homes and wider community settings, as part of cultural, media and digital literacy practices. Marsh cites a survey of 1852 parents and caregivers of children aged birth to 6 years in England which found the following:

- Children spent an average of 2 hours 6 minutes engaged with a screen each day (TV, DVD, computers, games, etc).
- 22 per cent of children can turn the TV on by age 1; 49 per cent can do it by age 2.
- 53 per cent of children used a computer at home on a typical day.
- 27 per cent below 4 years used a computer independently at home.
- 47 per cent could use a mouse and click by age 4.
- 27 per cent had used a digital camera to take photos by age 6.
- 15 per cent had used a video camera by age 6.

Although the survey revealed significant use of ICT by children at home, a survey of these children's teachers revealed that many were uncomfortable with the use of digital technologies in the classroom. In particular, 25 per cent of teachers did not plan to use computers in the early childhood setting, 74 per cent never planned to use digital cameras and 81 per cent never planned to use video cameras. In addition, 83 per cent said that they would never plan for children to visit websites during their time in early childhood eduction. Marsh views this mismatch of home and centre or school experiences as a concern for children's developing knowledge and skills.

In a recent Australian study, Zevenbergen and Logan (2008) found that 95 per cent of 4 to 5-year-old children had access to computers somewhere outside the educational setting, with 87.31 per cent having access to a computer in the home. The highest levels of use were for educational games (59.9 per cent), non-educational games (79.54 per cent) and drawing (48.92 per cent), with some use of software packages, pre-writing activities, modelling or copying of others, internet searching and free play. According to parents, these children were developing a range of computer-related skills, such as using a mouse, finding letters and numbers on a keyboard, using drawing tools, loading CDs and DVDs and using a printer. Boys were more frequent users of computer technologies and were more likely to play games, both educational and non-educational.

The implications of both these studies are obvious: children are entering early years settings with a range of skills, abilities and experiences that children of the past did not have, so teachers of the future need to both understand ICT, and use them in the classroom if they are going to provide a curriculum that is culturally and socially meaningful to children.

A CASE STUDY

(extract from *Tukutuku Korero/Education Gazette*, 21 August 2006, p. 5)

As part of the New Zealand E-Learning Teachers Fellowships program, Liz Fitzsimmons worked with the Port Ahuriri new entrant classroom on the impact of ICT on young children's learning.

continued »

A case study continued »

For her e-fellow project, Liz has been working with a class of Year 1 children and their teacher. Within that context, Liz is following the learning journeys of six case study children as she works with them to use the ICTs to create and use resources. She is looking at the attributes of meaningful learning as described in the constructivist theory. A literacy focus was chosen for the research. Working closely with the classroom teacher, Liz helped to plan a unit based around the work of the children's author, Lynley Dodd. The main learning objective was to develop rich language through the creation of three resources.

'We used Lynley Dodd's picture books to help the children develop an awareness of the descriptive language that this author is so well known for, and we wanted that to be developed in the children's written and oral language. ICT was going to be an area that supported this development.'

First the children were immersed in the literature of Lynley Dodd. The teacher worked with the children to build up a rich vocabulary of words from the books that were used to describe characters. Their awareness of Dodd's use of descriptive language began to be transferred into their own writing.

The first resource created was an animated PowerPoint book made by the class in which each child had responsibility for one slide. This involved each child taking a photo for the background, drawing animal pictures using Paint, and inserting them onto the background and animating them. They then composed a caption using rich language, inserted the text and made an audio recording.

'The whole process was very literacy oriented – it was visual, had movement, spoken word and written word, and when they recorded their scripts, they had to be very precise in their oral reading.'

The second resource built on the descriptive language and skills of the first but also focused on the retelling and sequencing of a story and made use of ArtRage. In the last resource created, each child made their own book. This involved first planning their stories and pictures with a story board, and then creating a digital PowerPoint story. The stories were then printed and burned onto a CD that the children could take home. Liz says that while the children initially had to learn new skills in order to create resources, she was 'absolutely astounded' by how quickly they learned to use the tools.

Hill and Mulhearn (2007) argue that the term 'multiliteracies' is a useful way to combine understandings of the ways in which print-based literacy and digital technologies combine. As they state:

Functional user	Meaning maker
♦ Locating, code breaking, using signs and icons ♦ Selecting and operating equipment ♦ Moving between mediums: cameras, videos, computers	♦ Understanding multimodal meanings ♦ Purpose of text and text form ♦ Connecting to prior knowledge
Critical analyser	**Transformer**
♦ Discourse analysis ♦ Equity ♦ Power and position ♦ Appropriate software/hardware	♦ Using skills and knowledge in new ways ♦ Designing texts ♦ Producing new texts

Figure 10.4 Map from Hill & Mulhearn 2007, p. 62

> Digital literacies and print based literacy are not oppositional concepts, both are required. In fact, traditional print based reading and writing was found to be vitally important. For example, writing was significantly important as a memory tool, for planning, designing and recording ideas and information. Reading was critically important for predicting, scanning, interpreting, analysing and selecting from the abundance of information. Interestingly the children switched effortlessly between genres, scanning material for information, following procedures, searching by scrolling through menus, and interpreting icons and written instructions on tool bars. In other words, although reading, writing, listening and speaking are paramount, today's students must be able to do more, as they decipher, code break, achieve meaning and express ideas through a range of media, incorporating design, layout, colour, graphics and information (p. 61).

Building on these ideas, Hill and Mulhearn (2007, p. 62) provide a 'multiliteracies map', a framework for conceptualising literacy in the curriculum.

Some interesting things to do with digital technologies (from Marsh 2005):

- Examine short extracts of film and discuss camera angles, sound, setting and lighting;

- Watch film with the sound turned down and ask children to create a soundtrack;
- Watch the beginning of a film and stop it to get children to predict what might happen next; and
- Get children to produce a story board which outlines the beginning, middle and end of a film narrative they have watched.

Many of these activities are simply variations on activities that teachers would do with print-based materials. Incorporating ICT in the classroom is about embracing and using new cultural tools, rather than reinventing pedagogy. This cultural-historical view of incorporating technologies into an early childhood centre reflects the bringing together of everyday and schooled concepts because children's experiences in the home and community are drawn upon to further the acquisition of multiliteracies.

REFLECTION 10.2

Using the model shown in Figure 9.5 take one of the literacy concepts discussed earlier and identify an everyday context in which the literacy concepts would arise. Then generate an example of the type of conversation and interaction that would result (mediation) so that the child's everyday practice is transformed (i.e. the child thinks consciously about the concept in practice). Once you have done this, look at the example provided in Figure 10.3.

LITERACY CONCEPTS

- concepts and conventions of print;
- ability to produce narratives; and
- ability to produce pre-conventional spellings.

The example below is based on research conducted for the *Foundations for Discovery* ICT pilot project at Pukerua Bay Kindergarten, near Wellington, New Zealand. Discussing the value of ICT in the classroom, Allen and Wightman (2009) give the following example:

> An example . . . is the value of email for sharing images and stories. What was one family's discovery of a shark on a local beach became a whole community investigation of the event; the emailed photographs being

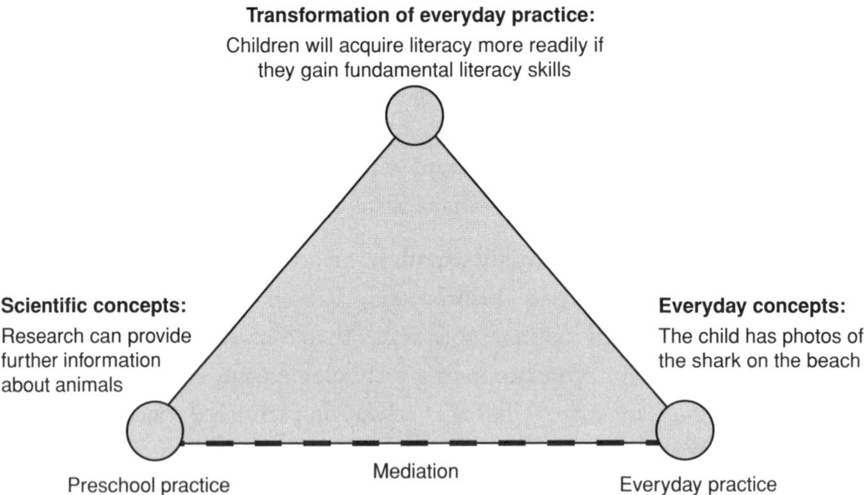
Transformation of everyday practice:
Children will acquire literacy more readily if they gain fundamental literacy skills
Scientific concepts:
Research can provide further information about animals
Everyday concepts:
The child has photos of the shark on the beach
Preschool practice
Mediation
Everyday practice
In this example, the teacher works with the child's interest in the sharks on the beach and helps the child to use classroom resources (the computer) to search for further information about sharks. This is further developed into story writing, thus extending the child's fundamental literacy skills.

Figure 10.5 Transformation of everyday practice: Sharks at kindergarten

> the link to communicate what happened. One family e-mailed pictures to Kindergarten to share. This led to other families visiting the shark on the beach and sharing their photos too. These emailed images also allowed those who never saw the shark to access a shared starting point for their own investigations. They could more easily be included in the excitement and engage with aspects of sharks' physiology, relative sizes, habitat and behaviours, in a wide range of Kindergarten environmental curriculum spaces, including the ICT suite (Allen & Wightman 2009).

As this example clearly illustrates, the use of ICT in meaningful ways in the early childhood setting can build on children's conceptual knowledge in science, as well as helping the child learn fundamental research and literacy skills, whilst maintaining children's interest and motivation to learn.

Summary

This chapter has examined some of the issues associated with languages, literacies and digital technologies in the modern early childhood classroom/centre. In order to ensure that children have optimal opportunities to learn, teachers need to know about the language, literacy and digital technology experiences that children have had prior to entering the educational setting, regardless of age of the child, and to then build on these experiences with meaningful and interesting activities. Some children, especially those who speak a different language or who have identified learning needs, will require extra support in order to become confident and competent with language, literacy and ICT.

References

Allen, A. & Wightman, G. (2009). ICT transforms wonder. *Early Education*, 45, pp. 21–24.

Anthony, J.L. & Francis, D.J. (2005). Development of phonological awareness. *Current Directions in Psychological Science*, 14, pp. 255–59.

Blanton, W.E., Moorman, G.B., Hayes, B.A. & Warner, M. (2000). Effects of participation in the Fifth Dimension on far transfer. http://129.171.53.1/blantonw/5dClhsepublications/tech/effects/effects.html, retrieved 9 August 2003.

Cunningham, A.E., Perry, K.E., Stanovich, K.E. & Stanovich, P.J. (2004). Disciplinary knowledge of K–3 teachers and their knowledge calibration in the domain of early literacy. *Annals of Dyslexia*, 54(1), pp. 139–66.

Foulin, J. (2005). Why is letter-name knowledge such a good predictor of learning to read? *Reading and Writing*, 18, pp. 129–55.

Gee, J.P. (2004). *Situated language and learning: A critique of traditional schooling*. Routledge: London.

Gregory, E. & Kenner, C. (2003). The out-of school schooling of literacy. In N. Hall, J. Larson & J. Marsh (eds), *Handbook of early childhood literacy*. London: Sage, pp. 75–84.

Harris, P. (2007). Reading contexts and practices in the early years. In L. Makin, C. Jones Díaz & C. McLachlan (eds), *Literacies in childhood: Changing views, challenging practices*. Sydney: MacLennan & Petty/Elsevier, pp. 153–67.

Heath, S.B. (1983). *Ways with words: Language, life and work in community and classrooms*. Cambridge MA: Cambridge University Press.

Hicks, D. (2002). *Reading lives: Working class children and literacy learning*. New York: Teachers College Press.

Hill, S. & Mulhearn, G. (2007). Children of the new millennium: Research and professional learning into practice. *Journal of Australian Research in Early Childhood Education*, 14(1), pp. 57–67.

Knobel, M. & Lankshear, C. (2003). Researching young children's out-of-school literacy practices. In N. Hall, J. Larson & J. Marsh (eds), *Handbook of early childhood literacy*. London: Sage, pp. 51–65.

Kravtsova, E.E. (2008). *Zone of Potential Development and subject positioning*. Paper presented at Monash University, Peninsula campus, 15 December.

Makin, L., Jones Díaz, C. & McLachlan, C. (eds) (2007). *Literacies in childhood: Changing views, challenging practice*. 2nd edn. Sydney: MacLennan & Petty/Elsevier.

Marsh, J. (2005). Cultural icons: Popular culture, media and new technologies in early childhood. *Every Child*, 11(4), pp. 14–15.

McNaughton, S. (2002). *Meeting of minds*. Wellington: Learning Media.

Neuman, S. (2004). The effect of print rich classroom environments on early literacy growth. *Reading Teacher*, 58(1), pp. 89–91.

Nicholson, T. (2005). *At the cutting edge: The importance of phonemic awareness in learning to read and spell*. Wellington: NZCER Press.

Oldridge, L. (2007). Debunking the myths: ICT and young children. *Early Education*, 42, Spring/Summer, pp. 9–11.

Pahl, K. (2002). Ephemera, mess and miscellaneous piles: Texts and practices in families. *Journal of Early Childhood Literacy*, 2(2), pp. 145–66.

Snow, C.E., Burns, M.S. & Griffin, P. (eds) (1998). *Preventing reading difficulties in young children*. Washington DC: National Academy Press.

Tabors, O. & Snow, C. (2001). Young bilingual children and early literacy development. In S.B. Neuman & D.K. Dickinson (eds), *Handbook of early literacy research*. New York: The Guilford Press.

Tafa, E. (2008). Kindergarten reading and writing curricula in the European Union. *Literacy*, 42(3), pp. 162–70.

Tagoilelagi-Leota, F., McNaughton, S., MacDonald, S. & Ferry, S. (2005). Bilingual and biliteracy development over the transition to school. *International Journal of Bilingual Education and Bilingualism*, 8(5), pp. 455–79.

Tunmer, W.E., Chapman, J.W. & Prochnow, J.E. (2006). Literate cultural capital at school entry predicts later reading achievement: A seven year longitudinal study. *New Zealand Journal of Educational Studies*, 41, pp. 183–204.

Volk, D. & de Acosta, M. (2001). 'Many differing ladders, many ways to climb . . .': Literacy events in the bilingual classroom, homes and communities of three Puerto Rican kindergartners. *Journal of Early Childhood Literacy*, 1(2), pp. 193–223.

Vygotsky, L.S. (1962). *Thought and language*. Cambridge MA: MIT Press.

Vygotsky, L.S. (1978). *Mind in society: The development of higher psychological processes*. In M. Cole, V. John-Steiner, S. Scribner & E. Souberman (eds). Cambridge MA: Harvard University Press.

Vygotsky, L.S. (1987). *The collected works of L.S. Vygotsky*. R.W. Rieber & A.S. Carton (eds), prologue by J.S. Bruner, translated and with an introduction by N. Minick. New York: Plenum Press.

Whitehurst, G.J. & Lonigan, C.J. (1998). Child development and emergent literacy. *Child Development*, 69, pp. 848–72.

Yelland, N. (2006). New technologies and young children: Technology in early childhood education. *Teacher Learning Network*, 13(3), pp. 10–13.

Zevenbergen, R. & Logan, H. (2008). Computer use by preschool children: Rethinking practice as digital natives come to preschool. *Australian Journal of Early Childhood*, 33(1), pp. 37–44.

Chapter 11

Content knowledge: The arts and health, wellbeing and physical activity

In this chapter the theory and the practice of Vygotsky's (1987) work on concept formation will be further discussed. The content areas of arts and health, wellbeing and physical education will be used to illustrate the importance of conceptual knowledge in the early childhood curriculum.

On the face of it, this sounds like an unusual combination, but as we hope this chapter shows, much of the concept formation associated with these domains of knowledge involves the interrelationship of cognitive abilities and psychomotor skills. For the purposes of simplicity only, the arts in this discussion include the visual arts, dance and music. The focus is on concept formation that involves developing physical abilities, such as drawing, painting, playing a musical instrument, singing, dancing, and playing on the jungle gym, playing ball games and other games with rules.

Health, wellbeing and physical activity

If we think about concept formation for physical activity, we probably see how this subject area too can be thought about in terms of cultural-historical theory, as many aspects of children's everyday knowledge about these things from the home setting can be integrated with research on health, wellbeing and physical activity.

In this area of children's knowledge, learning how to be healthy, maintain a strong sense of their own identity and remain physically active are essential skills for a lifelong sense of wellbeing. Helping children to grow up fit, healthy and physically capable is a fundamental aim of most teachers, and regular physical activity is mandated in most curricula. For example, in the *Hong Kong*

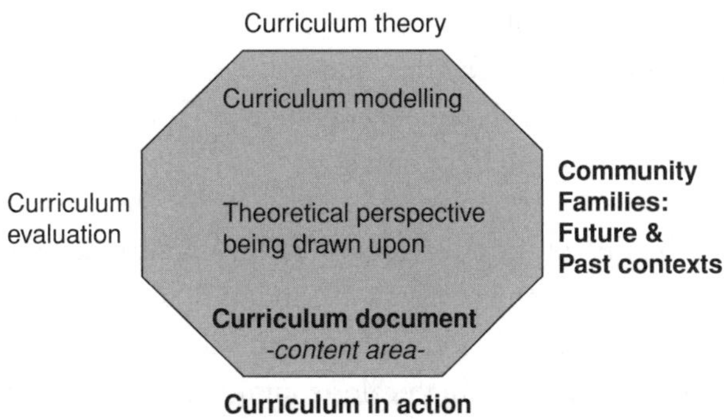

Figure 11.1 Curriculum development pathway – content knowledge

Guide to the Pre-Primary Curriculum (The Education and Manpower Bureau 2006), the learning area Physical Fitness and Health includes these core concepts:

> children develop a healthy life-style by cultivating good habits and awareness of personal and public hygiene; children develop self care ability; children develop interest in and the habit of participating in physical activities; and children know how to protect themselves by understanding basic health and safety issues (p. 23).

The reasons for supporting children's physical health and development are made very clear in the medical literature. As Hills, King and Armstrong (2007) state:

> During childhood and adolescence, nutrition and physical activity influence the growth and development of numerous body tissues, including body fat, skeletal muscle tissue and bone. It is important to bear in mind that growth and maturation will continue even when physical activity is limited, whereas nutrition (ideally in combination with physical activity) is essential for optimal growth and development. Children who experience appropriate nutrition and regular physical activity may be expected to display healthy patterns of physical maturation consistent with their genetic potential. Unfortunately the opportunity to be physically active has reduced over time – probably due to a series of changing environmental factors. The environment exerts a strong influence on physical activity (p. 534).

As providers of children's early childhood environments, parents and teachers must ensure that children receive adequate opportunities and support to become physically active. Bredekamp and Copple (1997), in the NAEYC position statement, state that physical activity serves three primary purposes:

- stimulating physiological development;
- creating functional motor abilities; and
- organising the brain for subsequent cognitive processing in all three domains (physical, social-emotional, cognitive).

With regard to the first purpose, lack of physical activity may result in incomplete physiological development (Stork & Sanders 2008), as physical activity in early childhood is needed for normal bone growth and muscle development. Lack of physical activity plus a high calorie intake leads to obesity, an increasingly important issue in relation to young children. Childhood obesity leads to obesity in adolescence and adulthood, which results in increased incidence of heart disease, diabetes and cancer.

Children's physical abilities are the result of the maturation of the nervous and skeletal systems, which over time and in stages enable increasingly complex motor activity. Children need to use cognitive and physical effort in order to learn and master fundamental motor skills such as throwing, catching, hopping, skipping and twisting. These early childhood physical skills underpin adult ones, which are achieved with experience, practice and physiological development. As with all other areas of development, there is a need to 'hard-wire' the necessary skills and abilities in the early childhood period, so that these activities can be more readily managed in adolescence and adulthood. Hills, King and Armstrong (2007, p. 536) state that 'The first years of life represent an intense period of motor learning that provides foundation for later, more complex and skilled performance.'

Hills, King and Armstrong (2007) note that various sorts of physical activity are important parts of physical health and should be a normal part of growth and development. Regular weight-bearing exercise, for example, is needed, because it:

- contributes to the growth and maintenance of a healthy musculoskeletal system;
- helps maintain a desirable body composition by controlling weight and minimising body fat; and
- helps to prevent and reduce high blood pressure.

In addition, they argue, regular participation in physical activity plays a key part in the social and emotional development of young children, and that physical activity leads to a reduction in depression and is associated with improved motor skills and development. They argue that the fundamental motor patterns of crawling, standing, walking, running and jumping are fostered through play, and that without regular opportunities to practise, these habitual (and vital) physical activity and skills can be compromised.

Stork and Sanders (2008) argue that because of the decrease in the amount of time that children spend on incidental physical activity, caused by changes in family structures and a more hurried lifestyle, there is an increased need to promote both physical education and physical activity in early childhood settings. They contend that there is little research on physical education in early childhood settings, but that what there is suggests that physical education is worth the effort because of the improvement it makes in children's physical abilities.

They also note that free play in early childhood may involve limited opportunities for a number of physical skills to develop, and that teacher-led physical games may involve considerable waiting around for turn taking, which does not lead to the amount of physical activity that is needed for skill and mastery to develop. Although neither of these activities should be discouraged, planned and regular physical education sessions will yield greater results in terms of physical and motor development. They cite research (Kelly, Dagger & Walkley 1989; Goodway & Branta 2003) which shows that modest interventions of physical education – 45–50 minutes twice a week over a 12-week period – with children aged 3 to 5 years lead to increases in motor skill development in hopping, galloping, ball bouncing, kicking, catching and throwing. These motor skill improvements did not occur in the control groups in both studies.

Stork and Sanders (2008) also point out that although children can learn these fundamental skills with simple tuition, the pedagogy needs to be right. It should be appropriate to the age and physical abilities of the children and based on pedagogy of play, which relies on concrete experiences, imitation and experimentation. Children must be actively involved in order to learn; mere observation, in this area, will not lead to learning. Stork and Sanders (2008) promote the SKILL program (Successful Kinaesthetic Instruction for Lifelong Learning) (Goodway & Savage 2001) and Project SKIP (Successful Kinaesthetic Instruction for Preschoolers) (Goodway & Robinson 2006) as using appropriate pedagogy for young children: these programs are based on a 'mastery climate' in which tasks are differentiated for individual children and children have choices which put them in control of their own learning. Stork and Sanders (2008) consider that both programs increase children's motor abilities and their sense of physical competence. In addition, children who are involved in physical activity are more likely to become comfortable with the effects that accompany physical exertion, such as perspiration, increased heart rate and strenuous muscle contractions.

Clearly, children will enter early childhood settings having experienced a range of physical activities in the home environment, and the task, as previously argued, is to find out what forms the child is already familiar with as the basis for curriculum design. The teacher's role in terms of promoting physical skill is to provide a positive, caring environment in which there are many interesting and stimulating things to do (Bredekamp & Copple 1997) and in which there are a range of situations, challenges and activities that allow children to develop skills and learn about their own potential for movement, under the guidance of an adult (Stork & Sanders 2008). Stork & Sanders (2008) argue that the research literature shows that teachers need the following pedagogical skills:

1. Arrange tasks in progressions that yield high rates of success while maintaining a necessary degree of challenge.
2. Use physical and verbal cues to shape and refine motor performance.
3. Individualise tasks to accommodate differences in ability and interest.
4. Model the form and nature of physical actions with a clarity and simplicity that allows children to grasp key elements.
5. Employ a wide range of strategies for inviting children to believe they can improve through practice and effort, can make decisions about their own motor performances, and, above all, can enjoy the pleasures of success (p. 202).

Although children will have used a diverse range of equipment in their home settings, Stork and Sanders (2008) argue that the equipment children can use most readily is soft, flexible, graspable and slow moving, to accommodate their slower reaction time and lack of tactile coordination and overall agility. There should be sufficient equipment and enough variety so that all the children can be active at the same time.

There is evidence that children need adequate physical space in which to be physically active, so that they can swing a bat, kick a ball or skip safely. For playgrounds to incorporate active motor play, approximately 40 square metres per child is seen as a reasonable minimum (Greenman 1988). In addition, there are guidelines on the amount and type of physical activity that young children should engage in (NASPE 2009). These guidelines were developed to help raise awareness of the need for physical activity in young children, and to prevent the 'push down' of physical education practices used in primary schools into early childhood settings. The emphasis is on children getting the right sort of physical activity, in the right amounts, in an appropriately resourced environment, from a competent and confident teacher. Given the diversity of types of physical activity that children experience at home, there are many ways in which physical activity could be encouraged in the early childhood setting – dance, forms of martial arts and yoga, and ball games, for example.

Pellegrini and Smith (1998) found three dominant types of physical activity play in young children:

1. **Rhythmic stereotypes** – gross motor movements that do not appear to have a purpose, e.g. foot kicking or body rocking. This type of play peaks in the middle of the first year, with around 40 per cent of infants observed to engage in this sort of physical play.
2. **Exercise play** – gross motor movements which are mainly associated with physical vigour. This type of play increases from the toddler age onwards and peaks between 4 and 5 years. At 4 years of age, 20 per cent of children's play is typically physically vigorous.
3. **Rough and tumble play** – refers to the vigorous behaviours such as wrestling, kicking and tumbling. Initially often supported by parents in early childhood, it peaks at around 8–10 years of age.

In the US, the National Association for Sport & Physical Education (2002) provides the following position statement: All children birth to age five should engage in daily physical activity that promotes health-related fitness and movement skills. They divide the position statement into a set of guidelines with accompanying advice on appropriate activities for infants (birth to 12 months), toddlers (12 to 36 months) and preschoolers (3 to 5 years):

Guidelines for infants

1. Infants should interact with parents and/or caregivers in daily activities that are dedicated to promoting the exploration of their environment.
2. Infants should be placed in safe settings that facilitate physical activity and do not restrict movement for prolonged periods of time.
3. Infants' physical activity should promote the development of movement skills.
4. Infants should have an environment that meets or exceeds recommended safety standards for performing large muscle activities.
5. Individuals responsible for the wellbeing of infants should be aware of the importance of physical activity and facilitate the child's movement skills.

Guidelines for toddlers

1. Toddlers should accumulate at least 30 minutes of structured physical activity per day.
2. Toddlers should engage in at least 60 minutes and up to several hours per day of unstructured physical activity and should not be sedentary for more than 60 minutes at a time except when sleeping.

3. Toddlers should develop movement skills that are building blocks for more complex movement tasks.
4. Toddlers should have indoor and outdoor areas that meet or exceed recommended safety standards for performing large muscle activities.
5. Individuals responsible for the wellbeing of toddlers should be aware of the importance of physical activity and facilitate the child's movement skills.

Guidelines for preschoolers

1. Preschoolers should accumulate at least 60 minutes of structured physical activity per day.
2. Preschoolers should engage in at least 60 minutes and up to several hours per day of unstructured physical activity and should not be sedentary for more than 60 minutes at a time except when sleeping.
3. Preschoolers should develop competence in movement skills that are building blocks for more complex movement tasks.
4. Preschoolers should have indoor and outdoor areas that meet or exceed recommended safety standards for performing large muscle activities.
5. Individuals responsible for the wellbeing of preschoolers should be aware of the importance of physical activity and facilitate the child's movement skills.

In Chapter 2, it was noted that physical activity was featured in most of the curricula summarised. In some it was separated out (in the US, for instance) and in others it was integrated (in Hong Kong, for instance).

In Chapter 9, a curriculum model for bringing together everyday concepts and scientific or mathematical concepts was introduced. We will use this same model for thinking about health, wellbeing and physical activity, so that we can combine understandings that occur in homes and communities with children's learning and concept formation in the early childhood setting.

REFLECTION 11.1

Using the model shown in Figure 9.5, take one of the physical education concepts shown below and identify an everyday context in which the physical education concepts would arise. Then generate an example of the type of conversation and interaction that would result (mediation) so that the child's everyday practice is transformed (i.e. the child thinks consciously about the concept in practice). Once you have done this, look at the example provided in Figure 11.2.

Physical education concepts

- Sustained physical activity builds fitness
- Physical activity every day is good for health
- Practising movement skills leads to mastery
- Fundamental motor skills such as throwing, catching, hopping, skipping, and twisting lay foundations for complex motor skills.

In this example, the child has told the teacher that he likes to kick a ball with his brother at home. The teacher can follow up on this to introduce a range of other things that the child and his peers can do with a ball, such as throw it, roll it, catch it, play games with rules, along with experimenting with balls of different sizes. What starts as a home activity is thus transformed into a regular opportunity for physical activity every day; this activity also consolidates both knowledge of how to play with balls and skills for kicking, rolling, catching and throwing a ball, which are required for many sports with rules.

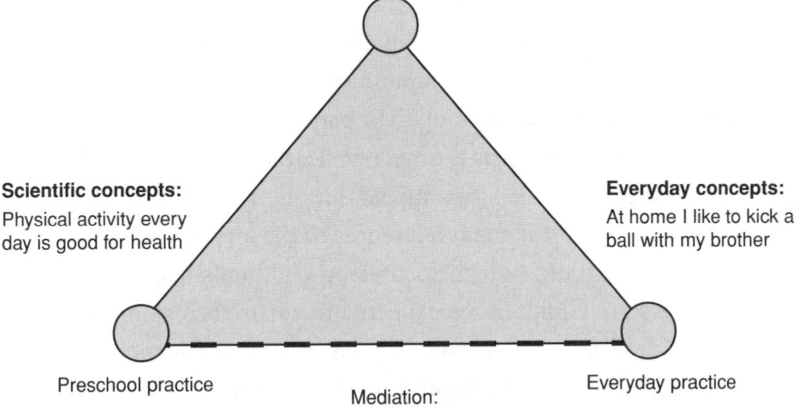
Transformation of everyday practice:
Learning a range of physical games will enable children to participate more fully in the life of the early childhood centre and build or maintain health
Scientific concepts:
Physical activity every day is good for health
Everyday concepts:
At home I like to kick a ball with my brother
Preschool practice
Everyday practice
Mediation:
The teacher introduces a ball into the outdoor programme and together the children and teacher work out many other ways to use the equipment, i.e. roll, throw, catch.

Figure 11.2 Transformation of everyday practice: Ball skills

The arts

As mentioned earlier in this chapter, many aspects of the arts are based on children's achievement of higher level psychomotor skills; these help children achieve in the arts and physical activity at the same time. Eisner (2002) argues that through active engagement with arts experiences children can develop their senses and their imagination:

> The senses provide the material for the creation of consciousness, and we, in turn, use the content of consciousness and the sensory potential of various materials to mediate, transform, and transport our consciousness into worlds beyond ourselves (Eisner 1994, pp. 17–18).

Eisner (1994) further argues that human beings use their senses to create and interpret codes of representation, which symbolise experiences. Eisner argues that one key purpose of including the arts in education is to help children understand the various codes of representation and use them for themselves to create meaning.

As discussed in the previous chapter, children bring to their early childhood education a range of experiences of electronic media, such as TV, video, and computer, along with a vast range of traditional forms of arts from their homes and communities, including Indigenous and immigrant forms of visual arts, drama, dance, and music. In the Singaporean curriculum, the arts encompass dance, drama, music and the visual arts, and often these are taught in interrelated ways. For example, children may experience drama, dance and music as they practise a performance they are preparing for parents. Or they may script plays for books without words and sing their play.

Although the domain of the arts is often not clearly identified in early childhood curriculum documents, it often appears in other strands. For example, Terreni (2008) suggests that the main references to the arts in *Te Whāriki* occur in the communication strand, which focuses on children's language, literacy and creative expression. Children are expected to experience an environment in which they can develop 'an increasing familiarity with a selection of the art, craft, songs, music and stories, which are valued by the cultures in the community' (p. 80), in which 'skills and confidence with the processes of art and craft, such as cutting, drawing, collage, painting, print making, weaving, stitching, carving and constructing' are encouraged, and in which children 'experience the stories and symbols of their own and other cultures' (p. 80). In Korea, the arts appear in the *Creative inquiry* section, in Ontario, Canada, they are in the *Awareness of selves as artists* section, and in England they are mentioned in the *Creative development* section.

Niland (2007) notes that humans have, throughout history, communicated through arts such as storytelling, music and dance, and often use combinations of art forms to express ideas. Makin and Whitehead (2007) state that the responsiveness to music, in particular, begins before birth:

> Even before birth, children respond to aural sensations such as voices and music (Al-Qahanti 2005) and differentiate between their mother's voice and that of other people (Kisilevsky et al., 2003). Part of the intense physicality of a baby's life is the enjoyment that comes from rhythmic, patterned and predictable sounds such as lullabies, lap games, songs and rhymes. Gradually, layers of meaning map onto this physical enjoyment (p. 170).

Niland (2007) agrees that all children have been exposed to the arts in their homes and communities; however, she also argues that children whose exposure to the arts has been predominantly through electronic media have had passive experiences. Mediating children's home and educational experiences can help promote a love of the arts, as well as consolidating understanding and appreciation of a diverse range of art forms, including electronic media. Niland proposes the following methods of integrating music in particular into early childhood, as ways of consolidating children's understandings of the interrelatedness of music and other curriculum areas: adding sound to stories; singing stories instead of reading them; adding narrative to a song; adding song to a story; and adding music to rest times.

Although increasing children's appreciation of the diversity of the arts seems an obvious ideal, like other domain areas we have discussed, understanding of the arts is cultural-historical in nature. Andang'o and Mugo (2007), discussing music education in Kenya, contend that the education system itself limits the forms of music that children are exposed to. In Kenya, as (it could be argued) in Māori and Pasifika communities in New Zealand, there are four main venues that shape Kenyan children's music education: the home; the church; music festivals; and school. Andang'o and Mugo believe that traditional forms of singing with family members are dying out in urban areas of Kenya and other parts of Africa, as a result of the impact of television, mass-produced western music and other media. They stress that because early childhood centres play such a big role in children's lives, they must work in ways that support local forms of music. In this way, the early childhood setting complements the cultural heritage of the child, rather than competing with it. Andang'o and Mugo (2007) therefore argue strongly for aligning music in the curriculum with the indigenous practices of the local community.

With regard to the visual arts, Richards (2007) challenges the widely supported view that children's artistic abilities unfold in a natural and predictable developmental way – from early random mark making to realistic representations – and are best left unhindered. She argues instead that learning in the arts is a social, cultural and historical act and that many teachers' entrenched beliefs about not interfering with children's art are inconsistent with current cultural-historical theorising. In her view, teachers need to recognise the social and interactive nature of children's art experiences.

In a similar vein, Terreni argues vehemently against the notion that children will develop skills in visual art through maturation, or through participation in families and communities. Instead, Terreni proposes that

> rather than just setting up well-resourced art areas and then standing back from them, active teacher engagement in this domain creates important opportunities for children to 'talk about, critique and reflect upon their representation of their worlds' (Gunn 2000, p. 160) (p. 71).

Terreni suggests that children's sense of belonging, and their understanding of the visual arts, can be assisted by including culturally diverse art and artefacts from different cultures in the early childhood setting. In Pasifika cultures in particular, the art or artefact may be a bearer of cultural meaning or metaphors for larger social meanings (Aprill 2007), so teachers can mediate children's understandings by discussing, questioning and researching meanings as they encounter new forms of visual art.

Dyson (2008) similarly proposes that children need license in the early childhood curriculum in order to express their growing understandings:

> Drawing in particular is a primary way that many children, from varied cultures, represent, imagine and extend their experiences (Arnheim 2006; Fineberg 2006). As such, drawing can be an impetus for writing and for talk, but it requires much more than just 'planning'. It is a particular medium with possibilities and constraints, just as writing is. To become sophisticated participants in the multimedia texts of our times, children need to experience how meanings are transformed or revealed as they are differently articulated (e.g. in speaking, writing or drawing) (p. 25).

Think back again to Figure 9.5, adapted for thinking about the arts (based on Fleer & Raban 2007). This model uses cultural-historical theory to exemplify concept formation for young children.

REFLECTION 11.2

Using the model used previously in this chapter, take one of the musical concepts shown below and identify an everyday context in which the musical concepts would arise. Then generate an example of the type of conversation and interaction that would result (mediation) so that the child's everyday practice is transformed (i.e. the child thinks consciously about the concept in practice). Then take a look at the working example in Figure 11.3.

MUSICAL CONCEPTS

- Singing can be for fun
- Music is about rhythm
- We can dance to a beat
- We can use instruments to make loud and soft noises
- We can play a range of instruments in tune.

Encourage the children to bring a favourite song from home, with the words and music. Each child takes a turn to teach the other children their favourite song, along with any actions or typical musical accompaniment. Children may invite parents along to help teach their song.

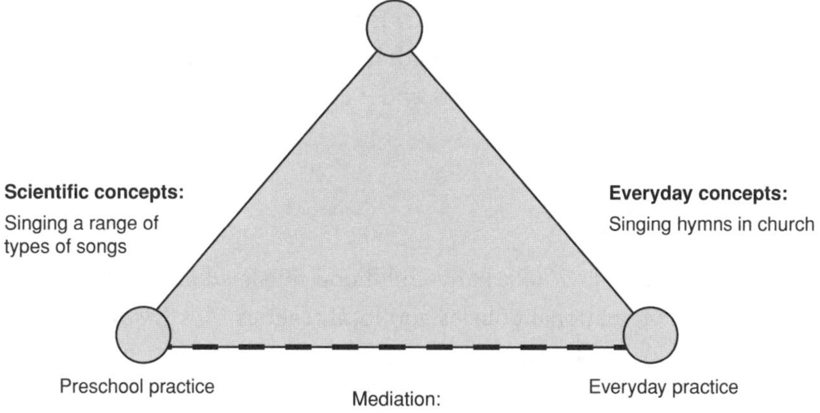
Transformation of everyday practice:
The child can participate more fully in the early childhood setting when they can take part in singing, dancing and musical activities
Scientific concepts:
Singing a range of types of songs
Everyday concepts:
Singing hymns in church
Preschool practice
Everyday practice
Mediation:
The teacher and children share songs from their families and communities

Figure 11.3 Transformation of everyday practice: Singing

In this example, the teacher has used the knowledge about singing that children and their families have to increase the types (and numbers) of songs that children know about and can sing, as well as their understanding of the role of singing in diverse family and cultural settings.

This example is beautifully exemplified in the DVD *Tuakana Teina: Keeping everyone on the waka* (Massey University 2008), where children lead the merging of arts concepts with everyday knowledge. In the *Tuakana Teina* DVD, an older boy comes over from the local Samoan early childhood centre and teaches all the children in the kindergarten some of the traditional Samoan dance routines. *Tuakana Teina* involves a sharing of expertise among children, regardless of age.

Summary

Clearly the challenge for these domains of children's learning is to merge the knowledge that teachers have of concepts that children will need to be successful learners with the cultural knowledge and skills that the children bring to their learning. As previously noted argued, McNaughton (2002) argues that the curriculum must be wide enough to incorporate the familiar while unlocking the unfamiliar. This is clearly true of all of the concepts discussed in this chapter. Children bring with them many understandings and experiences of the arts, and teachers can help them learn about other cultures' forms of the arts. Similarly, children will come to early childhood settings with experiences of health practices, approaches to wellbeing and understandings of the importance of physical activity. The task of the teacher is to reinforce the familiar and not judge family practices, while enabling children to critically examine alternative world views of health, personal identity and wellbeing and physical activity.

References

Anadang'o, E. & Mugo, J. (2007). Early childhood music education in Kenya: Between broad national policies and local realities. *Arts Education Policy Review*, 109(2), pp. 43–52.

Aprill, A. (2007). Letter from New Zealand: The postmodern marae. *ANZAEA*, 17(1).

Bredekamp, S. & Copple, C. (eds) (1997). *Developmentally appropriate practice in early childhood programs*. Washington DC: NAEYC.

Dyson, A.H. (2008). On listening to child composers: Beyond 'fix its'. In C. Genishi & A.L. Goodwin (eds), *Diversities in early childhood education: Rethinking and doing*. London: Routledge, pp. 13–28.

Eisner, E. (1994). *Cognition and the curriculum reconsidered*. New York: Teachers College Press.

Eisner, E. (2002). *The arts and the creation of the mind*. New Haven: Yale University Press.

Goodway, J.D. & Robinson, L.E. (2006, March). SKIPping toward an active start: Promoting physical activity in preschoolers. *Beyond the Journal*, 1–6 [online]. Available: http://www.journal.naeyc.org/btj/200605/GoodwayBTJ.pdf.

Goodway, J.D. & Savage, H. (2001). Environmental engineering in elementary physical education. *Teaching Elementary Physical Education*, 12(2), pp. 12–14.

Greenman, J. (1988). *Caring spaces, learning places: Children's environments that work*. Redman WA: Exchange Press.

Hills, A.P., King, N.A. & Armstrong, T.P. (2007). The contribution of physical activity and sedentary behaviours to the growth and development of children and adolescents. *Sports Medicine*, 37(6), pp. 533–45.

Makin, L. & Whiteman, P. (2007). Multiliteracies and the arts. In L. Makin, C. Jones Díaz & C. McLachlan (eds), *Literacies in childhood: Changing views, challenging practice*. 2nd edn. Sydney: Maclennan & Petty/Elsevier, pp. 168–82.

Massey University (2007). *Taukana Teina: Keeping everyone on the waka*. Palmerston North: Massey University. DVD available from Massey University College of Education.

McNaughton, S. (2002). *Meeting of minds*. Wellington: Learning Media.

Ministry of Education (1996). *Te Whāriki: Early childhood curriculum*. Wellington: Learning Media.

Ministry of Education (2007). *The New Zealand Curriculum*. Wellington: Learning Media.

Ministry of Education, Singapore (n.d). *Nurturing Early Learnings. A framework for a kindergarten curriculum in Singapore*. Singapore: Pre-school Education Unit.

National Association for Sport and Physical Education (2002). *Active Start: A statement of physical activity guidelines for children birth to five years*. Retrieved 25/02/2009 from http:www.aahperd.org/naspe/template.cfm?template=ns_active.html.

Niland, A. (2007). Musical stories: Strategies for intergrating music and literature for young children. *Australian Journal of Early Childhood*, 32(4), pp. 7–11.

Pellegrini, A.D. & Smith, P.K.(1998). Physical activity play: The nature and function of a neglected aspect of play. *Child Development*, 69(3), pp. 577–98.

Richards, R.D. (2007). Outdated relics on hallowed ground: Unearthing attitudes about beliefs about young children's art. *Australian Journal of Early Childhood*, 32(4), pp. 22–30.

Stork, S. & Sanders, S.W. (2008). Physical education in early childhood. *The Elementary School Journal*, 108(3), pp. 197–206.

Terreni, L. (2008). Providing visual arts education in early childhood settings that is responsive to cultural diversity. *Australian Art Education*, 31(1), pp. 66–79.

The Education and Manpower Bureau (2006). *Guide to the Pre-Primary Curriculum*. Hong Kong: The Curriculum Development Council.

CHAPTER 12

CONCLUSIONS

Setting: A university tutorial room

Timing: The last class for the year

Participants: An international group of 3rd year BEd (Early Years) students and their lecturer

Subject: Curriculum in the early childhood setting

Lecturer: It seems incredible that we are finally at the end of the course! What I'd like to do today, as part of wrapping up this course and helping to prepare you for your new careers as teachers, is to check that you have a good understanding now of the term 'curriculum' and what it means in terms of your teaching practice. If you think back to the beginning of this course, I asked you to define what you understood by the term 'curriculum' and it was evident in that early discussion that as a group we had a range of different opinions about it and also quite a bit of confusion about what 'curriculum' might mean for us as teachers. We've spent a lot of time on this topic and we've looked at many aspects of it. Take about 15 minutes to discuss this now and then we will discuss it as a group. Get someone from your group to record your ideas, so that we can share them.

Students move off into groups of about six people and begin the task set by the lecturer.

Anna: I remember this activity – we were all over the place about what we thought a curriculum is.

continued »

continued »

Kelly: Yes, we were – and to be honest, I didn't want to take this course, but it has been useful in terms of clarifying my thinking about curriculum.

Kiri: Yes, it has. I've realised now that the curriculum I'm used to using is similar in lots of ways to other curriculum documents, but it really represents the social, educational, political and economic aims each community or country has for their children.

Hui Lee: Yes, indeed – I can now think quite critically about my own curriculum and I am able to question some of the assumptions about children that underpin the curriculum used in Singapore. It's good to be able to put the focus of the curriculum into a bigger context of what a curriculum is striving to achieve.

Mandy: I agree – I can see why the new Australian curriculum is taking the form it is taking, although I wonder really how this will work in relation to all the curriculum documents that exist in the states and territories. Do you think that people will take notice of the national curriculum when they are used to using their own state curriculum, or of the things they learnt when they did their teacher education program?

Kiri: That's a good question – I think we all know how many of our Associate Teachers find it hard enough to deal with all the new ideas that we are being taught at university, without having to deal with a whole new curriculum. I reckon it will take some time before teachers right across the country work out what the new curriculum in Australia means for them and what theories they need to know about in order to teach within the curriculum framework.

Sam: It has been interesting to think about curriculum in this way – I can see now that Canada's approach is probably too prescriptive about what children will learn, but it does give some guidance on what sorts of conceptual knowledge the community wants. I guess I can understand how that has come about now.

Gwendolyne: I've also thought quite a lot about the curriculum in Malawi and how it talks about which concepts I should be teaching. This course has been quite helpful for making me think through how important it is for me to help children develop conceptual knowledge around

continued »

continued »

literacy, numeracy, science, physical education and so forth, but I can't do this in isolation of what children already know. What I need to do is find out what conceptual knowledge children already have and find ways to further their knowledge and make links to conceptual knowledge that we know the research says that children need.

Gemma: I still think that the curriculum document itself is a guide to what we should be trying to achieve within the classroom. What I've taken out of this course is that I have to work much more closely than I thought I would with the families and communities, so that I know what I need to include in my curriculum to help children learn.

Kelly: Yes, I think Gemma is right. I started out thinking that the curriculum document would tell me what to do, but I've realised that it just provides a framework which sort of encompasses my practice. The curriculum itself is based around my knowledge of the children in the classroom or centre, my observations and other assessments of their learning and my planning of the sorts of activities that I think would help them learn.

Anna: I suppose in some ways my Associate Teacher, the one who said that she planned on the trot, was right to a certain extent, but I think I've got a clearer idea, through studying cultural-historical curriculum this semester, that what I am trying to do is provide both spontaneous and planned activities that really relate to where children are in their learning. Some days, I might plan something that I think will build on their interests, while on other days I will simply seize the moment and talk with children about how else we might find out further information. What is really important is that I find out what children bring with them into the classroom and make sure that anything I plan is meaningful and culturally relevant to them.

Arohia: Yes, that's right. I guess I had never thought about the fact that not all children will respond the same way to the things I do in the classroom. I found the sessions on curriculum as a cultural broker really eye-opening, and they've made me think quite a lot about how I need to talk to parents about how children are used to learning at home and in their community groups.

Kiri: If we think back to that original question about curriculum being constructed and contested, I think I understand now that it really is. We

continued »

continued »

have to construct the curriculum with the children, the parents and other members of the community, where appropriate, and all these groups have a say in what our curriculum can and should be. It will also be different from year to year, depending on who is in our classroom or centre.

Gemma: Remember what I said to you about parents needing to have an active role in planning the curriculum right at the start?

Anna: Yes, and you were right, although I don't think the rest of us saw that then. Although this is a really good idea, I can see that it might be challenging to achieve in practice in communities where families are not used to talking with teachers about curriculum or where parents think they can just dump the kids and run, because they are busy. I think the relationship formation issues around working with parents will require quite a lot of work.

Kelly: I talked about assessment last time and this course has really made me rethink how I will go about assessing what children have learnt. I think, if I'm honest, that I have probably worked on the assumption that if the children were busy and seemed happy the curriculum was effective, but I can see now that I actually have to keep my subject content knowledge at a high level, so that I can recognise what children have learnt already and can work out where and how to challenge their thinking and extend their learning. To think that I thought teaching younger children would be easier than other levels of teaching!

Arohia: I guess I can see better now how the cultural-historical curriculum we have been talking about this semester fits with co-construction of children's learning, which our practicum lecturer is so passionate about. This approach can be a useful method of extending children's learning.

Anna: I think the idea of co-construction is similar to the ideas around evaluation that we have talked about. In this model, the expertise and responsibility for evaluation belongs to the teaching team, the families and communities. In a funny sort of way, we have to co-construct how we will evaluate with that group, rather than dreaming it up ourselves or just relying on external evaluation agencies, like the Education Review Office or Ofsted.

Lecturer: Can you come back into the whole group now? First, can you tell me how your group defined what a curriculum is?

Like our group of students, we have reached the end of our course of study on this topic. Before we go on to talk about what we think we have discussed in the chapters in this book, take a moment and think back to the question we posed to you at the outset.

REFLECTION 12.1

Take a moment and think about what you understand by the term 'curriculum'.

We asked you the following questions about curriculum at the outset:

- Is it a model?
- Is it a document?
- Is it the way the environment is organised?
- Is it the way people plan for children's learning?
- Is it the day-to-day decisions that teachers make about children and their learning?
- Is it what is negotiated with parents, community and external agencies?
- Is it what external evaluation agencies want to see?

We hope the answer you have arrived at is that it is all of these things, but conceptualised, organised and managed in different ways according to the social, educational, cultural, political and economic drivers of each community at a particular moment in time. In this way, we can understand that curriculum is a cultural and historical construction.

We've argued that all curriculums have answers to the following questions:

1. **Aims, goals, objectives or outcome statements** – what do we want this curriculum to achieve, what would we expect to be the outcomes as a result of participating in the implementation of that curriculum?
2. **Content, domains, or subject matter** – what will we include or exclude from our curriculum?
3. **Methods or procedures** – what teaching methods or approaches will we use to achieve our goals or outcomes?
4. **Evaluation and assessment** – how will we know when we have achieved them?

We have used a diagram throughout each chapter which demonstrates what we consider to be the core components of a cultural-historical curriculum. Although all aspects of curriculum are related to each other, we have highlighted particular parts of the diagram in various chapters to indicate the particular features being addressed in each topic.

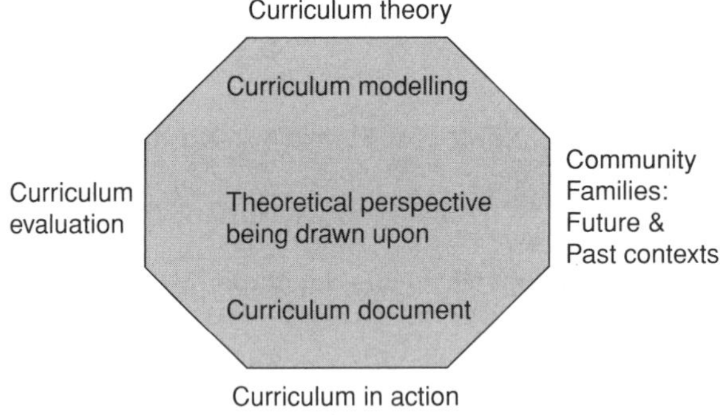

Figure 12.1 Curriculum development pathway – content knowledge

In addition, we have argued that any curriculum statement or document has answers to the following questions about children:

- How are children viewed in the document? What language is used to describe them?
- What content is valued? – e.g. democracy, subject knowledge, domains such as social and emotional, etc
- How is knowledge framed? – e.g. divided into areas, holistic, absolute, general, detailed and specific, related to community, politically oriented, culturally diverse, etc
- How is progression organised (or not)? – e.g. stages, journey, community-defined and embedded, related to school-based curricula, development as traditionally defined through ages and stages, etc
- Who decides on the content? – e.g. government, licensing agencies, community, professional associations, the early childhood professional delivering the program, etc.

In our view, the answers to these questions are as follows:

How are children viewed? What language is used to describe them?

Children are viewed as active learners, who are competent and capable and bring a wealth of social, cultural and historical knowledge from their homes and communities to bear upon their learning in educational settings, such as centres and schools. There is understanding that children will learn in different ways in their families and communities and it is the task of the teacher to find out how children are used to learning and build on these skills.

What content is valued?

Content that is valued stems from both community knowledge and wisdom and evidence from research and scholarship around what conceptual knowledge helps children succeed at school and in life. We have highlighted some of the current research evidence around conceptual knowledge and skills that teachers can help children gain in centres and schools.

How is knowledge framed?

Knowledge is framed around the learning that children bring to educational settings, along with their emerging interests. In addition, the curriculum is a vehicle for helping children gain 'schooled knowledge' that will be helpful to them throughout their educational career.

How is progression organised (or not)?

Progression is organised around the child's strengths. A method of 'potentive assessment' (Fleer 2010) is used to identify learning and development and to determine how the child can be challenged in their thinking and learning. Children's development is determined by their experiences, the interactions they have with people and their community's expectations of them. The effectiveness of the curriculum is evaluated by children, teachers, administrators, families and communities, all of whom have a stake in the outcomes of the curriculum.

Who decides on the content?

Content is collaboratively decided by the children, teachers, parents and community and in relation to any formal curriculum documents, regulatory or legislative requirements. In this model, concept formation in children should be thought about as two interrelated levels: the everyday level and the scientific or 'schooled' level. In curriculum development and planning in early childhood settings, it is important to know about these two levels and how they relate to each other, because these ideas help teachers build content and the learning of content into play-based approaches to early learning. We have

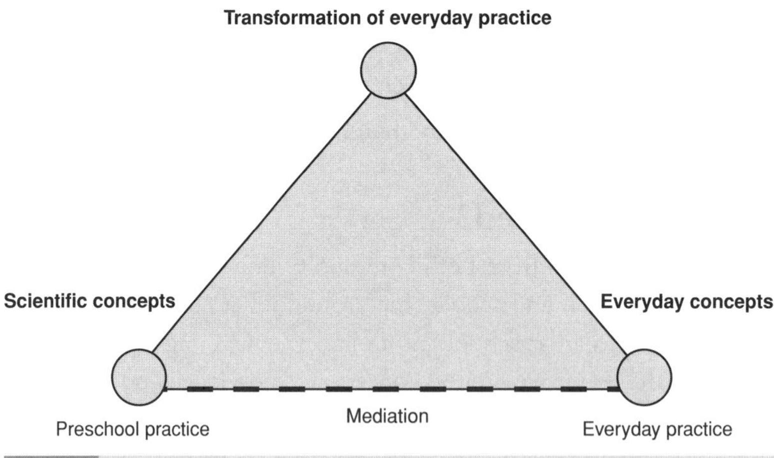

Figure 12.2 Curriculum development model

used the model of teaching and learning proposed by Fleer and Raban (2007) to explain this process in terms of domain areas of knowledge, such as maths, science, literacy, ICT, physical education and the arts. The role of the teacher is to act as mediator between the child's everyday understandings and 'schooled' concepts.

In conclusion, we hope you have enjoyed this journey into thinking about curriculum in the early childhood setting. We consider curriculum quite a challenging topic, and we hope that we have provided you with a framework for thinking about curriculum decision making and children's learning. We hope we have provided you with food for thought about how to plan, implement and assess curriculum for young children.

References

Fleer, M. (2010). *Early Learning and Development: Cultural–historical concepts in play*. Melbourne: Cambridge University Press.

Fleer, M. & Raban, B. (2007). *Early childhood literacy and numeracy: Building good practice*. Canberra: Department of Education, Science and Training.

INDEX

b denotes box, **f** denotes figure, **t** denotes table